SHARING

YOUR

FAITH

WITH A

BUDDHIST

Books by
Madasamy Thirumalai

Sharing Your Faith With a Buddhist
Sharing Your Faith With a Hindu

SHARING YOUR FAITH WITH A BUDDHIST

MADASAMY THIRUMALAI

BETHANYHOUSE
MINNEAPOLIS, MINNESOTA

Published by Bethany House Publishers
11400 Hampshire Avenue South
Bloomington, Minnesota 55438
www.bethanyhouse.com

Bethany House Publishers is a Division of
Baker Book House Company, Grand Rapids, Michigan.

Printed in the United States of America

Library of Congress Cataloging-in-Publication Data

Thirumalai, M. S., 1940-
    Sharing your faith with a Buddhist / by Madasamy Thirumalai.
        p.   cm.
Includes bibliographical references.
    ISBN 0-7642-2791-2 (pbk.)
    1. Buddhism. 2. Buddhism—Relations—Christianity. 3. Missions to Buddhists.
I. Title.
    BQ4012.T45   2003
    294.3—dc22   2003014251

MADASAMY THIRUMALAI is a professor of world religions and linguistics, is the academic dean at Bethany College of Missions, has taught at universities in India, and is a widely published author. A native of India, he has a master's degree from the University of Hawaii and a Ph.D. in linguistics from the University of Calcutta. He and his family live near Minneapolis, Minnesota.

ACKNOWLEDGMENTS

Our Lord Jesus Christ has blessed me with a number of friends, and through them I personally experienced His grace while writing this book. Mike Leeming, Professor of Missions and Biblical Studies at Bethany College of Missions, read the entire manuscript and made several suggestions to improve its presentation. Christopher Soderstrom, my editor, went beyond the call of duty and personally helped me design and redesign the format of the book, discussed the contents of the manuscript in great detail, and improved my style and presentation. My wife, Swarna, read portions of the manuscript in several stages and gave tremendous help to ensure that I finished on time.

My friends Dave and Hoinu Bunce, John and Michelle Pandian, John and Sheila Bjorklund, Stan Schmidt, Vangie Kelstrup, and Steve and Denise Darula were a great source of strength and encouragement. I have spent many hours with Stan Schmidt, Alec Brooks, and Tom Bates discussing Buddhism in relation to the Word of God. Dave Hicks, President of Bethany Fellowship International, has blessed me with his prayers and words of encouragement. His exhortation that I do my best for the glory of God is a great blessing.

I have true help in Paul Hartford, Director of Bethany College of Missions, who encourages all his colleagues (whom I am among) to do their best for the expansion of God's kingdom. My gratefulness is due Terry Donnelly, Vice-President of Bethany Fellowship International, who very kindly helped me by sorting out several administrative problems concerning my role as an author within the organization. I would like to make special mention of Paul Strand, Ed Dudek, Tom Shetler, Tony Hedrick, Joel Anantharaz, and Seelan Mathiaparanam, who took special interest in this project and helped me with insights of their own based on their field experience. I also owe a sense of appreciation to Steve Laube, former Editorial Director of Nonfiction for Bethany House Publishers, and Julie Smith, Managing Editor of Nonfiction for Bethany House Publishers, for all their help.

During the period when I was finishing this book, I had to undergo open-heart surgery for several bypasses and a mitral valve repair! Because of the grace of our Lord Jesus Christ, I had the best team of doctors. I am grateful to Dr. Eric Veum, my physician, Dr. William Northrup III, cardiac and thoracic surgeon, and Dr. Robert Ketroser, cardiologist. I am indeed grateful to them for getting me back to normal life! My grandchildren, Joshua, Selvi, and Anna, helped me so much in this process.

Last but not the least, I am grateful to the members of my cell group, led by John and Jodene Anderson (Kjell and Carol Garborg, Jonathan and Deirdre Thompson, Randy and Rebecca Theesfield, Elaine Linder, Bettye Johnson, and Jan Schnyder), who prayed for me and showered their love upon me.

—M. S. Thirumalai

CONTENTS

INTRODUCTION

My acquaintance with Buddhism began when I was a high school student in a small town in southern India. The history books that we read in school had many favorable references to Gautama Buddha (sometimes referred to as Siddhartha Gautama) and portrayed him as a selfless person who preached (and seemed to be the embodiment of) nonviolence and peace. Allegedly, he forsook his kingdom and his position as a prince to seek "true" knowledge of the meaning of life. Indian leaders, small and great, regional and national, would always refer to him as a great philosopher, full of divinity, who impacted the whole world as no other person has. Buddhism is the greatest Indian contribution to humanity, they would declare, pointing out the many countries in Asia that eventually embraced Buddhism as their own religion. Little did I realize at that time that the didactic literature dealing with morals and ethics in my mother tongue, Tamil, actually is based mainly on Buddhism, even though these books were all supposed to have been written by Hindus.

I was brought up a Hindu. I believed in and worshiped idols, and I sought the favor of gods and spirits through animal sacrifices, sorcery, divination, and witchcraft. Like many of my classmates and other friends, I always put pictures or images of Gautama Buddha, that serene face, on the wall in my parents' home. There was no objection to this practice from my parents, who took the Buddha to be one of the many gods that we might worship.

Vegetarianism, a distinguishing mark of the upper castes in southern India, was reinforced with the study and knowledge that the Buddha was against the killing of animals. Some of the highly regarded Tamil literary works raised the question, "How could one consider himself merciful if he eats the flesh of another (animal) to fatten his own flesh?" The argument, put as it was in this perspective, was so convincing that

I was persuaded to become a vegetarian for a number of years.

Over time I began to look at Gautama Buddha as both an incarnation of a divine being and a great social reformer because he preached against the rituals of the Brahman priests, who dominated the Hindu religion, and offered a plan of nirvana for even the members of the lowly communities. As a person coming from an agriculturist non-Brahman caste, I started seeing validity in the Buddha's arguments against caste practices. Here was an Indian philosopher, a "divine" person, who sought to change Indian society; this appealed strongly to me, as it did to many other educated persons who were dissatisfied with the socioeconomic and political situation in India (and throughout the world). In the midst of all this, however, I never thought that my spiritual experience would be enhanced or improved if I read and followed Gautama Buddha's teaching.

Rather, I felt attracted to the implications of the Buddha's teaching toward our local conditions. Mahatma Gandhi spoke about nonviolence as the major tool for social transformation, and most of us who were drawn to the Buddha in India were already agnostic, indifferent to and not believing in the existence or nonexistence of God (or a god). Buddha's argument in favor of right conduct, right thinking, and right speech was a social program, and thus rationalists and agnostics felt very much at home with him.

Later on I realized that the entire scope of Buddhism is geared more toward individuals than toward society. The disciplines recommended in Buddhism are aimed at the nirvana of the individual. The distinction between the laity and the clergy (monks) bestowed some special worth on the latter, while degrading the hard work of the peasants and laborers as not leading to nirvana. Those who did not want anything to do with karma in Hinduism were now faced with another type of karma that simply enslaved the individual in this life.

That man cannot live by bread alone or by the meditative disciplines alone, and that he needs the grace of God for his salvation, became clear to me once I came to know who Jesus is. While my Buddhist friends and their exemplary Buddha tried to avoid suffering through their efforts, I saw Jesus standing up to the Evil One and overcoming him for our benefit. I saw Jesus suffering for us and with us: He is not the One who simply shows the way but actually walks with us throughout our life.

I found in Jesus a friend who loves me, cares for me, counsels me, and participates in my life for my sake. He says, "Here I am! I stand at the door and knock. If anyone hears my voice and opens the door, I will come in and eat with him, and he with me" (Revelation 3:20). He assures me that I will find rest for my soul if I take His yoke upon me and learn from Him. His yoke is easy, and His burden is light (see Matthew 11:29–30).

This is not all. He assures me that if I ask anything in His name, He will do it (John 14:14). He came to serve you and me and all of us—His creation—and to give His life as a ransom for us (see Mark 10:45). He offers us eternal life, and if we receive it we shall never perish (see John 10:28). We live on forever, while Gautama Buddha's way focuses on extinction.

Jesus is always with us, even to the very end of the age (see Matthew 28:20). I don't have to carry my burdens on my own; Jesus is always there to help me. Through His death on the cross and through His resurrection, He enables me to live a life that is pleasing to God the Father, and by His grace, not by my meritorious works, I am assured of my salvation. He forgives my sins, and He does not even remember them anymore (see Hebrews 8:12). So in Jesus the question of my suffering in the life beyond does not arise at all.

Gautama Buddha, on the other hand, offers no such help. The Buddha tells me that it is futile for me to seek the help of anyone on my journey toward nirvana. I should achieve it on my own, with no help from others. He tells me that I cannot escape from the operation of karma (past acts defining my eternity, in some sense), that I must continue to suffer because of my karma, and that there is no hope for me in this life.

The grace of the Lord Jesus is available to us not only as individuals but also as members of His community—even in this life. The Lord Jesus Christ gives us the confidence that we will "see the goodness of the LORD in the land of the living" (Psalm 27:13). There is no need to torture ourselves in order to become God's children.

Even as I can make a list of good things that flow from my faith in Jesus Christ as the Lord and Savior of all, I know in my spirit that God is worthy of praise and adoration regardless of circumstance. We worship Him for who He is and not simply for what He gives us. Surrendering ourselves totally to His will gives us rest and peace beyond description.

The Word of God is concerned with the well-being of God's creation. God wants us to be stewards of what He has made because we are made in His image. He wants to be with us because He is our Father—He loves us like no other. In due course, He will transform us into holy and fit vessels worthy of His name and worthy to worship and praise

Him. Recitation or repetition of words, both meaningful and obscure, is of no consequence to Him. What He wants are contrite hearts. He offers love, hope, and security.

My prayer is that our Buddhist friends will come to know God as their Father, worship Jesus as their Lord and Savior, and be led by the Holy Spirit to come to the true faith, giving up their image worship and other similar practices.

The name of Jesus is alive. Thousands like me are hearing of Him, and many are admitting that He is gracious, caring, mighty, and worthy of our worship. The Holy Spirit stirs desire in the hearts of the people He has created, and these stirrings in the hearts of Buddhists need to be nourished. It is my hope and prayer that this book will serve the function of helping us to become co-laborers with the Spirit in His ministry of saving souls.

BUDDHA AND BUDDHISM

Buddhism, the world's fourth-largest religion, originated in India, but it has very few followers in that land. The *World Christian Encyclopedia* (Barrett et al.—see bibliography for full citations of all sources) reports that there are 362 million Buddhists, comprising about 6 percent of the earth's total population.

Buddhism is an international religion, being the official or dominant religion in Sri Lanka, Myanmar (Burma), Thailand, Cambodia, Laos, Vietnam, Tibet, Bhutan, Mongolia, Korea, Japan, and China. Along with Hinduism, Buddhist thought, worldview, and way of living have had the greatest hold over Asian peoples, not excluding the most populous Islamic nation of the world, Indonesia.

There are three major divisions (or sects) within Buddhism: *Theravada* (or *Hinayana*), *Mahayana,* and *Vajrayana* (Tibetan). Each has its own folk traditions, which blend native pre-Buddhist tradition with Buddhism. Theravada Buddhism is practiced mainly in Sri Lanka, Myanmar, Thailand, Cambodia, Laos, and partly in Vietnam. Mahayana Buddhism is found in China, Japan, Korea, and Vietnam. Vajrayana Buddhism is largely in Tibet, Mongolia, Nepal, Bhutan, and two Himalayan (northeastern) Indian states. Buddhists are found on every inhabited continent, and in recent decades this religion is attracting new adherents in Western nations among the "elite."

While Buddhism has lost its place in India, it has retained a pervasive influence among the Hindu intellectuals who admire its values and philosophy. In Southeast Asia, Buddhism continues to thrive as a national religion, fueling the flames of loyalism, patriotism, and nationalism. In their struggle against Western colonialism, the people of Southeast Asia often took recourse by asserting their Buddhist religious identity.

After World War II, many of these countries came under the

influence of communism. Like the Eastern Orthodox Christian groups, Buddhists were subjected to state-sponsored ideology. Buddhism has not died under the rule of communists because Buddhism is not a mere religion, having long ago become a way of life. With its emphasis on self-help in human salvation, Buddhism is seeking markets of currency elsewhere, particularly in the industrialized Western and Japanese societies. At present, Buddhist monks are quite opposed to Christianity and are doing their best to appeal to the people, in the name of nationalism, not to accept faith in Christ. And yet, by God's abundant grace, the gospel is received by many in all these nations.

The spectacular growth within the last few decades of the church in Korea galvanizes the servants of God in these nations into more concerted action to draw people to Christ. The communist regimes have failed to deliver the goods of economic prosperity they promised. There is frustration everywhere.

THE ORIGIN OF BUDDHISM

Buddhism is an offshoot of Hinduism; in fact, it arose as an ideology against Brahmanical Hinduism. This started in an eastern province of India, in about the fifth century B.C., spreading all over India, and then in other countries east, north, and south of India "with great rapidity, not by force of arms, or coercion of any kind, like Muhammadanism, but by the sheer persuasiveness of its doctrine" (Monier-Williams, 72).

The ritualism of the Brahmans, their claim of supremacy over the other castes, the pernicious operation and consequences of the caste system, the subtle conflict between the priestly and princely classes, and the revulsion felt against the sacrificial system were some of the reasons that led to the emergence and spread of Buddhism in India. Buddhism coexisted with Brahmanical Hinduism and influenced its philosophy in several ways.

> Brahmanism has taken from Buddhism the abolition of sacrifices, great tenderness toward animal life, great intensity of belief in the doctrine of salvation by works, and in the efficacy of abstract meditation as a source of power in accelerating progress toward final emancipation. It has received from Buddhism a tendency to recognize caste as an evil, or at least as an imperfection to be got rid of under certain circumstances and on certain occasions. (Monier-Williams, 80)

WHAT IS THE MEANING OF "BUDDHA"?

Buddha is a Sanskrit or Pali word (these are classical languages, ordinarily not spoken now), an honorific title that refers to a person who is awakened or enlightened, who has reached a higher level of consciousness. This term is related to another word, *buddhi,* meaning "intelligence" or "understanding."

Buddha is also a generic word that may be applied to a higher class of people who have an understanding into reality and, through this insight, can be liberated or transformed from the cyclical bondage of birth, death, and rebirth (*samsara*). There are other words in Sanskrit (or Pali) that refer to concepts such as *teacher, lord,* or *master,* but *Buddha* is a special word. A Buddha may be a teacher, a lord, or a master, but his special and most important characteristic is the awakening or enlightenment that he has received that can effect his transformation and liberation from samsara.

The word *Buddha* may refer to the historical Buddha (Gautama Buddha or Siddhartha Buddha), or it may be used to refer to a series of Buddhas, including the historical Buddha, who attained *moksha* or nirvana (meaning release from this world of rebirths), who have been liberated from samsara. There are thousands of such Buddhas recognized in Buddhism; some are lesser, having liberated only themselves from samsara, while others are greater, having attained the same for the benefit of many.

Multiplicity of Buddhas is accepted, and thus, polytheism is ingrained in the theology and practice of this religion. In the very conception of the "Buddha" lies the belief that there are many agencies that can help an individual achieve his liberation.

WHO IS GAUTAMA BUDDHA?

The founder of the Buddhist community was a man called Siddhartha ("One Who Has Reached His Goal") or Gautama (his family name), born at Kapilavastu, a city and kingdom at the foot of the mountains of Nepal, around 566 B.C. (various schools within Buddhism have suggested different dates for his life). Gautama Buddha is also *Sakyamuni,* the sage of the Sakya clan or kingdom. (Buddhism abounds in the enormous number of epithets for Gautama and various other Buddhas. To maintain consistency, we will refer to the historical Buddha as "Gautama Buddha" throughout this book.)

Buddhists do not look upon Gautama Buddha as the founder of the Buddhist faith or religion; he is one among the *many* Buddhas who received the "awakening" in ages past and is recognized to be the Buddha of *this* age. There were supposedly many Buddhas before him, so it is important for us to remember that our Buddhist friends tend to minimize the importance of Gautama as *the* Buddha. However, in real-life situations, often he comes to dominate the thoughts, discussions, and emulations of ordinary Buddhists.

Scholars have observed that the period in which Gautama Buddha was born was a remarkable time in the history of humankind, including a great interest in knowing and seeking the truth. Gautama, Mahavira (the founder of another ascetic Indian religion), Zoroaster (the founder of Zoroastrianism), Socrates, Confucius, Isaiah, and the composers of the Hindu Upanishads all seemed to be stirred by a desire to know who God was. In every way during this era, people were beginning to raise doubts about the efficacy of rituals and sacrifices. New thinking and new expectations were in the air.

Gautama Buddha was born (in the Hindu Kshatriya caste) to an aristocratic family near the present border of India-Nepal (recent archaeological excavations, sponsored by the United Nations, claim to have located the chamber of his birth in Nepal, two hundred miles southwest of Katmandu). He is said to have attained nirvana (supreme knowledge) under a bodhi tree, or "tree of wisdom," in 486 B.C. He may have commenced preaching his new faith at Varanasi (Benares), the most important sacred place of Hindus, around 500 B.C.

Buddhacarita (the *Biography of Buddha*), a highly regarded Buddhist scripture detailing Gautama Buddha's birth, says,

> [He] came out of his mother's side, without causing her pain or injury. . . . He did not enter the world in the usual manner, and he appeared like one descended from the sky. And since he had for many eons been engaged in the practice of meditation, he now was born in full awareness, and not thoughtless and bewildered as other people are. (Conze, 35)

The Buddhist texts say that Gautama had already endured countless births through incalculable eons, and that through the cycle of samsara he had been perfected and made ready to attain *parinirvana* (total liberation and nonexistence, "perfect nirvana") at the end of this incarnation (as Gautama Buddha).

His parents doted on him and held him dear to their hearts; they did not want their child to suffer for any reason. Everything around him was beautiful and pleasant, and so Gautama grew up without knowing what pain was. He had no idea whatsoever about the darker side of life, and he married when he was still in his teens, provided with all the finest things that affluence could offer. His parents built him a palace, and he and his wife lived there happily.

However, one day on his way to the park, he observed an old man with wrinkles and all the outward appearances of old age, with attendant helplessness and great sickness. Gautama had never suffered from illness, nor had he ever seen an ugly old man. He also saw a deceased body being carried away for cremation, and he had never before seen a dead man, nor did he know what death was. He likewise noticed a man begging (perhaps a monk), and he could not process the meaning of what he saw—he was shocked and did not know what to make of these things. He was so secluded by his parents (from the natural world, outside the palaces in which he lived) that he did not realize that this earth was full of such elements, and he was very much troubled in his heart.

At the same time, the story continues, he also took note of an ascetic on the street who was nonchalant, quiet, and undisturbed by the events happening around him. The combination of these sights forced Gautama to ponder the meaning of life and why man had to suffer all these miseries in this world. He came to the conclusion that the only thing worthy of pursuit in this life was to find the answer for the riddle of existence. Sickness, old age, poverty, and death awakened in him a resolve to know the truth about life and to seek ways to overcome all suffering.

Gautama Buddha was twenty-nine years old when one night he quietly left his wife and son (an only child) while they were sleeping. He married his wife, a beautiful princess, when he was nineteen, and his son was born ten years later. It was hard indeed for him to leave them, but he "overcame the temptation to stay and get involved in the affairs of this world." He renounced his inheritance, his family, and everything he had, cutting his hair and becoming a monk.

Gautama's subsequent experiment with Hindu philosophical inquiry did not lead him to pure knowledge, so he tried the asceticism of the Jainist sages. It is claimed that he then lived on one sesame seed or one grain a day and tortured his body and soul in every possible ascetic mode, and that he was initiated and practiced several disciplines of meditation under the instruction of two Brahman teachers. He found that the ascetic life only added more suffering and did not lead him to the knowledge he sought, so he became a hermit.

Finally, after six long years of searching for truth, Gautama found the alleged cause and cure for all human suffering while in meditation one night under a bo tree ("bodhi" or "pipal" tree, a large tree that survives many generations, *Ficus religiosa*), nearby the town presently known as Bodh Gaya, in the Indian state of Bihar. His realization consisted of *four noble truths* and then an *eightfold noble path* (discussed in chapter 2) to attain those truths.

Gautama Buddha died at the age of eighty, and Buddhists believe that in his death he reached his total liberation (parinirvana); he achieved the goal of all beings of becoming totally extinct (no longer existing). In the farewell address he is said to have given to his disciples, he was very emphatic that they should seek salvation on their own, without help from others:

> Therefore, O Ananda [the chief disciple of Buddha], be ye lamps unto yourselves. Rely on yourselves, and do not rely on external help. . . . Those who, either now or after I am dead, shall be a lamp unto themselves, relying upon themselves only and not relying upon any external help, but holding fast to the truth as their lamp, and seeking their salvation in the truth alone, shall not look for assistance to anyone besides themselves, it is they, Ananda, among my bhikshus [monks], who shall reach the very topmost height! But they must be anxious to learn. (Burtt, 49–50)

Buddha in actuality was almost agnostic, but after his death he became so venerated that he was deified. His followers admired him for his wisdom, his simplicity, his compassion, and for relinquishing his royal inheritance to seek real truth and happiness. Stories were afoot that narrated how Brahma (the Hindu god of creation) himself, with his heavenly host, went and worshiped Buddha as the Great One.

It was then claimed that there were miracles when Gautama Buddha was born. The eyes of the blind were opened so they could see his glorious birth. The deaf began to hear, the hunchbacks were straightened, and the lame started walking. Similar miracles were seen when he realized the Ultimate Truth (attained nirvana) under the bo tree. In the theological speculation of Buddhist monks, he became the savior of the world: he was preexistent, incarnate as planned, supernaturally conceived, and miraculously born. Sinless, yet suffering inexplicably, he entered the world with a redemptive purpose, all-knowing and all-seeing, everlasting, the savior of gods and of men.

Idols of Gautama Buddha sprang up everywhere, standardized in relation to the attributes that theology bestowed upon him. Ironically, the man who did not want the world to depend upon any mysterious Divine Being for salvation, the man who preached that the individual can and should achieve his own salvation without assistance, was made a god and was worshiped as such.

Meanwhile, Brahmanical Hinduism was absorbing the various tenets of Gautama's preaching as its own, and finally it elevated him as one of the ten *avatars* (incarnations) of Vishnu (the preservation-god of Hinduism, one among its three chief deities, the other two being the aforementioned creator-god, Brahma, and the destructor-god, Shiva).

BUDDHIST TRUTHS, PATHS, AND PROHIBITIONS

2

THE FOUR NOBLE TRUTHS

Enlightenment led Gautama Buddha to enunciate four truths that underlie Buddhism and its worldview.

1. Suffering permeates all existence.
2. Desire—for possessions, enjoyment, separate identity, existence—is the root cause of all suffering. All of these foster further involvement in life, which only brings suffering.
3. Suffering will cease if we suppress all our desires.
4. Cessation of suffering is possible only if we follow the eightfold noble path (also called "the Middle Way"), avoiding both self-indulgence and self-mortification.

THE EIGHTFOLD NOBLE PATH

1. Right vision/views
2. Right thoughts/aspirations (including a determination to achieve nirvana)
3. Right speech
4. Right action/conduct
5. Right mode of livelihood/living as a monk
6. Right effort/application to the study of the Law (Dharma)
7. Right awareness/memory in recollecting the Law (Dharma)
8. Right concentration/meditation

It is difficult for human beings to follow all eight aspects of the path in this life; only a select few can do so. Therefore, those who cannot *completely* adhere to the eightfold path may at least follow, in this life, the first four (right vision, right thoughts, right speech, and right action) and then work on the others as they go through the cycle of births and rebirths. The last four are reserved for clergy, and thus, there are two classes of men recognized: laymen, who are still attached to this worldly life, and *bhikshus* (monks).

In the Buddhist tradition followed in India and Sri Lanka, women were admitted to the order of nuns for several centuries. It is reported that Gautama Buddha, at the persistent request of his aunt or foster mother, finally agreed to this during the fifth year of his nirvana, setting up a few special rules of behavior for women that asserted the precedence of clerical males (bhikshus) over females (bhikshunis). These included the declaration that bhikshus could admonish bhikshunis but not vice versa. The practice of inducting women into the Buddhist Order died out around the tenth century amid widespread criticism of the misuse of this provision, among other things.

A common belief among Buddhists is that in rebirths men are born as men and women are born as women—only negative karma makes a man to be reborn as a woman. In certain circles it is believed that there are both male and female Buddhas (persons who have attained or who are eligible to attain nirvana), and at present an attempt is being made to revive this tradition. The Chinese branch of Buddhism (Mahayana) continues to have nuns.

The bhikshus, then, are the ones who will obtain their nirvana; the laity will not. By becoming a monk, an individual facilitates his progress toward nirvana faster than the path pursued by a layman. Thus from the beginning the emphasis was to call upon people to become monks so that they could advance. Gautama Buddha, according to a scriptural text, saw at least two good things come out of monkhood, even in this life: that superior social status is accorded by the laity, and also that when "a householder or one of his children, or a man of inferior birth in any class listens to" the truth from the monks, he develops his faith "in the one who found the truth" (Burtt, 103).

The Ten Prohibitions

Five of the Buddhist prohibitions (1–5) are meant for all, and the rest (6–10) are meant only for the monks (Monier-Williams, 78–79).

1. Kill not.

2. Steal not.
3. Commit no adultery.
4. Lie not.
5. Drink no strong/intoxicating drink.
6. Eat no food, except at stated times.
7. Abstain from dances, theatres, songs, and music.
8. Use no ornaments or perfumes.
9. Use no luxurious beds.
10. Receive neither gold nor silver.

THE EIGHTEEN POSITIVE INJUNCTIONS

Injunctions 1–6 are incumbent upon all, and the rest (7–18) are meant for monks only (Monier-Williams, 79).

1. Charity (benevolence)
2. Virtue (moral goodness)
3. Patience (forbearance)
4. Fortitude
5. Meditation
6. Knowledge
7. Dress only in coats of rags.
8. Have a coat in three pieces, sewn together with the owner's own hands.
9. Cover the coat of rags with a yellow cloak.
10. Eat only one meal daily.
11. Never eat after noon.
12. Live only on food collected from door to door in a wooden bowl.
13. Live for part of the year in woods and jungles.
14. Have no other shelter but the leaves of trees.
15. Have no other furniture but a carpet.
16. Sit, rather than lie down, on this carpet during sleep.
17. Sit, otherwise, with no support except the trunk of a tree.
18. Frequent cemeteries and burning-grounds every month for meditation on the vanity of life.

Nonviolence and benevolence (toward all forms of life), deliberate bearing of injuries and humiliation, and patient suffering against all odds are highlighted for observance.

KARMA

Buddhist karma is an important concept derived from Hinduism, with some significant modification. A major difference between Hindu karma and Buddhist karma is that in the former, karma is closely linked to the caste system, according to which a person may be born in a lower or upper caste as a consequence of karma. Buddhism does not posit a caste connection.

Karma means "deeds" or "acts" or "works": one's thoughts, words, and actions in this life have a consequence in the next. Also, emotions that one experiences in this life are a result of what he or she did in previous lives. Karma, then, results in appropriate future reward or punishment.

> *Karma* is a principle of moral reaction applied to both good and evil actions. As a man sows, so shall he reap. Bad actions reap suffering and bondage to human existence. Good actions lead to freedom from this bondage. . . . According to Karmic law, a man may be reborn as a god, as a member of a higher or lower caste, or as an animal, according to his every thought, word, and act. Each man, therefore, carries with him his past; in fact, he is his own past. . . . Similarly the mental and moral tendencies of this life will work themselves out in the next . . . the state of each creature in any particular life being dependent on the good or evil actions of preceding lives. (Nicholls, 142–43)

The results of karma cannot be avoided by any other means—even the gods, Bodhisattvas, or Arhats cannot help a person to overcome its consequences. (A *Bodhisattva* is a being who has reached the stage of attaining nirvana for himself [through samsara] but has chosen, out of compassion, not to enter nirvana until all beings are helped to attain nirvana. An *Arhat* is someone who has been "made perfect" by following all the disciplines needed for nirvana.)

Karma has been a convenient justification for the poverty and other ills faced by various Buddhists. While, as mentioned earlier, Buddhism (except in Sri Lanka) does not follow the caste categorization followed in Hinduism, Buddhist texts inform us that the change from an ordinary person to the status of a Bodhisattva is marked by five advantages accrued by the latter:

> [The Bodhisattva] is [1] no more reborn in the States of woe, but always among gods and men; he is [2] never again born in poor or low-class families; he is [3] always a male, and never a woman; he is [4] always well-built, and free from physical defects; [and] he can [5] remember his past lives, and no more forgets them again. (Conze, 31)

Thus, social, economic, and physical well-being is shown to be a result of karma. The social stratification in the Theravada Buddhist nations (such as Sri Lanka, Myanmar, and Thailand—see chapter 5) is justified on the principle of karma, although there is some freedom to move from the low social groups to higher ones. Even in Buddhism, *karma helps and extends the perpetuation of discrimination.*

Karma also glorifies good works as a source of liberation from the unending cycle of samsara (birth, death, and rebirth). Karma is used to explain all suffering: if a person is born deformed, it is because of karma in his past life; if a person wants to have happiness in a future life, he must work for it right now, regardless of the situation in which he is placed. He must suffer for his acts of commission and omission; there is no such concept as forgiveness, so he must achieve his salvation through his own efforts.

Unfortunately, we all know that no human being can be perfect while living on earth; all of us will commit sin in our thinking, speech, and actions. No amount of hard work and conscious effort can purify us. Although the principle of karma may be an enticing one for intellectually oriented skeptics of Christ, it is totally flawed. Works alone cannot save anyone.

The Order of Buddhist Clergy

We have already made several references to the order of monks and their special status in relation to laymen. At the time Gautama Buddha preached his first sermon, there were only five listeners who embraced his teaching. Soon there were sixty young people, all from noble and wealthy families, who dedicated their lives to his teaching and who carried his message to other nations. Buddhism was quickly accepted in parts of southern India and Sri Lanka, and with the spread of the Buddha's teaching came the need and responsibility to organize his disciples into a congregation.

Young men who were not afflicted with diseases (such as leprosy, boils, consumption, or seizures) were admitted into the order. They had to be free from debts, and they could not give up royal service to enter the order. They had to receive parental consent, they had to be more than twenty years old, and their alms-bowl and robes had to be in good condition. (As already stated, women were admitted into the order in due course—in a position lower, however, than men.) The initiates took three vows, repeated constantly: "I take refuge in the Buddha. I take refuge in Dharma (the Law). I take refuge in Sangam (the Order)."

They were also required, every two weeks, to repeat 227 rules in the monastic assembly.

There is actually no proper "priesthood" in Buddhism—the monks are *teachers*. As already pointed out, the monks scrupulously obey the ten prohibitions and strive to practice the eighteen positive injunctions. They do not do physical labor, which would get them involved in worldly affairs or perhaps even cause injury or death to other beings (such as worms), thus leading to the accumulation of more karma. Monks live on alms collected and gifts given without any solicitation. They confess sins to one another every two weeks. (This description applies more fully to the clergy of the Theravada nations—see chapter 5.)

THE PLACE OF WORKS IN THE PLAN OF SALVATION THROUGH JESUS

God certainly wants us to do good works. He even helps us and blesses us as we do them: "Let your light shine before men, that they may see your good deeds and praise your Father in heaven" (Matthew 5:16). "We are God's workmanship, created in Christ Jesus to do good works, which God prepared in advance for us to do" (Ephesians 2:10).

Jesus himself is an example: "God anointed Jesus of Nazareth with the Holy Spirit and power, and . . . he went around doing good and healing all who were under the power of the devil, because God was with him" (Acts 10:38).

The Bible says that God remembers good works: "God is not unjust; he will not forget your work and the love you have shown him as you have helped his people and continue to help them" (Hebrews 6:10).

It is clearly said, "We must all appear before the judgment seat of Christ, that each one may receive what is due him for the things done while in the body, whether good or bad" (2 Corinthians 5:10).

We are commanded:

> Be careful not to do your "acts of righteousness" before men, to be seen by them. If you do, you will have no reward from your Father in heaven. . . . But when you give to the needy, do not let your left hand know what your right hand is doing, so that your giving may be in secret. Then your Father, who sees what is done in secret, will reward you. (Matthew 6:1, 3–4)

Likewise,

May our Lord Jesus Christ himself and God our Father, who loved us and by his grace gave us eternal encouragement and good hope, encourage your hearts and strengthen you in every good deed and word. (2 Thessalonians 2:16–17)

In a large house there are articles not only of gold and silver, but also of wood and clay; some are for noble purposes and some for ignoble. If a man cleanses himself from the latter, he will be an instrument for noble purposes, made holy, useful to the Master and prepared to do any good work. (2 Timothy 2:20–21)

At one time we too were foolish, disobedient, deceived and enslaved by all kinds of passions and pleasures. We lived in malice and envy, being hated and hating one another. But when the kindness and love of God our Savior appeared, he saved us, not because of righteous things we had done, but because of his mercy. . . . Devote [yourselves, then,] to doing what is good. These things are excellent and profitable for everyone. (Titus 3:3–5, 8)

"Yes," says the Spirit, "they will rest from their labor, for their deeds will follow them" (Revelation 14:13).

THE INSUFFICIENCY OF WORKS FOR SALVATION

God has asked us to do good works toward each other and to live a sanctified life; He has assured us that all our good works will be rewarded. Although it is said that we will receive suitable punishment for evil deeds that are not confessed, God is merciful and gracious—He wants us to repent of our sins and put our trust in Him, not in our works. If we do this, He will save us. However, *doing good works does not lead to salvation; neither does it ensure a better life in the future.* Good works are thoroughly insufficient to save us; it is God who redeems our life from the grave (see Psalm 49:15).

No man can redeem the life of another or give to God a ransom for him—the ransom for a life is costly, no payment is ever enough—that he should live on forever and not see decay. (Psalm 49:7–9)

All of us have become like one who is unclean, and all our righteous acts are like filthy rags; we all shrivel up like a leaf, and like the wind our sins sweep us away. (Isaiah 64:6)

I will expose your righteousness and your works, and they

will not benefit you. (Isaiah 57:12)

Therefore, son of man, say to your countrymen, "The righteousness of the righteous man will not save him when he disobeys, and the wickedness of the wicked man will not cause him to fall when he turns from it" (Ezekiel 33:12).

Two men went up to the temple to pray, one a Pharisee and the other a tax collector. The Pharisee stood up and prayed about himself: "God, I thank you that I am not like other men—robbers, evildoers, adulterers—or even like this tax collector. I fast twice a week and give a tenth of all I get." But the tax collector stood at a distance. He would not even look up to heaven, but beat his breast and said, "God, have mercy on me, a sinner." I tell you that this man, rather than the other, went home justified before God. For everyone who exalts himself will be humbled, and he who humbles himself will be exalted. (Luke 18:9–14)

Therefore, my brothers, I want you to know that through Jesus the forgiveness of sins is proclaimed to you. Through him everyone who believes is justified from everything you could not be justified from by the law of Moses. (Acts 13:38–39)

What then shall we say that Abraham, our forefather, discovered in this matter? If, in fact, Abraham was justified by works, he had something to boast about—but not before God. What does the Scripture say? "Abraham believed God, and it was credited to him as righteousness" (Romans 4:1–3).

It does not, therefore, depend on man's desire or effort, but on God's mercy. (Romans 9:16)

If [salvation is] by grace, then it is no longer by works; if it were, grace would no longer be grace. (Romans 11:6)

A man is not justified by observing the law, but by faith in Jesus Christ. (Galatians 2:16)

It is by grace you have been saved, through faith—and this not from yourselves, it is the gift of God—not by works, so that no one can boast. (Ephesians 2:8–9)

NIRVANA

Nirvana, appearing at the end of karma, is a condition of total freedom—total annihilation of self—beyond which there is no future birth.

It is the total extinction of all desire and a final, complete release from suffering, including no consciousness (there is total peace, but no consciousness of peace). *This is the goal of human beings—to have no existence.*

According to Theravada Buddhism, laymen have to go through many births and rebirths, whereas it is perhaps possible for monks to progress more quickly. Mahayana Buddhism, practiced in nations such as China and Japan (see chapter 6), says that all have the opportunity to eventually attain nirvana, while Vajrayana (or Tibetan) Buddhism (see chapter 7) suggests that one may be able to attain nirvana even in this birth itself. Regardless, everyone must achieve his own salvation.

SAMSARA—THE TRANSMIGRATION OF SOULS IN ENDLESS REBIRTHS

Transmigration of souls, or reincarnation in endless rebirths, is a cornerstone of Buddhist and Hindu belief. In Hinduism, souls are eternal and are reborn in new bodies. Buddhism does not believe in the existence of souls after death; what remains is the karma accumulated by an individual in his past lives. The *energies* or *forces* associated with the soul survive, operate within the karmic rule, and are given another appropriate body in the next birth. Rebirth may be in any form; a dead person's karma may be born again in the body of any living thing, and consequently, there is no guarantee that a human will be reborn as a human. Transmigration offers a progressive evolution from the lowest to the highest birth, toward Bodhisattva status. There are, however, endless possibilities for backsliding in status. Humanity is involved in a game of chutes and ladders.

The ultimate goal, liberation into nirvana, appears impossible—again, everyone commits sin. Since there is no forgiveness provided, and since karma operates unrelentingly, anyone who commits *any* kind of sin is liable to suffer the consequence in his next life. For example, you are certain to be punished in your next life if you have a sinful thought in this one. Even the smallest of all sins or errors would ensure that you have a rebirth and suffer the consequence of what you have already committed.

There is no way, then, that any person can really obtain the much-desired liberation; only mythical characters can achieve it. *In the absence of the operation of forgiveness and mercy through grace, it is impossible for any person to become saved within Buddhism.* Even though Buddhists believe there may be living Buddhas and Bodhisattvas in their midst to help them in this process, karma is unavoidable, and one is bound to be reincarnated in some form after death and thus be ensured of the continuity of struggle. Hence, life is fatalistically viewed as a dreary recycling of more suffering and pain; release from samsara is supposed to be achieved through self-help, and fatalism works in exactly the opposite direction, discouraging every effort due to the inevitable failure.

Buddhist and Hindu literature and thinking is replete with the hope that what could not be achieved or is missed in this life may perhaps be attained in the next; these writings point to tragic heroes who have risen high in their next rebirth and are given the comfort they sought in their earlier lives. This suggests enticing opportunities, but unfortunately it is quite misleading, for it justifies the present without enabling people to seek the forgiveness of God, whose Word plainly says that we have only one life and that we are judged after death based on what we do now. Since God is gracious, He *will* forgive our sins if we repent and make amends. It is our *faith* in Him that justifies us.

Once again, the writer of Hebrews makes it plain that we have only one life, the present one: "Just as man is destined to die once, and after that to face judgment, so Christ was sacrificed once to take away the sins of many people" (9:27–28).

> We . . . would prefer to be away from the body and at home with the Lord. So we make it our goal to please him, whether we are at home in the body or away from it. For we must all appear before the judgment seat of Christ, that each one may receive what is due him for the things done while in the body, whether good or bad. (2 Corinthians 5:8–10)

The story of the rich man and Lazarus (Luke 16:19–31) plainly mentions that those who have died are not born again into this world but are judged according to their deeds. Consider also Isaiah 14:9–11 and Revelation 20:11–15.

SCRIPTURES OF BUDDHISM

Gautama Buddha did not himself record or write down his thoughts. However, after his death some five hundred disciples are said to have put together, in verse form suitable for recitation, his sayings uttered on about three hundred occasions. The sacred texts of Buddhism commonly followed in Theravada nations (see chapter 5) are called *Tripitaka*, "the three baskets," composed of *Sutra*, *Abhidharma*, and *Vinaya*.

Sutra contains the preaching of Buddha, including Dhamma-pada ("the Way of Virtue"); Abhidharma contains the "higher doctrine" that discusses what exists beyond (or cannot be understood by) our senses; Vinaya contains the rules for the people who wish to (or have) become monks. The Theravada scriptures are in the Pali language, while the Mahayana and Vajrayana scriptures are in Sanskrit, Chinese, and Tibetan.

Buddhism has a strong tradition of orally transmitting its scriptures, even though they were written very early in its history. Buddhist monasteries (and their education of laypeople) have always emphasized *memorization* and *recitation*—even today these skills are highly valued, and in some sects (such as Zen Buddhism—see chapter 6) this is the dominant and preferred form of transmission. Participants in monastic debates can hope to win only if they are proficient in these two areas.

One of the ways to develop your friendship with a Theravada Buddhist is to ask him to recite some of his favorite verses and explain to you their meaning. Often such verses focus on the importance of monastic life, the need to obtain one's own salvation, and the praise of Arhats or Bodhisattvas; and many have memorized the utterances of Gautama Buddha. These verses would certainly offer you an opportunity not only to discuss (in depth) their meanings but also to compare and contrast them with verses from the Bible.

THE PROBLEM OF PAIN AND SUFFERING IN BUDDHISM

The "four noble truths" enunciated by Gautama Buddha all revolve around suffering; Buddhism teaches that our life is nothing else. Suffering is caused by our desires, which lead us to get involved in the process of life, which brings further suffering. We can win our fight against suffering only if we suppress our desires, avoid involvement in life, and pursue a middle path between self-indulgence and self-mortification. Desire, then, may be considered (in Buddhism), if not a sin, *at least* as a vehicle to bring only harm to us.

In his first preaching after his enlightenment, Gautama Buddha declared:

> Now this, monks, is the noble truth of pain: birth is painful, old age is painful, sickness is painful, death is painful, sorrow, lamentation, dejection, and despair are painful. Contact with unpleasant things is painful, not getting what one wishes is painful. (Burtt, 30)

Pain and suffering can be overcome, he maintained, by the eightfold noble path, but one may have to undergo innumerable births, deaths, and rebirths before this is achieved (even according to legend, this was true for him, as well).

In essence, according to Buddhism, the goal of humankind is to release itself (ultimately, by seeking extinction) from pain and suffering, which are to be detested and avoided through appropriate conduct.

Even though Christians know that suffering, both physical and mental, is real, suffering is never treated as something good in Christianity. Otherwise, the Lord Jesus Christ would not have gone about reducing and eliminating it whenever He came across people who were hurting. He actually calls the weary and sick to come to Him to find rest and peace from their pain. However, according to the Christian faith, suffering is not *merely* something that causes pain; God also allows it as a means of providing an opportunity for edification. Suffering *can be* a mode of punishment for one's acts of commission and omission, but it also has the function of uplifting and cleansing the one who suffers.

Pain is often felt on an individual basis, even though one person may share in the suffering of another when there is love or moral agreement between the two. Suffering is also widely distributed, not restricted to any specific category of people (or demographic). Modern science attempts to reduce or eliminate pain, but it does not go away completely. The question often raised is, "Why should I suffer, or why should there be suffering at all, in a world created by God?" Often we are not able to adduce any specific reason.

Job suffered enormous pain and various manifestations on his body, and his wife's (as well as his friends') pursuit of answers or sources for his suffering did not lead anywhere. We find that "those who suffer [God] delivers in their suffering; he speaks to them in their affliction" (Job 36:15).

The Word of God tells us that God will refine us "in the furnace of affliction" (Isaiah 48:10). Suffering is caused not *exclusively* as a consequence of sin but also as a result of our intention to do good or even from actually doing good. For example, Joseph was obeying God when he ran from the temptations of Potiphar's wife, and yet he went to prison as a result. Jesus endured indescribable pain because He bore our sins. Likewise, when we bear the burden of others, we may suffer.

Moreover, the Lord blesses righteous desire (see Proverbs 10:24): "The desire of the righteous ends only in good" (Proverbs 11:23). Desire is not evil in itself, nor does it cause only suffering and disadvantage. The sin of an individual is seen in his wickedness and his evil desires. The psalmist says, "The LORD examines the righteous, but the wicked and those who love violence his soul hates" (Psalm 11:5).

There is no better statement than the verses of Isaiah 53 to declare how God himself (in Jesus) suffered for our sake: "He was despised and rejected by men, a man of sorrows, and familiar with suffering" (v. 3). God's suffering *for* us and *with* us is a great assurance that we have in Jesus Christ: "In all their distress he too was distressed, and the angel of his presence saved them" (Isaiah 63:9).

God was also pained to see His creation going astray:

> The LORD saw how great man's wickedness on the earth had become, and that every inclination of the thoughts of his heart was only evil all the time. The LORD was grieved that he had made man on the earth, and his heart was filled with pain. (Genesis 6:5–6)

> At the same time the Lord promises that if we call upon Him, "I will answer [you]; I will be with [you] in trouble, I will deliver [you] and honor [you]. With long life will I satisfy [you] and show [you] my salvation" (Psalm 91:15–16).

Suffering can come from various sources. We may bring it upon ourselves by our own actions:

> Do not be deceived: God cannot be mocked. A man reaps what he sows. The one who sows to please his sinful nature, from that nature will reap destruction; the one who sows to please the Spirit, from the Spirit will reap eternal life. (Galatians 6:7–9)

However, *it is not true that suffering is always a result of our sin.* For example, Jesus, in John 9, said the blind man's affliction was not caused by sin but was allowed for the purpose of bringing glory to God (vv. 1–3). This is in clear contrast to what Buddhism teaches (namely, that karma is the source of all suffering, including physical deformity).

Paul reminded the Roman Christians,

> We also rejoice in our sufferings, because we know that suffering produces perseverance; perseverance, character; and character, hope. And hope does not disappoint us, because God has poured out his love into our hearts by the Holy Spirit, whom he has given us. (Romans 5:3–5)

The writer of the letter to the Hebrews exhorts us to endure hardship as discipline:

> Let us fix our eyes on Jesus, the author and perfecter of our faith, who for the joy set before him endured the cross, scorning its shame, and sat down at the right hand of the throne of God. Consider him who endured such opposition from sinful men, so that you will not grow weary and lose heart. (12:2–3)

The apostle James also encouraged us:

> Consider it pure joy . . . whenever you face trials of many kinds, because you know that the testing of your faith develops perseverance. Perseverance must finish its work so that you may be mature and complete, not lacking anything. (James 1:2–4)

You can mention to your Buddhist friend that since God suffered for us at Calvary and now intercedes on our behalf, we have the consolation that we are not alone in our difficulties. We also have the hope that the Lord will carry us through every hardship, using each as a means to bring us into knowledge of Him and love for Him, thereby purifying our hearts. Mention that we agree with his (Buddhist) belief that suffering is inevitable and unavoidable *as long as we live in this world*.

For some acts of suffering, we may be able to find an immediate answer. For others, we may not. Either way, suffering cannot be avoided, even though we may have knowledge of *why* we suffer; and suffering cannot be overcome by our efforts alone (*or* through avoiding our desires and following the right paths). It is our dependence upon God and our trust in Him that He will carry us through that helps us grow in maturity.

Please remember that giving advice (or even encouragement) does not reduce the burden of suffering for a friend. In fact, talking about suffering (or rationalizing/justifying it on one ground or another) often annoys and wounds. She could begin to feel that you are more interested in asserting your viewpoint than in participating in her suffering. Often, more than conversation (at a given moment), the sufferer needs companionship, silent support, or a distraction that does not focus on suffering.

My suggestion is that you remember the theological rationale and function of suffering, but never try to expound on it when you are with a person who is hurting. Only when he is ready to receive such knowledge should you talk to him about what the Word of God says about suffering. Meanwhile, the best course is to pray for *and* with him for an effective remedy or solution. Stories of healing and victory from the lives of anointed Christians, by the grace of the Lord from the Word of God, might help your friend at some point, as well. These can illustrate what the apostle Paul wrote to the Corinthians: "Just as the sufferings of Christ flow over into our lives, so also through Christ our comfort overflows" (2 Corinthians 1:5).

It is indeed difficult for a person who is suffering to fully believe in the assurance that "in all things God works for the good of those who love him" (Romans 8:28). This faith can come only by the grace of the Lord, never by human effort.

An early Christian teacher, Irenaeus (c. A.D. 120–202), wrote,

> Perfect knowledge cannot be attained in the present life: many questions must be submissively left in the hands of God. . . . If, however, we cannot discover explanations of all those things in Scripture which are made the subject of investigation, yet let us not on that account seek after any other God besides Him who really exists. (Roberts and Donaldson, 399)

THE BEGINNINGS OF BUDDHISM

3

As we have seen, Buddhism began as a belief system within Hinduism. The members of the Buddhist community deliberately approached life in a way that was distinctive from the manner in which Hindus approached it, although there were many similarities.

HINDUISM AND BUDDHISM

The *distinctiveness* of this new sectarian group revolved around a few clearly distinguished features, as again, the rationale for and plan of salvation suggested by the Buddha had four distinctive elements:

(1) This world is full of suffering. (This assumption is now very commonplace among Hindus and was perhaps shared by them, to some extent, in the past.)
(2) The root cause of all suffering is desire.
(3) Suffering can be brought to an end.
(4) This end can be achieved through one's own individual effort, and for this there is a definite path (the elimination of desire and, ultimately, self).

In Buddhist nirvana, the gods have no role to play. The Buddha was not sure about the real existence (or role) of the gods in the process—again, he was rather agnostic and even anti-god—but at the same time he also was against the Brahmanical rituals and castes. Gautama criticized the Brahman class on several occasions. He asked who had ever seen Brahma face to face. He asked whether the bank of the river Akirvati (in northern India) would move and be placed elsewhere by invoking and praying to Brahma. He insisted that the talk of the Brahmans was ridiculous, mere words, a vain and empty thing.

At one time he declared:

> I do not call a man a Brahmana (Brahman) because of his origin or of his mother. He is indeed arrogant, and he is wealthy: But the poor who is free from all attachments, him I call indeed a Brahmana. (Burtt, 71)

Note, however, that there is an *ideal person* (or *candidate for salvation*) even in Gautama Buddha's teaching (that is, one who overcomes all desire). He was not *eliminating* distinctions between persons but rather *reinterpreting* them (going from an emphasis on birth or wealth to spiritual discipline).

Gautama Buddha also (deliberately, it seems) used colloquial language or dialect rather than Sanskrit, the "sanctified language of the gods," in his discourses. Sanskrit was not permitted to be taught to the lower castes, and the Hindu sacred scriptures (in Sanskrit) were taboo for them. Gautama Buddha was reaching out to all, irrespective of their castes, although in the beginning more people from the intellectually oriented Hindu communities joined the sect.

For devout Buddhists, Gautama Buddha appeals to those who are individualistic in their thinking, belief, and practice. Like most other personages about whom we read (in both nonfiction and fiction), *independence* distinguishes the life history of the Buddha, whose teaching resonates greatly with Westerners who insist on individual freedom that takes precedence over the demands of society and community.

BUDDHISM ON THE MARCH

These features were sufficiently revolutionary to distinguish Buddhists from orthodox Hindus, and throughout the centuries they would be suitably altered for the communities to which the "monk missionaries" took the message. In addition, as a simple strategy, the clergy would initiate a process of accommodation with, and adjustment to, local belief systems, incorporating them as part of the new religion at its lower levels. For instance, many of the nuances that we find in the teachings of the present Dalai Lama are taken from Christian thought and then interwoven as part of the new type of Buddhism he preaches to Westerners. Most Buddhists have no problem with this time-honored process, as their history is full of such alterations and amendments.

It is important for us to see how opposing Brahmanical hierarchy (and replacing it with a distinction between clergy and laity) has not really led to change in the treatment meted out to commoners. Buddhism, both within and outside of India, has made accommodation with the hierarchical organization of the communities.

In the beginning, membership to the Buddhist community was open only to those who did not have any physical deformity. *Removal of caste from the influence or consequence of karma was revolutionary, but it did not eliminate other ills of the worldview obtained through the Hindu looking-glass.* Many adjustments in social values brought about by the novel ideas of Gautama Buddha were nullified through accommodation and adjustment.

BUDDHIST CLERGY

Monks were itinerant preachers and teachers with multilingual skills. The ones who were associated with royal families served the aristocrats and lived in the cities, while the ordinary monks and laypersons who served the masses lived in both cities and rural areas, directly involved in the day-to-day lives of those who depended on their rituals. Even now the clergy recite the 227 monastic rules of discipline as part of their worship, and this recitation is viewed with awe by the laypeople, establishing the monks as spiritually superior.

(The monastic elite—people like the Dalai Lama [now in exile]—and scores of meditationists have come to influence movie stars, politicians, high-profile officials, and famous athletes, who in turn, influence other Westerners. The stage is now set for the re-creation of the international Buddhist community.)

Thus, the most crucial Buddhist distinctions are, first, between clergy and laity and, second, between intellectuals/philosophers and laypersons. Both divisions are seen as acceptable and complementary, so it is possible to view the practices of folk religion in no pejorative sense whatsoever. Even so, monks are believed to have superior spiritual value, and therefore, Buddhism "nevertheless accepted an inequality of spiritual achievement among human beings and their consequent ranking on the basis of karmic action in past lives and in the present" (Tambiah, 11).

WORSHIP

Although the clergy and the laity worship Gautama Buddha together, there are distinctions. For example, the gathering of the sangha (monastic community) is an important local event. Monks convene biweekly (in conjunction with the lunar cycle) to recite the rules of the community. During the rainy season a ceremony is held that focuses on the confession of commissions and omissions, and people offer new robes to the monks.

Festivals and rituals indirectly highlight the importance of the clergy in Buddhist society. They go door to door every morning to receive voluntary alms from laypeople, who consider this gift-giving a merit that will help them eventually to be reborn to better conditions. It is also perceived that the monks themselves receive merit by their mendicant actions because they are helping others to accumulate it, as well.

MEDITATION AND RECITATION AS WORSHIP

With the establishment of various schools of faith and practice, the Buddhist disciplines, especially meditation, became significant rituals. These include the day-to-day activities of life, such as reciting the three vows (see chapter 2), walking through villages and receiving alms, giving lessons to pupils, sitting, solving puzzles and riddles, debating, reciting the verses, and figuring out the meaning of utterances. (Living in a monastery is a discipline in itself.) Among the monks, there are orders that are stricter in the observance of disciplines than others.

WORSHIP OF RELICS AND SITES

Worship of the relics of the Buddha and his disciples plays a more important role in the lives of ordinary people than most other acts of piety—coupled with pilgrimage, this worship is perhaps the most intense of all spiritual experiences for the laity. Relics are placed in caskets, which are kept in a stupa (a tall pillarlike structure) or caitya (a tumulus, mound over a grave), and people visit these monuments to burn incense and make offerings. (Gradually, the containers of the relics were also considered to be sacred, whether they contained anything or not.)

This time-honored practice began with the adoration of the sacred sites associated with the birth, awakening, first preaching, and death of the Buddha, and other places, events, and objects associated with his immediate disciples were added in due course, a process continued with the display of the supposedly original body parts and other objects associated with Gautama Buddha and other important personages. Since this occurred wherever Buddhism was taken, growing mythology ensured there would be sacred places that merited pilgrimage—such as trees, hills, rivers, and waterfalls—in every Buddhist nation.

The Buddhist focuses on Gautama Buddha, his individual disciples, and the spirits in and around his locality of worship. He goes around the stupa (or temple, or casket) several times in prayerful mode. Again, local pre-Buddhist or non-Buddhist belief systems are easily integrated into the worship ritual. For example, in Sri Lanka, some of the Hindu places were included as places of Buddhist worship. In Japan, the kami (nature spirits) adored in Shinto (native Japanese religion) were identified with the Buddha and Bodhisattvas. In China, Manjusri (a great Bodhisattva with the sword of wisdom who was reputed to have performed miraculous acts and who could bestow intellectual skills to his devotees) was treated as an inhabitant of mountains that were considered to be sacred even before Buddhism arrived—popular pilgrimage centers were given new Buddhist meaning within the Chinese context, and the Bodhisattvas were transformed into Chinese Bodhisattvas, so to speak. In Burma and Thailand, the footprints of Gautama Buddha were associated with indigenous spirits that were guardians of pilgrimage sites.

The tree commonly shown in Buddhist sculptures and paintings represents the tree under which Gautama Buddha received his awakening. (The throne also represents the awakening.) The stupa represents his nirvana, and the wheel represents the doctrine of samsara (cycle of birth, death, and rebirth). These symbols likewise represent the folk beliefs derived from mythologies and local traditions.

THE BUDDHIST CALENDAR

In addition to appropriating the sacred places of pre-Buddhist and non-Buddhist belief as its own, Buddhism also adopted local calendars as its own and added new Buddhist meaning, including festivals organized in honor of great Buddhist leaders during local pre-Buddhist celebrations. For example, the All Soul's festival in China is supplemented with Buddhist elements. In Sri Lanka, there are festivals honoring the Buddha in various stages of his life, as well as one celebrating the arrival of the earliest Buddhist missionaries. The Indian emperor Asoka [270–232 B.C.], who was instrumental in the spread of Buddhism in India and beyond, after his conversion sent his son Mahindra as a Buddhist missionary to Sri Lanka.

In Tibet and in Tibetan cultural areas (such as Bhutan), the celebration of the arrival of Buddhism is an integral part of the calendar. The defeat of local demons with the advent of Buddhism is celebrated as a tremendous festival, and Buddhist deities and leaders in the history of Tibetan Buddhism are celebrated, with the integration of Buddhist and indigenous spiritist traditions.

RITUALS

The rituals connected with the initiation of a Buddhist male into adulthood are common in several Buddhist nations, especially in Southeast Asia, and these are being copied in other nations where they had not earlier been practiced. Initiation of a non-Buddhist to the Dharma (Law) is fine-tuned with several rituals, including the recitation of the vows (or verses from the teachings of Gautama Buddha) or other sectarian vows and mantras and the total shaving of the head. Children from Buddhist homes may be taught in the monasteries, and in Thailand and Burma, some may take temporary initiation to the order as part of their entry into adulthood, while others may opt for initiation into the full monastic order.

Cremation is the most common form of funeral rite in Theravada countries, following a supposedly original (and very particular) order of rites performed when Gautama Buddha was consumed by fire. Elitist, noble, and rich families (and clergy) are thus cremated; rituals, care, and adoration for the dead are elaborate in both the Theravada and Mahayana traditions, and the merit that one obtains through right conduct and rituals can allegedly be transferred to the deceased relatives.

New and impressive Buddhist rituals attracted attention in the communities the monks entered; they received the Buddhist rituals in addition to their own, and hence there was no real competition between the two. Once the religion was established in the new community, rituals became prestigious hallmarks, becoming synonymous with the religion itself.

Buddhist literature tells us, though, that there were controversies related to ritualistic practice. Some argued that making offerings to sangha (the community of monks) has more merit than worshiping the symbols, insisting that while relics are the remainders of a dead person, the sangha is a thriving association of living persons. Moreover, it was said, supporting the sangha is supporting the community—both clergy and laity. Others argued, in contrast, that the worship of Gautama Buddha in any form—stupa, bodhi, throne, etc.—is far superior to serving a living monk because the Buddha is already in a state of nirvana, superior to others who have not reached it.

The rituals performed in the Mahayana tradition (see chapter 6) focus on three aspects:

1. declaring individual faults;
2. rejoicing over the merit others have acquired through meritorious service; and

3. pleading with and praying to all Bodhisattvas to remain in this world in order to help suffering beings.

A Mahayana Buddhist may perform these rituals three times during the day and three times during the night (six times daily). Worship, offered with incense, centers on praying to the Bodhisattvas to save the petitioners from danger and to improve their spiritual and material well-being. Also, images of Gautama Buddha and others are bathed in perfume, clothed, and carried around in musical procession. Meditation likewise plays an important role, although not for the common people, who are encouraged to follow the worship and rituals.

BUDDHISM AS A MISSIONARY RELIGION

Buddhism was a missionary movement almost from the beginning. The disciples of Gautama Buddha traveled far and wide, taking with them their master's ideals. They denounced the Hindu idea of pollution between social groups. For example, members of the Hindu upper castes would not dine together with the members of the lower castes. Small groups traveled throughout India and beyond, establishing themselves as sanghas in the popular trade routes, often in cities or nearby camps. They mostly merged with local populations and, again, generally approved, adopted, or accepted beliefs and practices. However, at least in Tibet and Mongolia, Buddhist monks ruthlessly suppressed pre-Buddhist religion (not with great success).

Because assimilation, adoption, and accommodation of indigenous communal beliefs was a hallmark of Buddhist missionary effort, local chieftains, businessmen, princes, and kings supported the monasteries, which functioned also as centers of learning. The sanghas were adored for the serenity of their surroundings and for their rejection of worldly life in favor of spiritual pursuits.

A WAY OF LIFE, NOT A RELIGION?

Buddhism presented itself as a way of life that served various groups of people: asceticism and contemplation for some, moral discipline and right modes of living for the ordinary majority, devotion to objects of worship for commoners, and magic, alchemy, and exorcism for the masses who depended on the curative processes offered by the monks. Methods or modes of choice for making progress in a spiritual journey are individual, each Buddhist being expected to chart his or her own course of salvation (the pace of achievement varying from one individual to another).

It was during the reign of the Indian emperor Asoka that the sanghas became more involved with the laity, and the Buddhist state became an instrument in the hands of communities to preach Buddhism as a way of life for other nations. Asoka, in addition to sending missionaries, encouraged the practice of meditation and pilgrimage, laying great emphasis on the proper and effective functioning of the sanghas and also protecting and honoring them as the chief means of propagating Buddhist teaching.

Throughout history, Buddhism has leaned heavily on royal power, attracting elites at the helm of national affairs, and, through their good offices, has been able to reach out to the masses. This does not, however, minimize the importance of missionary efforts. Buddhism was preached as a way of life for the community even as it offered explicit methods for seeking salvation.

Even though Hinduism and Buddhism are apparently divergent religions, there was and is a common strand in the acceptance of karma, samsara, idolatry, asceticism, emphasis on ritual as a means to gain spiritual merit, and magic. These similarities help modern Hindus and Buddhists interested in self-oriented salvation to forge a united front in preaching their ideals to Western societies. Nevertheless, conflicts between caste-oriented Hinduism and relatively casteless Buddhism are being highlighted through the mass conversion of lower castes to Buddhism, especially the so-called "untouchables" (the Dalits) in modern India. Buddhism, both past and present, is actually redesigning the caste institution rather than eliminating it (explained elsewhere).

With the secularization of the Western world, it has become possible for people of other faiths to live in Western society without being influenced or changed by Christianity. Christians are now primarily in the position of *responding* in order to counter what is presented and propagated by non-Christians. On the other hand, in parts of Asia and Africa, people more regularly value their religious faith, identifying the practice of it with patriotism and national fervor, which leaves opportunity for Buddhist expansion.

THE ATTRIBUTES OF BUDDHA

4

There are three important ways by which the Buddha is made known. *First,* the Buddhist scriptures often use descriptive words or phrases rather than his personal names (Gautama or Siddhartha); these are the epithets used to describe his nature. *Second,* the life stories that narrate the Buddha's ministry and enlightenment are told. *Third,* the images that visually represent Gautama Buddha reinforce his character in the minds of Buddhists.

EPITHETS

The terms that refer to Gautama Buddha focus on his characteristics, his person, his immanence, and his transcendence. "Buddha" (meaning "the Enlightened One") is the most commonly used epithet, and he is also called "the teacher of gods and men." His earthly lineage is used in the term *Sakyamuni* (sage of the Sakya clan or kingdom). The name "Siddhartha" means "the person whose goals (or aims) are achieved." He was called a *mahapurusha,* a "great person," and referred to as the "emperor," "monarch," or "lord" (*bhagvan*) of the universe. One of the most popular epithets is *tathagata,* meaning "such and such, come and gone."

Of the hundred or more classical epithets referring to the Buddha, most create in the user a sense of mystery, with no explicitly describable meaning. Ambiguity, metaphor, and mystery are three prominent elements of not only the epithets of Buddha but also the descriptions of Buddhist theology. Polysemy (multiple meanings of a word) and the pun are two important techniques adopted by Buddhist commentators.

No wonder, then, that Buddhists consider this life to be a riddle (and solving riddles to be an instrument of meditation).

Repetitive recitation and memorization of the names of Gautama Buddha help Buddhists to mentally shape and visualize his image—these are forms of meditation and, therefore, spiritual works.

LIFE STORIES

The narratives that illustrate the ministry and enlightenment of Gautama Buddha have been embellished throughout history. With the spread of Buddhism in Asian nations, these stories began to portray Gautama as a superhuman, magical, mythical, and transcendent being, to the neglect of his human nature (along with his human deficiencies). He is said to have preached not only to his disciples but to future Buddhas as well—from the mountaintops to nature around him and to those in other worlds of the heavenly realm. The Buddhist chronicles do not focus only on his ministry in the person of Gautama Buddha but also on all the lives he had until he attained total liberation.

Buddhists mix the historical and the mythical (fictitious, nonexistent, or imaginary) elements in their meditation on and worship of the Buddha. Thus, while sharing our faith with our Buddhist friends, we need to carefully distinguish between the teaching of the *historical* Gautama Buddha, who lived on this earth as a human being, and the episodes in the life of the *mythical* Buddha. We deal with the former based on what he is said to have spoken and on the theological assumptions illustrated in his teachings; the latter needs to be considered as representing spirits, similar to those attached to idols. (The Bible calls these idols worthless even as it recognizes the spirits that reside in them.) While untruth in Gautama's words can be countered through analysis, the spirits of mythology must be checked with fervent prayer.

The modern tendency to look at Gautama Buddha as a social philosopher, rationalistic in his approach and revolutionary in his handling of socioeconomic disparities of his era, is taken to an extreme level: *This is an attempt to separate, in an idealized manner, the historical Buddha from the mythical Buddha.* In the day-to-day life of a Buddhist, historical characteristics (social reformation and philosophy) often take a backseat to the supposed powers of myth and miracle.

IMAGES

Images and relics of the Buddha play a crucial role in the continuity of Buddhism. These concrete objects bring the transcendent Buddha nearer to the people; seeing an image is seeing Gautama Buddha alive.

Buddhist theology is imparted through portraits and representations, and it is assumed that the essence of the Buddha actually resides in them.

While images are prominent, objects associated with the life history of Gautama Buddha, such as the bodhi tree and the wheel of dharma (generally speaking, a graphic representation of the eightfold path in the form of a wheel with eight spokes), may also be used as vehicles of meditation. Images and symbols are offered flowers, incense, music, food, clothes, and drink, just as we find in Hindu temples.

Visits to the holy places are extremely important for the pious Buddhist. Once again, apart from the renowned pilgrimage sites associated with Gautama Buddha's birth, renunciation, enlightenment, first sermon, and ministry, every Buddhist nation abounds in sites that are supposed to have preserved original relics of Gautama Buddha or even early ambassadors of Buddhist doctrine.

How Many Buddhas?

According to a time-honored Buddhist text (written by Nagarjuna in the first century), Gautama is only one among the thousands of Buddhas before and after him (an old belief noted even in the early Buddhist writings—we have no choice but to treat these Buddhas as mythological persons). An interesting insight is the belief that they *all* followed the same route to enlightenment: they were brought up in luxury, they later confronted the realities of life, they gave up their wealth to become wandering monks, and they attained enlightenment through contemplation. According to Buddhist tradition, they also chose to preach what they experienced and taught the same truth as Gautama Buddha. The persons who attained the status of "Buddha" are diverse, but their life history, experience, and enlightenment process followed the same series of events in each case.

A Buddha appears in the world under various circumstances. According to the Theravada scriptures (among other sources), a Buddha is recognized by special marks on his body and limbs, miraculous signs at his birth, his demonstration of magical powers, his calm mental posture, his speech and purity, etc. *The world can have only one Buddha at a time, and for the present age, Gautama Buddha is the Buddha.* A new Buddha is born (or arrives) only when the teachings of the earlier Buddha are forgotten; he is born not in the beginning of an eon (*kalpa* in Sanskrit) because at that point people may live happily without sickness, aging, suffering, or death. *Only when suffering increases in the world do people begin to seek ways to overcome it,* and when they are ready to receive a Buddha, then one is born for that age. Tradition and texts teach that a Buddha is born only in Jambudvipa (India), either in a family of priests (the Brahman [highest] caste) or in a family of nobles (the Kshatriya [second-highest] caste).

Buddhist texts assume that there are numerous (or even an infinite number of) future Buddhas waiting to be born. In the Theravada tradition (see chapter 5), the future Buddha or Bodhisattva is called *Maitreya*, which means "the friendly one." At this time he is a Bodhisattva (a person on the path to buddhahood), waiting for the time of his birth, when he will begin the new era of peace, prosperity, and salvation.

In the Mahayana tradition (see chapter 6), the future Buddha or Bodhisattva is called *Amitabha*, which means "boundless or unlimited light." Amitabha had already attained enlightenment but decided to postpone his nirvana so he could help other creatures attain their peace.

Some pious Buddhists (mostly folk practitioners) also believe there are "living Buddhas" ("great gurus") in this world, persons who may have attained Buddha status through secret (esoteric) practices and have comprehended the meaning of hidden texts, revealing their hidden truth (interpretation) to help others move forward in their own enlightenment journey. Commentators, monks, teachers, and missionaries were often treated as living Buddhas, seen to be incarnations of some heavenly Buddha.

Buddhist texts insist that once a person attains buddhahood, there is no distinction between him and other Buddhas. However, this is at the *theological* level; in the life of the ordinary Buddhist, each Buddha is perceived as having special and distinctive merit and is, consequently, in a unique position (with specific powers and abilities) to help his devotees in their journey.

Buddhists view Gautama as a great soul, noble in character and diligent in his pursuit of enlightenment, a man who sacrificed personal luxury to seek truth. They look to him as their leader even as they view him to be divine (at least in some manner). Nevertheless, while the idea that Gautama and his teachings are there to assist in the achievement of salvation is an attractive picture painted in the minds of sincere Buddhists, the portrait is fuzzy and misleading in many ways.

THE PROBLEM OF POLYTHEISM

Polytheism (belief in/worship of more than one deity) is something we need to discuss with our Buddhist friends since, as mentioned above, supposedly there are thousands of Buddhas. The Bible condemns polytheism because it cheapens the glory of God and wrongly elevates spirits, persons, and other beings and objects, which do not deserve to be worshiped or praised, to His level. Idolatry occurs when *natural* cultural elements are imposed on the *supernatural,* which means the divine is seen through human values.

A Buddha, at best, is a leader whom a person may emulate; he does not participate in the life of the individual, as does Jesus. The decision of the Bodhisattva that he will not immediately enter the final liberation stage (total nirvana, the ultimate stage beyond enlightenment) is laudable as a grand theme, but this in no way helps people in their journey—he is merely a model. (This is one of the reasons, perhaps, that Buddhist theology had to work out an elaborate code of conduct for people on the road to salvation, on which Bodhisattvas become objects of meditation.) At any rate, *if Bodhisattvas have to be shown as active participants in our efforts at salvation, helping us in some tangible way, then the self-help salvation scheme of Buddhism falls apart.*

Jesus, in contrast, is an ever-present companion and does not keep himself aloof (see Matthew 11:28). When we have an opportunity to present our faith in Him as Lord and Savior, this might be the most important point to bring to the attention of our Buddhist friends. We need to tell them that the Lord Jesus wants to transform us into His image. His unconditional love and unceasing grace for *all* of us is the model that brings complete peace, not ritual, sacrifice, or asceticism. The presence in our midst of the Holy Spirit, the Comforter left behind for us after the earthly ministry of Jesus, not only convicts us regarding our actions, thoughts, and words but also separates us from the evil surrounding us.

RENUNCIATION OF THIS WORLD?

This world and all we find in it are created by God and therefore originally good. Marriage is instituted by God and is likewise good. Leaving one's own wife and children behind in order to seek salvation may be justified in Buddhist social, cultural, and theological terms, but when seen from the viewpoint of others—such as the wife and children—it amounts to putting others through suffering. Consequently, a Buddha who wants to liberate himself from suffering puts those who love him through more suffering. Furthermore, even though Buddhism started in objection to the Brahmanic rituals and caste hierarchy practiced among the Hindus, Buddhist texts suggest that Buddhas are born only in the higher castes and only in certain lands.

The worship and adoration of the images and relics of Gautama Buddha come into conflict with the Bible, which condemns idolatry and consequent rituals, offerings, and sacrifices. Your Buddhist friend may have great difficulty understanding and following this, as images have had great centrality in his life—giving up his devotion in this area will seem to mean he is giving up his being. The matter, then, must be raised with tremendous care and without showing disrespect for the objects or images.

BUDDHA AND JESUS

A major Buddhist problem is that at one level a Buddha is treated only as a human being, while at another level he is treated as an incarnation. At one level, a Buddha is not a god, but at another level, he is treated as a god, capable of answering the supplications of faithful petitioners and performing miracles.

Jesus came from heaven to live among us as a man. He is fully divine *and* totally human, God in His incarnation as Jesus the Christ. The Word of God also suggests that the Trinity—the Father, the Son, and the Holy Spirit—are co-eternal, while a Buddha is part of the cycle of birth, death, and rebirth, man being elevated (at times) to the level of a god.

The ministry of Jesus was, is, and will ever be for those who are lacking in spirit and body. Gautama Buddha represents an elaborate philosophical superiority, whereas Jesus represents the selfless servanthood that focuses on the poor, the needy, and the dregs of society. This *does not* mean Gautama Buddha was haughty or boastful about his caste or his socioeconomic background or his spiritual attainment. It *does* mean his dominant feature was intellectualism, not service to others.

Gautama Buddha exemplified the use of intellect in improving one's spiritual position. Jesus' appeal is to our hearts, full of emotions, passions, sins, and love. Intelligence is not the chief criterion for becoming a disciple of Christ, nor is a beautiful or perfect human body. Even during the ministry of Gautama Buddha, the blind and the lame and the infirm were not taken into the order of his followers. On the other hand, *all* were and are fully welcomed to be disciples of Jesus.

In terms of evangelism, this comparison of the goals of the ministries of Jesus and of Buddha should be presented (1) in a manner that applies to the immediate needs of your Buddhist friend, and (2) in such a way that he can relate to the ministry of Jesus and the social positions of his family, friends, and the poor and needy Buddhists in his home country.

Even with endless births and deaths and rebirths, there is no guarantee that one would ever attain ultimate enlightenment simply by following the behavioral and disciplinary codes laid down within Buddhism. The risk is enormous, and the mere thought of the enormity of the venture makes one give up hope. Therefore, is it the goal of Buddhist teaching to filter out people from the salvation path—from salvation itself—and condemn them to samsara? A hopeless situation, indeed!

THERAVADA BUDDHISM

5

MAJOR SCHOOLS OR DIVISIONS OF BUDDHISM

As we have seen, Buddhism started as a small sectarian community, but over the centuries it has grown to be a religion of many nations. There are references to Buddhist practices in the writings of the early church fathers, and while Buddhism is largely an Asian religion, it has followers all over the world.

Since Buddhism has many independent divisions, we can easily miss something, or focus on one aspect over another, when we try to define what Buddhism is. A true picture of Buddhism may emerge not merely from a comprehension of its established philosophy or theology but also from an understanding of the communal beliefs and practices of Buddhists. Since written as well as unwritten traditions and practices dominate the lives of its adherents, Buddhism is more a way of life, like Hinduism, than a single religion with uniform theology and practice.

Knowing this fact helps us when we wish to share our faith with a Buddhist. Often a Buddhist is one who believes in a number of systems—some from the orthodox faiths, some from his or her ethnic group, and others from his or her region. These may be in conflict with or even contradictory to one another, but this is considered acceptable. More often than not, the Buddhist is governed by belief and teaching that is a combination of (1) dominant ethnic and national beliefs and (2) traditions appropriated from the substratum of ancient folk beliefs. Your Buddhist friend is a conscious and deliberate member of a community, even though he or she may be living abroad, away from home.

GENERAL CHARACTERISTICS OF BUDDHIST COMMUNITIES

In every Buddhist society, the most significant person is Gautama Buddha. Despite the fact that there are many Buddhas, the point of reference in all Buddhism somehow relates to this historical person—a model, a teacher, and a deity to be worshiped. Other important elements are nonviolence, monastic organization (sangha), the goal of attaining nirvana through the practice of various disciplines, becoming totally empty (sunyata), and nonself (total extinction). The process in achieving these is deliberate, and a person may receive some assistance from others, but it is primarily axiomatic that self-help is the way to achieve nirvana.

WHO IS A THERAVADA (OR HINAYANA) BUDDHIST?

A Theravada or Hinayana Buddhist is *ordinarily* a native of Sri Lanka, Myanmar, Thailand, Laos, or Cambodia. "Theravada" means "the teaching of the elders." People may refer to Theravada as "Southern Buddhism" in contrast to Mahayana (see chapter 6), which is called "Northern Buddhism." The word *Hinayana* may be translated "lesser or smaller vehicle" (of salvation), while *Mahayana* means "greater vehicle" (of salvation). Early Mahayana writers used the word *Hinayana* as a derogatory term, and Theravada Buddhists do not generally like to be referred to this way.

There are several major differences between Theravada and Mahayana, but one worth mentioning here is the assumption of Mahayana that salvation is available to both clergy and laity. Theravada, on the other hand, emphasizes the likelier possibility of salvation for monks.

OFFICIAL RELIGION OF SEVERAL NATIONS

Theravada Buddhism is more or less the official religion of Myanmar, Cambodia, Laos, and Thailand (in Sri Lanka it has government support); thus, Theravada has great influence over civil and military authority in these nations. This is another key difference: Mahayana does not have this kind of sway in China, Japan, Korea, Taiwan, and Vietnam, though widely practiced, and even though the governments may recognize it.

PRIDE IN THE HERITAGE

Theravada is probably the oldest/earliest expression of Buddhism. Naturally, then, a Theravada Buddhist feels proud of and zealous for his heritage and may consider himself to be "orthodox" in holding to the means of salvation shown by Gautama Buddha himself. Even so, he agrees with the other Buddhists in acknowledging many similarities among the practitioners of Buddhism despite different nationalities or linguistic groups. Therefore, at one level the Theravada Buddhist may see himself to be distinct from people practicing forms of Buddhism other than his own, while at the same time maintaining that they are also Buddhists.

Most of the sacred Theravada texts are in Pali, believed to be a language (or dialect) spoken by the Buddha himself (recall that *Sanskrit* was considered prestigious and "elite"). Pali is no longer used in day-to-day life and is inaccessible except through these texts. So even in the choice of dialect, a Theravada Buddhist sees in religious discourses the need to use a medium that is accessible to everyone.

MAINTAINING A DISTINCT IDENTITY

Theravada has many similar beliefs to Mahayana, but the Theravada Buddhist always tries to keep himself distinct from the latter, particularly with morals and ethics. The followers of Theravada know that there are fascinating mythologies surrounding the worship of Mahayana deities, and they recognize that Mahayana has developed new expressions and impressive philosophy, yet most Theravada Buddhists are not attracted to Mahayana.

The exemplary model for a Theravada Buddhist is the Arhat (or Arhant), a person (such as the disciples of Gautama Buddha) who has successfully (and individually) worked out his salvation. Another difference between Theravada and Mahayana is the former's belief that monastic life helps in this process, equipping a person to be detached from this world and giving him freedom to practice the Buddhist disciplines, thus living a life that enhances the chances of salvation (nirvana).

So your Theravada Buddhist friend may even have had some monastic life experience as part of his adult initiation. He will try, whenever possible, to emulate asceticism (at least temporarily). When an opportunity presents itself, gently point out that neither rituals nor disciplines nor any other type of works—including meditation, almsgiving, and image worship—will help us attain salvation. (Related scriptural references are included later.)

Though you can expect to see your Theravada Buddhist friend as an intensely individualistic person, this does not mean that he is anti-social. Even while remaining a member or part of a group, actively participating and contributing, a Theravada Buddhist is usually aloof, for he believes that ultimately it is he, on his own, who should bear the burden of his salvation.

INDIVIDUALISM AND TOLERANCE

Individualism is the core of Theravada Buddhism, and adherents, even monks, may be discipled or mentored only in a superficial sense.

Accordingly, you should not approach your friend with an explicit posture of mentoring or discipling. One of the chief characteristics of a Theravada Buddhist is to accept and tolerate differences as a way of life while holding on to his own.

If your Theravada friend is educated well in her religion, she will consider the details of religious debates (between various monks and schools) to be very important. However, if she comes from a folk religious family that *acknowledges* the importance of debated knowledge for salvation but does not *focus* on it, then she may simply smile when theological issues are raised. In such a case, she does not feel the need to study the details because she looks at life as a slow (samsara-based) progression toward nirvana.

THERAVADA BUDDHISM IN SRI LANKA

If your Buddhist friend comes from Sri Lanka, you need to find out if he or she is a Sinhalese, Tamil, Muslim, or Burgher. Tamil names usually reveal whether a person is a Hindu, Christian, or Muslim—there are hardly any Buddhists among them. Sinhalese are mostly Buddhists and sometimes have names that resemble Portuguese or other European names.

Sri Lankan Buddhists believe Gautama Buddha himself preached there, and as mentioned, Emperor Asoka sent his close relatives to them as Buddhist missionaries. (Theravada spread eastward from Sri Lanka to Myanmar, Thailand, Laos, and Cambodia.) Buddha's footprint in stone is worshiped on one of the Sri Lankan peaks, and it is claimed that one of his teeth is in one of the island's towns. Furthermore, Theravada Buddhists in Sri Lanka adore a tree believed to have grown out of the shoot (or branch) of the tree under which Gautama Buddha is claimed to have attained his enlightenment. Buddhist images and pictures (receiving daily offerings and prayers) adorn Sinhalese homes, and shrines are common. People in large numbers visit Buddhist temples and go on pilgrimages to Buddhist sacred centers.

The Sri Lankan Sinhalese population—which comprises nearly 75 percent of the Sri Lankan population, and of which nearly 95 percent are Buddhist—has been Buddhist for at least two thousand years. There is a continued emphasis on the identity of the Sinhalese as Theravada Buddhists; rituals, schooling, literature, folklore, and secular activities encourage the continuation and maintenance of this inseparable identity between the two. A major part of sharing your faith with a Sri Lankan Theravada Buddhist would revolve around praying fervently that he or she would see that accepting Jesus as Lord and Savior is not a threat to ethnic identity and culture.

Ethnic Strife

Sri Lanka has two major nationalities, namely, the Tamil minority and the Sinhalese majority. As we said, Tamils are non-Buddhist (predominantly Hindu, with a significant number of Muslim and Christian communities), whereas again, the vast majority of the Sinhalese population is Buddhist. (There are also other groups, including a small community called Veddah that claims to be or is considered to be the island's original inhabitants before the Sinhalese arrived from northern [or eastern] India.)

For centuries the Sinhalese and Tamil communities were at war to establish themselves as the dominant Sri Lankan group. Ethnic identities got mixed up with linguistic and religious identities, and as a result, Buddhism has come to represent Sinhalese nationalism and patriotism for the Sinhalese majority—loyalty to Buddhism is loyalty to the Sinhalese cause, and thus, Buddhism is much more than a religious faith.

Religion and Politics

There is a strong unwritten historical relationship between the sangha, the laity, and the government in Sri Lanka. The monks take upon themselves the role of protector not only of Buddhism but also of its supremacy as the religion of the island. They have day-to-day contact with the laypeople, which ensures respect and reverence for Buddhism. Since they are seen to be self-sacrificing in their ways (they have "renounced the world"), and since they represent the traditional body of knowledge and wisdom, people continue to admire them and look to them for guidance in social and political matters. The government, in turn, is greatly influenced by the people.

With your Theravada friend, therefore, be sure you do not criticize the Buddhist order. As time passes, and when the opportunity presents itself, offer constructive information as to how the body of Christ becomes the support—spiritual and material—to those who follow Jesus as Lord and Savior. Show that our focus is on how we follow Jesus as He has commanded in the Word of God, and that this engenders love for all and a readiness to edify and encourage one another.

Your Theravada friend from Sri Lanka may not openly display prejudice against Hinduism, and he or she may even worship or pay obeisance to certain Hindu gods, but when it comes to discussing the Tamil issue, he or she is bound to be agitated. Do not focus your discussions on ethnic relations, but as a well-meaning Christian, use language of understanding and gentleness that enables your friend to look at the interracial rivalry from a position of love. Pray for the Sri Lankan church to be a leaven to bring amity between the warring Tamils and Sinhalese—we are called upon to be peacemakers.

Caste

Although Gautama Buddha preached against Hindu doctrine that placed one social group over another, caste and other divisions based on status still dominate the thinking of Theravada Buddhists in Sri Lanka. The Sinhalese avoided the classificatory order of peoples into Brahman (priestly caste), Kshatriya (the warrior class), Vaishya (the businessman/agriculturist class) and Sudra (the servant class), as well as the class of the so-called untouchables, but they still have a system that ranks people by their birth and occupation (and orders them to shun marriage outside of caste). While Buddhist loyalty is used to foster Sinhalese identity, insistence on internal caste distinctions divides rather than unites the Sinhalese people.

Everyone is born into a group, and *this* social position cannot be changed. The superiority or inferiority of a caste is based on the extent of the "purity" of the occupations pursued by its members. A person is born in a higher caste, allegedly, because of his purity in previous births, and he needs to protect this purity from pollution by contact with "less pure" people. Members of every caste should practice the norms of purity available to them so that their lot in future births will be better than what they have right now.

The ranking of the individuals within a caste depends upon many factors, including tradition and wealth. Strangely, even though "purity of birth" is supposedly based on karma, if members of the so-called lower castes prosper and accumulate wealth, *perception* about the social ranking of their castes among others may change.

Many people from the Karava (fisherman) caste, often found in the coastal areas, have been converted to Christianity. Because of the spread of Western education (mainly through the labor of Christian missionaries in the past) and secular democratic practices, the link between the castes and their professions is losing its significance. Nonetheless, a Theravada Buddhist who chooses to follow the Lord Jesus Christ may face the danger of becoming estranged from his close-knit extended family, losing his caste ranking, and not being able to find suitable spouses for his children within his caste.

There is no legal or governmental barrier against people choosing their own faith, but the collective pressure of Theravada society against following Jesus is a great hindrance. Despite these difficulties, Sri Lankan Buddhists were and are attracted to Christ; the vast majority of the Christians there have come mainly from this background, and there are influential churches and pastors among them.

Social Aspects

Most Sinhalese are monogamous; however, there is no theological barrier for a man to marry more than one woman, even when his wife is still alive. We also hear occasionally about a woman having more than one husband simultaneously. Divorce is easy to get but is not widely practiced; in fact, Sinhalese marriage is as stable as Hindu marriage in India. As in India, women form a substantial part of the labor force at the lower levels among the Sinhalese, working hard in the fields, as domestic servants, and in many different kinds of menial jobs. Women have also risen to hold powerful positions in government.

There are three major sects within Sri Lankan Theravada Buddhism: Goyigama (upper castes), the Amarapura sect of Karava (fishermen caste), and Ramanna Nikaya (no caste affiliation). There is no central spiritual authority: monasteries have their own independence, and their popularity among the laypeople varies (a clear distinction is maintained between clergy and laity). Supporting the monastic order, faithfully performing one's duties (both secular and religious), and showing compassion to all living organisms become the hallmark of laypeople on their way to nirvana in successive births (a journey that is accelerated by supporting the monks).

Folk Buddhism

Popular (or folk) Buddhism practiced in Sri Lanka is similar to folk Hinduism in India. Folk Buddhists treat Gautama Buddha as a god, elevating him to divine status, and their obeisance to the images of Buddha and his disciples are more in the form of deity worship than honoring or showing respect or reverence to accomplished individuals. There is widespread worship of images and relics, which are believed to have magical powers. For example, in one of the most popular and sacred Buddhist temples in Kandy, Buddha's image is worshiped with offerings of food and clothing, and to his followers he becomes a divine being with super spatio-temporal powers to control and supervise everyone and everything in this world and beyond.

Although Gautama Buddha was noncommittal or refused to comment on the existence and powers of divine beings, the laypeople believe in the pantheon of gods. Folk Theravada Buddhists believe that the Buddha allows smaller deities to regulate the worlds, operating within set boundaries. Since these spiritual beings are now endowed with the powers to regulate what happens within their authority, it is considered wise to pray to them for welfare and prosperity.

Small temples, close to the temples of Buddha, are set up for these spiritual beings, just as we find with the Hindus of southern India. Buddhist devotees visit the main temple and then pay their obeisance to these lesser deities, presenting their prayers and requests and making offerings. The deities that were popular in one generation may not be popular in another, again, similar to Hinduism. There is a widespread practice of propitiating the demons through rituals and exorcism. This is performed away from the temples but attracts large crowds of Theravada Buddhist spectators.

Ethnic Syncretism

Folk practices in Sri Lanka actually unite tension-ridden communities, so ethnic syncretism plays a significant role in the day-to-day life of a folk Theravada Buddhist, who accepts the deities of the Hindus and even some of the Muslim sages. As the lesser deities are common to both groups, Tamils and Sinhalese both visit their temples. Muslims have their shrines nearby and practice the folk beliefs of the Buddhist and Hindu ethnic groups with some variation.

Monasteries have provided education and discipline to all, but everyday Theravada Buddhist life is influenced more by the beliefs and practices of folk Buddhism, with its animism and spirit worship. So you need to know what animism is (see chapter 11) and why spirit worship is against the Word of God. Show your Buddhist friend that animistic beliefs and practices do not lead to the Lord, nor do they help people to attain salvation. Since a Theravada Buddhist considers himself to be practicing the orthodox (or original) religion, we could even use some of the thoughts and sayings of Gautama Buddha to demonstrate why we should not indulge in the worship of spirits.

In an indirect manner, find out whether your Sri Lankan friend worships only Gautama Buddha or the lesser deities, as well. In all probability, she makes no distinction because each of these appeals to her various needs. So your strategy should be to talk to her about how the Lord Jesus Christ cast out the demons and how, by His crucifixion, we are forever freed from our bondage to spiritual beings. When you have developed a closer relationship, pray for her and with her. Don't allow the "spiritual" or "religious" side to take an upper hand; it is attending to the practical elements of life that usually develops understanding between individuals.

More Sinhalese women than men are subjected to spirit possession and exorcism. If your friend is an unmarried Sinhalese woman, pray continuously for her peace of mind. An important point for discussion is how one can be released from the clutches of spirits. She is also likely to be concerned about her family, and since women are expected to wed and bear children, there is often some concern about marriage.

Rituals and Clerical Initiation

Theravada rituals are not as elaborate as those in Mahayana or Vajrayana, but Theravada has its own share of periodic rites in monasteries, shrines, and households. Monks chant verses to protect the nation, community, and individuals and their families from disasters. Festivals to remember the birth, enlightenment, and death of Gautama Buddha are celebrated with solemnity and majesty. Ceremonies for the initiation of Buddhist novices and for the ordination of monks are held. There are traditional rainy-season retreats in the monasteries, during which the laity offer cloth to the clergy (to enable them to make their robes), as well as monastic meetings according to new moons and full moons, and pilgrimages to sacred places—all of these are important in the life of a Theravada Buddhist.

Buddhist temples have strict traditional protocol as to rituals and participants. For example, in the Kandy Temple in Sri Lanka that houses the tooth-relic (the tooth of Gautama Buddha), there are rigid guidelines as to who is permitted to enter the various chambers. Social and political ranks are used as a yardstick. The methods for the *puja* (worship of the relics and images) are strictly followed. Processions around the city with various containers of holy objects, the opening of these in the presence of dignitaries, and the showing of the holy relics among the distinguished and elite are all done with magnificent devotion and paraphernalia—musical instruments, flags, etc.

(It must be noted that the Word of God is clearly against the performance of empty rituals. In the early part of the history of the Israelites, we read about their elaborate rites and sacrifices. When we begin to read the prophets, we realize how futile it is to perform rituals while failing to worship the Lord in spirit and truth. We will deal with the particular aspects of ritual in a later chapter.)

Monks are required to apply their heart and mind to the rituals—a single mistake, even by oversight, may render it ineffective. Even at their initiation, they must know, believe, and ponder the Buddhist teaching that the physical body will one day perish and that nirvana eventually awaits them. The body is seen to be a hindrance to this goal. Incidentally, most substance abuse, a common practice among ordinary Buddhists, occurs as an integral part of the various rituals, especially in Mahayana.

The yellow robes, the monks claim, are only to protect them from the vagaries of climate—cold and heat, gadflies and mosquitoes—when they travel and sleep. They are also protected from snakes, and the robes help them to avoid nudity. The monk will declare that the robe is not an ornament for show, nor does it proclaim purity or spiritual status.

Gautama Buddha emphasized on several occasions the need to have excellent language skills (fluent speech in particular) and diligent wisdom or knowledge. A monk who is both fluent and knowledgeable may be a student under another for only five years, at which time he must graduate to become a teacher himself. On the other hand, persons without fluency and knowledge will remain students all their lives.

Contrast this with the disciples of Jesus Christ: most of them were unlettered, but they had implicit faith in their Teacher. They made many mistakes, but ultimately their eyes were opened and they became exemplary followers of the Master, all because of their obedience to the words of the Lord.

It is difficult to excel in theological education, but what is needed is implicit obedience and willingness to follow the Master. This difference between the Buddhist insistence upon high attainments and the Christian demand for simple faith is bound to appeal to the Sinhalese who come from the poor, illiterate, less educated, and less fortunate families. *None of these things matter when you wish to serve the Lord!* Once you commit yourself to Him, He empowers in amazing ways. This is a message of hope and comfort rather than despair and fatalism. When your Sri Lankan Theravada Buddhist friend is perturbed about the problems he is currently facing, tell him how Jesus comes to our help through His Word.

At a monk's initiation, several questions are asked: Do you have your own alms-bowl? Do you have your own stole? Do you have an upper robe? Do you have an under robe? Do you have any diseases such as leprosy, boils, itching, asthma, or epilepsy? Are you a human being? Are you a male? Are you a free man? Are you free from debt? Are you permitted by the government not to join the military? Are you allowed by your parents to join the order? Are you twenty years old?

The candidate who is ready after his training to assume the role of a monk is told that he should collect food from households every day; it is required of him not to cook his own food. He lives by what others offer to him, and he should accept it without murmur or complaint. The robes are mandatory, and he should wear only these for as long as he lives. He is expected to stay under a tree, not under a shelter (except during the rainy season). He drinks cow's urine as his medicine, and he does not indulge in sexual intercourse if he wants to be a son of Gautama Buddha. He is never dishonest and never usurps anything from others, not even a blade of grass. He shall not knowingly kill *any* form of life. He should not take the life of even an ant. He shall not take life by causing abortion.

> A priest must not lay claim to more than human perfection, even by saying, "I delight in a solitary hut" or . . . [by] a state of mystic meditation, or freedom from passion, or perfect tranquility, or attainment of the four paths, or of the fruition of those paths, or else he ceases to be a priest, and is no longer a son of Sakya. (Gard, 165)

THERAVADA BUDDHISM IN MYANMAR

Among the various nationalities that live in Myanmar (formerly Burma), the well-settled Myanmarese (Burmese or Bama), who make up nearly 60 percent of the entire population, have adopted Theravada Buddhism as their own religion. As several other ethnic groups in Myanmar have done likewise, the overall Buddhist population is about 83 percent.

The Indian Buddhist missionaries did impact the people of Myanmar; however, Myanmarese exposure to and acceptance of Theravada was fortified by Sri Lankan developments. The Myanmarese Theravada Buddhist claims that he received original orthodox Buddhism through a visit by Gautama himself. From available records, we could conclude that Buddhism began flourishing in Myanmar at least fourteen hundred years ago. With such an ancestry, it is only expected that the Myanmarese would hold on to their Buddhist faith as a matter of national pride and identity.

Loyalty to Buddhism is strong, and successive governments have helped its growth in Myanmar. The first World Council of Buddhists, modeled after the ancient councils, was held in Myanmar (1954–56). This strengthened Buddhist identity and sparked a new missionary zeal among them.

Other Ethnic Communities

Among the other groups in Myanmar, the Karen and Chin peoples in the hills are mostly Christian, as are some among the Shan. The

Myanmarese Christians are few in number, and since the vast majority come from non-Myanmarese communities, usually occupying the hills (and traditionally treated as tribes and materially less advanced), Myanmarese Buddhists usually look down upon Christians. In addition, these tribal communities often agitate against the central and provincial governments for their rightful place in the country. With this stubborn resistance, the relationship between the major (Buddhist) and minor (Christian) communities is strained, to say the least. Your Myanmarese Theravada Buddhist friend thus will not only be governed by his loyalty to Buddhism but also by his determination to distinguish himself as an inheritor of a high religion. He is skeptical about the Christian communities in Myanmar, perceiving them as representing foreign values and religion.

Try to discover the ethnic background of the Myanmarese you encounter. There is nothing wrong with asking about this directly—people are often proud of their heritage and do not try to hide it from others. On the other hand, the social class division *within* an ethnic group is often concealed; a person may put himself in a "higher" social category than the one he actually inherited.

Sacred Sites

Myanmar is famous for its tall and exquisitely built Buddhist temples, pagodas, and monasteries. Theravada Buddhism rules the hearts of its men, women, and children. Myanmar has been under military rule for quite some time, and officially there is no religion adopted by the government, but Buddhism is as strong as ever, and the military regime that rules the country supports it.

The Buddhist temples and pagodas in Myanmar have small mirrors everywhere, as well as numerous images of Gautama Buddha and others. The temples and pagodas are painted in bright colors with little bells that jingle in the breeze. Large pipal trees are a common sight in the monasteries. Myanmarese homes also have their own shrines, before which images the household members pray daily, burn incense, and make offerings.

Clergy

As in Sri Lanka and other Theravada countries, in Myanmar the monks make daily rounds of their community, receiving alms. They do not eat everything but distribute the remaining food to the poor. They also assemble twice a day and chant the recitations as adoration of the Buddha and the way that he ordained.

One requirement that helps maintain the position of Buddhism as the main religion among the Myanmarese is that every male is expected to spend a few months in a monastery, either as part of his coming of age or later in his adult life. During this time, men are given focused instruction on the teachings of Buddhism and a taste of Buddhist disciplines, which they may or may not practice afterward. There is widespread respect shown to this arrangement.

Monasteries are looked upon as centers of education for the laity. Periodic readings from Buddhist texts for the benefit of laypeople are performed. Pali texts are translated for easy understanding. Families come to the monasteries to worship and to receive instruction and blessings. It is not unusual for a layman to function as a monk for a short while, even putting on the traditional yellow robe.

Belief in and Appeasement of Spirits

An important characteristic of Myanmar Buddhism is the belief in spirits. While this is found in all sections of Buddhism, Myanmarese Theravada Buddhism has developed its own arrangement. While intellectuals often deride such beliefs and argue that they are not part of orthodox Buddhism, the practical life of a Theravada Buddhist is governed by his belief in the *nats* (the term used to refer to the spirits).

Elaborate nat worship (or appeasement) is a distinguishing mark, and your Buddhist friend from Myanmar will not be an exception to this way of life. He may be highly educated and practice orthodox Theravada, yet he will be at least ambivalent about his belief in nats. Be familiar with how the Word of God deals with the spirit world (see also chapter 14).

The Gospels often speak about how Jesus drove out spirits and healed the people. Your Myanmarese friend will find it easy to compromise or make adjustment between his orthodox faith and the native nat culture. Pray for his release from this bondage. Spirits are real, and they continue to attract people and lead them to destruction. The Word of God is straightforward about denouncing spirits, spirit possession, exorcism, and the exorcist. We will discuss in a later chapter how the intent and ill effects of spirit possession may be made clear to a Myanmarese Buddhist.

According to Myanmarese belief, nats may be good or evil; people request the help of the good nats and try to appease the evil ones. Nats are portrayed in a vivid, descriptive manner in the monasteries and temples, which instills fear of them (especially in children). Again, according to orthodox Buddhism, the present life of a Buddhist is the result of his karma in his previous lives, and although Buddhist doctrine emphasizes that karma cannot be interfered with or altered, nat worship and appeasement offer benefits that may override the impact of past karma. (Myanmarese Buddhists, like others, try to acquire merit by good deeds and may perform works for the improvement of the karma of others, as well.)

Myanmarese nat belief is a native folk tradition that must have existed long before the arrival of Buddhism. As with other Southeast Asian Buddhist countries, native folk religion has become enmeshed with Buddhist practice, two traditions combined into one way of life. The same is true in Mahayana nations: In China we see that the Buddhist way of life is integrated with Confucianism and Taoism, and in Japan we observe the integration of the gods of Shinto and Buddhism even as they maintain their own distinctive functions and goals. *Religious syncretism is a hallmark of Buddhism wherever it is practiced.* This leads to divination, magic, sorcery, and alchemy—all condemned in the Word of God because the practitioners come under bondage and become fatalistic, denying the grace and sovereignty of God.

Myanmarese folk religion has four types of spiritual beings: ghosts, demons, witches, and nats. The first three are significant, but it is the nats that dominate Buddhist behavior. Neither modern education nor urban life seems to have had any effect on the elimination or reduction of the nat cult, which has its own organization, temples, priests, and rituals.

Anthropologist Melford Spiro, whose work on the spirits of Myanmar is still the best critical, analytical, and descriptive work on the subject, reports that the Myanmarese people believe there are two types of evil nats: nature spirits and the thirty-seven nats, both of which cause great harm. A third type, a category whose position within the nats' domain is somewhat ambiguous and unclear, are nats (or devas— roughly translated as "gods") that do good and are considered to be Buddhist personages. The existence of the nat cult is a bondage to the average Myanmarese, and the fact that professionals such as medical doctors diagnose conditions of illness, for example, by informing their patients that their illness is caused by the nats only empowers this stronghold.

The holy texts of Theravada Buddhism not only recognize the existence of various categories of evil and good spirits but also approve the appeasement and coercion of them through the recitation of certain verses. *Appeasement, coercion, and accommodation characterize the Buddhist view of the spiritual world.*

Nats, then, cause harm and suffering to humans, and suffering, according to Gautama Buddha, is the basic thing from which we should try to escape through our own efforts. Suffering is eliminated only when an individual attains nirvana through the seemingly endless cycle of rebirths; nat worship, however, tries to find a way to eliminate suffering (inevitable because of karma) in *this* life on the assumption that the nats may be the source of suffering. Thus, the role of an individual as the agent (karma) of his own suffering is somewhat downplayed. Of course, with the help of Buddhist rituals and scriptures, he can find release from the clutches of nats and consequently overcome suffering. In this way, there is a conflict between orthodox Theravada Buddhism, which emphasizes submission to karma on the one hand, and on the other, nat worship and appeasement, which seeks elimination of suffering in this life.

The sustained continuance of the nat cult in the life of every Myanmarese Buddhist only shows his or her dire (and realized) need to seek relief from pain and suffering right now, in this life, come what may. When the Buddhist personages—Gautama and the countless Buddhas that are adored, venerated, and worshiped—are unable to provide relief, and when highly respected teaching makes it necessary for the pious to view their pain, need, and suffering as a result of previous births, laypeople seek assistance from the nats and other spirits. *They need this tactical convenience because their doctrine does not provide for it.* Pray to the Lord Jesus for your friend, and also tell him or her that Jesus overcame pain and suffering once for all and that His promise to take care of us, even in this world, in this life, is still true.

Melford Spiro gives this graphic illustration of how an evil practitioner subdues and uses spirits to achieve his ends:

> To control ghosts, the master witch feeds them raw meat and, when they become dependent on him for their food supply, they carry out his bidding. Power over nats is acquired in a somewhat more complicated fashion. They must be made an offering consisting of opposite, sacred and profane, elements. Typically, the profane elements might consist of the beak of a crow, the penis of a dog, a woman's skirt, and earth from a cemetery, a latrine, and a nat shrine. The sacred elements might consist of a streamer adorning a Buddha image and earth taken from a Buddhist ordination chamber. The master witch then sets fire to this mixed offering under the shrine of the Mahagiri nat, a nat who is repelled by fire, and thereby gains control over the nat whom he has chosen as his agent.

Should this technique prove ineffectual, he smears the face of a nat image with this mixture, a technique that invariably succeeds in gaining control over the nat. (Spiro, 23)

Ghosts need to be appeased so that they will not continue to haunt one's place of residence and cause harm. A variety of amulets are specially prepared and worn for protection. Alchemy is also an important element in all Buddhist folk (and elitist Tibetan Buddhism) practices. In Myanmar, the help of alchemy is sought to prolong one's life, as protection against snakebites and other calamities that happen suddenly, and even to get precious metals from the baser ones. The rosary and the yellow robe of the monks are considered to be an effective way to ward off evil spirits.

As Spiro points out, the dilemma of a Buddhist intellectual, reared in the Buddha's teaching on suffering, seems to be a disadvantageous locking of horns with his own theological positions. It is not only the nat cult that comes into conflict with Buddhist theology but also the veneration of material objects and the offerings given to Buddhist personages in order to alleviate suffering in the present life, which according to the Buddhist scheme of karma, is supposed to override all other factors.

Remember, however, that you will be disappointed if you believe Buddhist reasoning can be countered by pointing out these contradictions. While purely theological discussion will fortify the newly converted Christian, the "debate approach" is *rarely* effective in winning people to Christ. You can politely point out such issues, but your Theravada Buddhist friend will come up with justification that is adequate from his or her point of view. Instead of continually belaboring this, we would do better to speak about how faith in Jesus liberates us from evil forces and sets us totally free.

Using one spirit to coerce another and appeasing a spirit to gain favor lead one into spiritual bondage. Our dealing with the spirit world then becomes a commercial proposition, which robs us of freedom. If one spirit is coerced, there are countless others that come into subsequent play, and we begin to sink into a bottomless pit. Pray for the needs of your Theravada friend and let him know that you are upholding him in your prayers. You will certainly see a breakthrough if you commit to continuous spiritual warfare.

THERAVADA BUDDHISM IN THAILAND

The kings of modern Thailand, who retained their distinctive identity as protectors and promoters of Theravada Buddhism, were not opposed to the influence of Western missionaries, being attracted to the additional benefits of trading, technology, and education. Geopolitical conditions in the second half of the twentieth century brought Thailand and the United States closer to each other. Thai rulers have been very adept at making peaceful overtures and accommodations in order to retain their freedom; however, the number of Christians among the Thais continues to be very low.

Thailand is a multiethnic country, but some homogeneity exists between its peoples. The age-old emphasis on Theravada Buddhism (including the idea of the king as a divine person with a divine mandate to rule) has helped foster allegiance to the nation. This does not mean there are no tensions between the various peoples of Thailand, but their unity amidst diversity is notable. Regional differences do continue to be important identity markers to the various peoples, most of whom use one dialect or another of the Thai language family.

The political relationship with the sangha (as well as the entire hierarchy of Theravada Buddhism) is so strong that Thailand is the only nation with a constitutional demand that the king be a Buddhist. Other Theravada nations, including Myanmar and Sri Lanka, have given up the monarchy and replaced it with other provisions, but in Thailand the king commands great respect and loyalty, perhaps also because as a person he has always shown his concern for, and dedication to, the people.

The modern rulers of Thailand (mostly from the armed forces), at the initiative of the present Thai king, have developed a policy to help the advancement of minority ethnic groups. There is a small Muslim community as well as several hill tribes that have responded in some measure to the gospel.

Arrival and Spread of Buddhism

Though there were ups and downs in the relationship between the two countries, the Thai people had close contact with the Khmer of Cambodia for centuries, and it appears that the gradual spread of Theravada Buddhism in Thailand was a result of this connection. Cambodia was the first and foremost nation to receive the impact of Hinduism and Buddhism from India, and the Khmer relationship with the Thai population was supplemented also by the influence brought on them through the Mon people, who settled in the central plain and northern highlands of Thailand. A present-day confluence of cultures, linguistic affiliations, and Theravada Buddhism is the visible result.

When Theravada was introduced as the official religion of a powerful kingdom (the Ayttaya, or Ayudhya, or Ayodhya), the door was opened for the arrival and establishment of Sri Lankan monks. In every walk of life—judicial, political, and social—Hindu-based Buddhism became the standard in the fourteenth century. Thais take great pride in their Theravada background, viewing it (as do others) as an emblem of loyalty and nationalism.

Social Stratification

The population of Thailand is stratified based on classes, such as (1) the royals and nobles; (2) military officers; (3) government officials, entrepreneurs, professionals, and small businessmen; and (4) the lower groups. Response to the gospel does not greatly vary among the classes, and there is enhanced flexibility of movement between them due to economic growth, education, and other opportunities. (One's family background is nevertheless important.) Buddhist clergy, occupying a unique position within the society, does not fall within any of these classes, offering an opening for those who wish to move upward in the social hierarchy.

Anthropologists note that Thai culture is somewhat organized on the patron-client relationship, in which the patron takes care of the client and the client performs services needed by the patron. A person who is a patron at one level may be a client at another level, and connection between patron and client is often governed by unwritten conventions. The client instinctively knows his role and the expectations of his patron; the patron's responsibility is to provide protection, support, and economic means to his client. At times, the patron-client relationship becomes a hereditary affair, to the disadvantage of the poor. While ethnic distinctions may play some role in determining the status of an individual or family, or even the community, frequently it is power (economic and political) that establishes "superior" and "inferior" status.

When seeking to learn the background of your Thai friend, ask what region of the country he comes from. (Most people who form the vanguard of Theravada in Thailand come from the central region.) The standard dialect of education and public office is the one spoken in central Thailand; if your Thai friend speaks more than one dialect, in all probability he comes from the other regions of the country in which there are substantial non-Thai ethnic communities.

Population Profile

Several communities in northern Thailand have been receptive to the gospel of Jesus Christ, and yet the peasants in all ethnic groups and regions are overwhelmingly Theravada Buddhists. Some of the ethnic groups that are not Thai are the Chinese (about 11 percent), Malay (about 3 percent), longtime Khmer residents, as well as recent refugees from Cambodia, and a few people groups that have direct affiliation with the Myanmarese. There are four major divisions of the Thai people based on regional distribution: the Central Thai, the Northeastern Thai, the Northern Thai, and the Southern Thai.

The Central Thai retain their identities and have political, social, cultural, and linguistic advantages. The Northeastern Thai are more accustomed to seeing Americans because of the U.S. military bases located in their region. If your friend is from the northeast, it is likely that he or she knows a little about Christianity but is not automatically receptive to the Good News. The Southern Thai are somewhat poorer than others. The south also has a concentration of Muslims and has been a center of Muslim insurgency in the past.

If you are going to Thailand for short-term missions, collect some background information about the dialect and dress code of the region or people group you will be serving. Thailand is deceptively homogeneous, especially for the Westerner; while there is much standardization of language, dress, and culture, the diversity is still there.

Temple Worship

Thai Theravada Buddhists are extremely faithful in attending the wat (temple). These temples are the centers of education and ritual, and attendance brings merit that assists in improving one's lot in future births. The temple is also where one seeks advice and comfort from the monks; those trained in magical arts help the laity to overcome their problems through various rituals and astrological predictions.

Monks discern the best (most auspicious) time to perform ceremonies, including marriages, and the laity seek their help for physical healing and exorcism. People can rent utensils from the wats for their familial and social functions, and they may even borrow money to meet their needs. Older men and women who have no relatives to support them sometimes go to the temple complex and take up residence there until they find alternative dwellings. The wat is also the center for Buddhist-approved communal entertainment.

Sexual Relations for Money

Visitors to Thailand quickly notice its saddest characteristic: prostitution. While many theories have been offered to explain the growth of this deplorable activity—ranging from alignment with the West and cheap imitation of Western culture to growing urban poverty—I believe there is some link between the patron-client relationship and the institution of sexual bondage. Thai laypeople disapprove of prostitution and wish that it were eradicated completely, but in ignorance they often inadvertently help its perpetuation. Prostitutes and pimps do not have any respectable social status, and the laity believe that they indulge in such evil activities because of their karma.

Don't raise these issues in early contacts with your Theravada Thai friend; there will be plenty of opportunities to talk about this pernicious practice once you are comfortable with each other. When the time comes, educate him regarding how prostitution debases all parties involved and how God detests it. From the harshest punishment (death) meted out to prostitutes (in Leviticus 21:9), the Word of God moves us to bestow the *compassion* and *grace* of the Lord Jesus on these unfortunate ones if they repent, reject their sin, and turn to God (John 8:7–11).

Monastic Life

The backbone of modern-day Theravada in Thailand is the vast rural population. Migrants to the city also contribute to the maintenance of Buddhist tradition by observing and participating in Theravada festivals and rituals in large numbers.

Joining a monastery for a short time (a few months at least) signifies the coming of age for Thai males. They may enter the monastic order in their early twenties but are not required to stay throughout their lives. Most males volitionally go to a monastery of their choice and have the freedom to determine the duration of their monastic self-training.

Monks get up around four o'clock, go through their morning ablutions (washing the body for ritual purposes), and put on their yellow robes. They go before the Buddha image, kneeling to burn incense sticks, adopting several postures, and chanting in praise of Buddha, the sangha, and the dharma. They meditate for a few minutes and then fall into pairs to confess each of the violations they may have committed the day before. Each day is filled with a variety of activities, including instruction, meditation, and exchange of ideas in the sanctuary. The ten prohibitions (see chapter 2) are repeatedly stressed and taught, and celibacy is mandatory, although not all the novices take these vows.

Accountability, strict adherence to traditions, morals, and ethics, and the performance of prescribed rituals play an important role in monastic life. Training places the initiates in at least seven grades (the seventh being the highest). However, most novices choose to leave the order after the ceremony in which they are officially ordained as monks through the offering of the yellow robes.

Monks are accorded a special status in Thai society; the sangha is hierarchically organized, and its leaders have great authority and influence both among the clergy and among the other Thai power groups. Monks usually abstain from directly influencing the political course of the nation, and yet political officers show unmistakable deference to the sangha as custodians of faith and culture. The government, for instance, encourages its officials to go on a paid leave of absence, at least once, to join the sangha for a period of three months.

Your Thai Theravada friend may have already gone through his training, and he may have been attracted to monastic life (at least as a cultural tradition). Encouraging him to tell you about his experience as a monk will open up an opportunity for you to get to know him and also to explain the futility of rituals and traditions (as laid out in the Word of God). Our transgressions cannot be washed away by our own efforts—we need to depend upon the true God, who looks upon us with both truth and love and accepts us in all of our human frailty. True spiritual experience does not require elaborate rituals; simple faith in God is all that is needed, and with faith comes a determination that helps us to obey.

Theravada Buddhists believe that merit is obtained by services and offerings given to the sangha, as well as by participation in religious ceremonies and construction and maintenance of (and visits to) the wats. Remember: achievement of nirvana is not the immediate goal for ordinary Buddhists—*correct living and gaining merit to improve one's lot in future births is the target of this life,* and the wats play a crucial role in this process.

Many ceremonies and festivals are celebrated in the wat. One very impressive ceremony is conducted in the home of the individual about to enter the sangha. The monks invite his life-soul to participate fully in this process (so that he will be successful in his future monastic role) and also make solemn declarations about the preparation of the candidate and his family, who are enthusiastically involved.

We saw a similar model in Sri Lankan Buddhism. The candidate is persuaded that by becoming a monk he not only brings merit to his own future but also to the future of his family members. Although theologically speaking every person is to work out his own nirvana, and even though Gautama Buddha himself declared that no one else could assist the individual on this journey, it is hard for the Theravada Buddhist not to assume that by his meritorious act he is also helping family members.

The Word of God does say "each one should carry his own load"

(Galatians 6:5), and it is likewise clear that you should "continue to work out your salvation with fear and trembling" (Philippians 2:12). We also read in the next verse, however, that "it is God who works in you to will and to act according to his good purpose." Thus, while we carry our own load, it is not by our efforts that we are saved but by the grace of the Lord, who helps us to live according to His plan.

We know that 2 Corinthians 5:10 instructs us to remember that everyone will "receive what is due him for the things done while in the body, whether good or bad." This can be completely misunderstood by your Buddhist friend, to the point that it supports his position. It is important for us to put this teaching in proper perspective: *God* forgives our sins, and "if you confess with your mouth, 'Jesus is Lord,' and believe in your heart that God raised him from the dead, you will be saved" (Romans 10:9). Expect your Theravada friend to find it difficult to accept this statement because of his understanding that only through strict disciplines, good deeds, and right conduct can he ultimately be saved. Not only is he not looking for salvation in his present life, conditioned to think that he must undergo endless births and deaths to achieve it, but he is not even given assurance that this will ever happen.

Do Monks Have Greater Spiritual Worth?

Since monastic orders are seen as the foundation of Theravada Buddhism, even a slight off-the-cuff remark against them will be offensive to your Thai friend. However, God does not distinguish between the priest and the plebian. What He looks for in us is a contrite heart and love toward one another.

Obviously, monasticism is not an exclusive characteristic of Buddhism. Several other religions—including some Christian denominations, such as the Roman Catholic Church and the Eastern Orthodox Church—have a strong monastic orientation. Clergy in almost every religion live an ascetic life, keeping themselves away from the world and its affairs and organizing themselves into an isolated community. They do have contacts in the world, but their lifestyle demonstrates that their life is distinctive from the lives of "ordinary" people. *This distinction does not mean that they possess special or superior spiritual worth.*

A simple life without hankering after name, fame, and wealth but with a focus on loving and helping others is the model the Word of God provides. For example, in Matthew 5:3 we read, "Blessed are the poor in spirit, for theirs is the kingdom of heaven." There is no demand to go to a jungle or a hilltop to practice asceticism.

Some have tried to present Matthew 7:14 ("Small is the gate and narrow the road that leads to life, and only a few find it") as a probable basis and justification for monasticism, but there is no scriptural indication that salvation is more possible for or readily available to those adhering to the monastic life. *The ministry of Jesus was one of involvement with the people in the world.* He was at hand for the sinners to bring repentance. He attended a marriage ceremony and other social events, and He nowhere declared that the life of a monk is better or has more spiritual worth than the life of anyone else.

Celibacy has its place but not over and against married status as the superior or preferred condition. The disciples said to Jesus, " 'If this is the situation between a husband and wife, it is better not to marry.' Jesus replied, 'Not everyone can accept this word, but only those to whom it has been given. . . . The one who can accept this should accept it' " (Matthew 19:10–12). Marriage and celibacy become matters of choice, not institutional requirements in the Word of God.

The apostle Paul makes the point clearly and addresses the issue directly:

> It is good for a man not to marry. But since there is so much immorality, each man should have his own wife, and each woman her own husband. . . . Do not deprive each other except by mutual consent and for a time, so that you may devote yourselves to prayer. Then come together again so that Satan will not tempt you because of your lack of self-control. I say this as a concession, not as a command. I wish that all men were as I am. But each man has his own gift from God; one has this gift, another has that. (1 Corinthians 7:1–2, 5–7)

One distinction between Christian monks and Buddhist monks is that the former are required to live by the labor of their hands, whereas the latter refrain. Christian monks are explicitly prohibited from participating in magical arts, alchemy, spirit possession, divination, etc., although some of them may still practice or allow such practices for the laity.

Consider these words from the apostle Peter: "You are well aware that it is against our law for a Jew to associate with a Gentile or visit him. But God has shown me that I should not call any man impure or unclean" (Acts 10:28). In Galatians 3:28 we read, "There is neither Jew nor Greek, slave nor free, male nor female, for you are all one in Christ Jesus." All of us, though, are to be vigilant: "You are all sons of the light and sons of the day. We do not belong to the night or to the darkness. So then, let us not be like others, who are asleep, but let us be alert and self-controlled" (1 Thessalonians 5:5–6).

The ascetic way of life *is* attractive to adventurous people, who may even sincerely believe that they are doing something noble and useful for the community. However, asceticism is manmade; it focuses on the disciplines and does not lead to the recognition and enjoyment of the Lord's love for us. Love of God, not love of oneself, should dominate our thinking and life.

Thai Folk Religion

An average Thai Theravada Buddhist has adopted the hallmarks of many folk practices to improve living conditions in this life: astrology, divination, exorcism, spirit possession, and worship and appeasement of various spirits (not officially sanctioned but widespread). Worship and appeasement are, in fact, the most frequent spiritual exercises for the ordinary people.

Phi is the Thai term used to refer to the host of spirits that impact human lives. Some of the phi reside in this world, while others are dead human beings; most are vicious, and they exist in all places. People who died an untimely as well as violent death become phi, as do those whose funeral rites were not properly conducted—these return to haunt the village and the household. The ghosts of people who led a morally righteous life are good and are thus called upon to enter the body of the medium.

The Theravada Buddhist performs rites for birth, death, marriage, and the construction of buildings and the prosperity of businesses. Most of these are modeled after or adopted from Hinduism. The monks are present when these rites are performed, chanting Buddhist scripture and offering holy waters for the sponsors and participants. Several of these rites may be conducted only in the homes of laypeople, rather than the wat. The dying person, for example, is encouraged to recite the Buddhist scriptures and focus on the Buddha for last-minute merits. The death of a person is followed by specific actions intended to bring greater merits to the dead.

Perceived Sources of Power

Anthropologist Stanley Tambiah gives an interesting and detailed description of Thai folk Buddhism, marked by abundant devotion to and worship of amulets. Amulets contain representations of Buddha and other personages; these are believed to be great powerhouses. Amulets are blessed by the clergy, and through these and other religious acts people believe that the amulets become objects of sustenance, protecting them and bestowing upon them prosperity. They come in different shapes, often in the form of medallions that are worn by millions of Thais inside their shirt or blouse and around their neck on necklaces or chains. These also may be carried inside the pocket or on the person. People often wear several amulets simultaneously, even sprinkling holy water on them. Great reverence is shown to these objects; Thais utter respectful words of apology to the amulets while handling them.

Amulets are also kept in homes and shown tremendous reverence and worship. All sections of Thai society—literate or illiterate, urban or rural, rich or poor—wear amulets. Stories are narrated in interpersonal conversations and newspapers about how amulets saved the narrator or helped him or her to obtain prosperity, succeed in examinations, obtain a job, etc.

Those who are conscious of their Buddhist theology treat amulets, relics, and images as reminders of Buddha's greatness and the need to emulate him in their daily lives. In reality, *these objects come to function not as representations but as idols having inherent power that is being transferred to the worshipers.*

In a friendly and discreet manner, find out from your Theravada friend whether he wears and/or highly regards amulets. Although he may be an educated and highly placed person, in all likelihood he may depend on the working of amulets for his personal needs. Such belief acquired early in life as part of one's culture and religion is not dissolved with modern education.

Discover whether he believes wearing amulets always leads to protection or success. More often than not, even those who wear amulets will tell you that this is not the case. You can raise the question of the dubious sacredness of material objects, explaining how the worship of tangible images degrades the sovereignty of God. The Bible clearly states, "[God is] against your magic charms . . . and [He] will tear them from your arms" (Ezekiel 13:20). When Buddhists think material objects have power in themselves, they begin to focus on these and not on God (not even on Buddha). When the Buddhist looks for spiritual power, things such as amulets function as super-spirits or deities, and he begins to give material objects the status of a mediator. The Word of God is clear: "There is one God and one mediator between God and men, the man Christ Jesus" (1 Timothy 2:5).

How do we reconcile the theological position that the Buddha has entered into nirvana (and no longer exists) with the Buddhist who is seeking blessing and power for his betterment in both this life and the ones to come? Since nonexistence (total extinction) is the ultimate goal, and since the Buddha has reached this level, how can we seek the help of one who is nonexistent (extinct)? Buddhists give some answers for this haunting question. For example: The symbolization causes goodness in those who pay obeisance to the relics, images, and objects (such as amulets) that have the representation of the Buddha and other meritorious Buddhist personages. These symbols are reminders of the Buddha and his victory, and they are powerhouses because they are associated with the Buddha and other meritorious Buddhists.

Notwithstanding this answer, it is plain that the laity begin to treat these objects as spiritual power sources, viewing them as imbued with the power of the Buddha and other "worthy" Buddhist figures. *Worshiping material objects as spiritual centers and drawing powers from these spiritual centers are prohibited in the Word of God.* We deal with this matter in detail in chapter 10.

THERAVADA BUDDHISM IN CAMBODIA

Cambodia has a lengthy recorded history, dating back at least two thousand years, and its popular Hindu-based Buddhism stems from the influence of India and Sri Lanka. In recent years Cambodia faced the worst human tragedy in Southeast Asia since Nagasaki and Hiroshima. *Operation World* (2001) reports,

> [Cambodia was] a tragic victim of the Vietnam War (1970–75) which opened the way for the extreme Marxist Khmer Rouge take-over in 1975, followed by one of the most savage slaughters in the 20th Century. Almost all former military personnel, civil servants, educated or wealthy people and their families were killed, and the nation turned into a vast labour camp. . . . The Khmer Rouge sought to eradicate all religion; 90% of Buddhist monks and most Christians perished. [Buddhist clergy were forced to do manual labor much against their vows. They were also coerced into supporting the communist ideology.] Since 1978 there have been periods of more tolerance, but only since 1990 have Christians been allowed to worship openly. There is increasing freedom of religion for Cambodians. (Johnstone and Mandryk, 137)

Just over 1 percent of Cambodians profess Christian faith.

Cambodian refugees in the United States continue to hold on to Theravada worship. There are wats in various areas; not long ago, a particularly large one was constructed and consecrated in Washington, D.C., endowed with the power of ordination and highly regarded by Cambodian-Americans.

The present population of Cambodia is estimated to be around twelve million, with almost 87 percent belonging to the Mon-Khmer stock (including several ethnic groups). There are also a few smaller communities, including the Malay (some of whom are Muslims).

Impact of Buddhism

Nearly sixteen hundred years ago, Hindu merchants, priests, and other religiously oriented intellectuals began to influence Cambodians; the elitists, especially—including members of the royal family, nobility, and military personnel—were attracted to Hinduism's rituals, learning, and modes of living. Sanskrit became the mark of elitism among Cambodians, and the Hindu legal code (composed by the Hindu sage Manu), which laid down social behavior and obligation, was adopted. However, caste hierarchy was not introduced, although the categories of the Brahmans and of the Achars (or Acharyas—ritual-performing individuals) were established. In this way, Hindu thinking became an integral part of Cambodian living as it received prestige and dignity through elitist support.

The social hierarchy of Cambodian society was slightly remodeled: as with Thailand, Theravada became imperial, and the king was considered to be divine (with a divine mandate to rule), owning both land and subjects, and the leader of the Buddhist clergy. Under him were a small number of Brahmans and other large classes of people (whose folk beliefs were easily blended). Along with Hinduism, Mahayana had a good following, although Theravada was the first practiced form of Buddhism in Cambodia and became dominant by the thirteenth century. So for over eight hundred years almost all Cambodians have adhered to Theravada (again, in cultural loyalty, equating it with their nation). Democracy and communism have brought some changes in the polity and thinking of the Buddhist population, but the people at large still view the king (and his mandate) as divine.

Monastic Life

The monastic orders common in Thailand are also common in Cambodia. The present government seeks to restrict day-to-day contact between the laity and the sangha, although some of the standard activities, such as the monks going through the village to receive food, are allowed. The difficulties of this current situation are compounded by the fact that the leading Buddhist clergy are from Vietnam, and the government views with suspicion the Vietnamese leadership of the institution.

There were numerous monasteries (bonzes) and temples (wats) in the past, and though there was some reduction during the Khmer Rouge oppression, these institutions are bouncing back with full support from the laity. Cambodia now has perhaps the most wats and bonzes of all the Theravada countries. Most Cambodian males serve as monks for a short period before leaving the orders, and older women and widows may become nuns, living in the wats, helping with daily monastic chores, and shaving their heads and eyebrows.

Monks do not vote in elections and do not participate in sensual activities (celibacy is required). The 227 vows are to be recited and followed, and participation in community rituals (performed by the Achars, the traditionally approved laity) is essential in establishing the sangha's approval of societal events. The monks pray, sprinkle holy water, counsel, use astrology, facilitate the gaining of merit through sangha-approved actions, and dispense medicines. They help in the process of exorcism, though they themselves may not actually perform it, and they assist in the spread of literacy (which is now an official government function).

Your Theravada Cambodian friend will likely have high regard for the monk order. In conversation, don't focus on the futility of the Buddhist sangha. Show how even in early Christian times, some church leaders lived in ways that are not approved in the Word of God, which does not approve of such partiality—*all* people are of equal spiritual worth. In Romans 2:11 we read, "God does not show favoritism." Colossians 3:25 tells us, "Anyone who does wrong will be repaid for his wrong, and there is no favoritism." Peter exhorts, "Since you call on a Father who judges each man's work impartially, live your lives as strangers here in reverent fear" (1 Peter 1:17).

The Task Is Twofold

The Cambodians you encounter may be antireligious, agnostic, or even atheistic. They have been impacted not only by Western thought but also by the intense propaganda of the Khmer Rouge, and they will probably be skeptical about anything that is spiritual, especially the claims of Christ.

So your task is twofold. *First,* speak (in spiritual terms) about how rituals, monastic superiority, reincarnations, samsara, worry over past infractions, alchemy, astrology, divination, image worship, and appeasement of evil forces and the dead bring people into spiritual bondage. Tell the story of Jesus in simple terms, centering on His ministry to the poor and needy as well as His justice and equanimity.

Christ's divine status may be *indicated* but not *highlighted*. Also make it a point not to focus on the Jewish or Middle-Eastern background of the man Jesus (because of nationalism and Buddhist loyalty). Light can be ignited in the heart and soul of your Cambodian friend when he hears how Jesus is an answer to prayer, how He saved the multitudes from their infirmities, how He is still with us through the Holy Spirit, and how His grace is sufficient for us. *The Word of God never returns empty.*

Second, if your friend is skeptical about all faith, explain that humans are spiritual by their very nature, that we all have the need for the presence of God in our life, and that human achievement does not yield permanent peace. While we need to be involved in this world, greater serenity and joy flow out of our dependence on the Lord, and if we trust in ourselves or in others (or in gods that cannot come to our aid or set us free), we will be forever enslaved to this world and the forces of evil. There is *no one* who does not know God in his heart, since, to paraphrase what Paul wrote, what may be known about God is plain, because He has made it plain to *all* of us (see Romans 1:19). We suppress this truth because of our own pride and self-righteousness, and no justification (based either on personal suffering or on social atrocities) is sufficient to reject our understanding and knowledge of God. Not only must we acknowledge God, but we must also be obedient to Him in response to His love.

Folk Religion and Spirits

Cambodian Theravada festivals are similar to those of nations we have already examined (one notable feature is the day to remember ancestors). For the laity, practical Theravada allows for the mixing of folk beliefs and practices with those of canonical Buddhism.

Belief in the spirits is widespread, and their assistance (through spirit practitioners) is sought for physical healing, financial aid, and the resolution of family problems. Spirits reside in temples, shrines, and households, often making sounds and causing unusual things to happen. Spirits recognized in Cambodian culture include common ghosts, evil spirits of those who died violently (and/or unexpectedly), malevolent female spirits, guardian spirits, spirits residing in material objects, ancestral spirits, and animal spirits. All of these must be appeased through proper rituals (often various offerings); without these, spirits will cause untold suffering and damage to those who ignore them.

There are several types of professional spiritists. The Achar (ritual performer in the wat) is important and influential. There are sorcerers, mediums, shamans, and amulet makers (highly respected, feared, and sought after) who prepare their objects and empower them through proper rites. Astrologers are also in great demand, particularly to determine auspicious times for all important events. Literate Cambodians follow the traditions of divination, sorcery, spirit worship, and other animistic beliefs—fear and appeasement dominate their thinking and practice, even though they often try to hide this from non-Cambodians and non-Buddhist persons for fear of being considered superstitious.

When you begin to dialogue with your Cambodian friend, state how belief in Jesus liberates us from these wrongs and gives us what we actually need. Listen to her, find out what she does in times of crisis, and offer to pray for her and her family. Know that the surrendering of spirit worship is a difficult process for a Cambodian. Share promises from God's Word that show how the Lord saves us from our troubles when we put our trust in Him.

What We Can Do

Animism, divination, astrology, and spirit possession are discussed later in this book. These topics are important for Cambodians, but their most urgent need is prayer for the healing of wounded souls who have suffered because of war and persecution. With utter chaos in the political and social system of their country, even Cambodians who live in far-off lands have gone through terrible trauma. They do not often show it, but they are hurting and deeply suspicious, and they have hidden anger in their hearts. Look for such signs and extend a healing touch to these people. Let them know that you are truly interested in them as people. Your main focus should be to touch them, in tangible ways, with the love of Christ. Let them see it, feel it, and believe it through your actions and words.

Remember, too, that Cambodia received Hinduism first and then adopted Buddhism. I believe it may be necessary for you to know something about Hinduism if you wish to minister to Cambodians.

THERAVADA BUDDHISM IN LAOS

Laos is a largely rural nation landlocked between Myanmar, Cambodia, Thailand, Vietnam, and China. In the past, Laos has been subjected to the hegemony of several Southeast Asian nations, as well as France, but always managed to bounce back to some sort of independence (through difficult political transitions). When Laos became a republic (under communist rule) in 1975, the monarchy came to an end.

Laos has a relatively small population (about 5.5 million), but a large number of Laotians live in Thailand, perhaps even more than in

Laos. There are very few Laotian Christians, yet now there is a wonderful opportunity to reach out to them because of relaxation in government restrictions on religious pursuits. Even so, the strong Theravada influence is a stumbling block, and there are very few missionaries devoted to Laotians.

Society and Religion

There are three major groups of Laotians. The Lao Sung, of Tibeto-Burman stock, reside in the highland ranges and make up approximately 10 percent of the population. The Lao Theung live in both the midland and highland ranges and are about 25 percent of the population. The Lao Loum occupy the lowland (fertile, good for rice cultivation) and constitute the majority at around 65 percent of the populace. (There are at least forty ethnic groups identified in the country.)

To open doors, ask your Laotian friend about his community of origin and the language he normally speaks in his household. Laotian ethnic differences have not led to large-scale strain or conflict, but there is an underlying mistrust among the various ethnic groups—the Lao Loum have traditionally dominated public life and enjoyed greater benefits. Know that even under the terms *Lao Sung, Lao Theung,* and *Lao Loum* there are several ethnic communities, so find out your friend's specific subgroup. (Also be aware that the Lao Theung have sometimes been labeled with derogatory terms.)

Among the smaller ethnic communities, the Hmong people are most widely known. Although Theravada is prominent, many groups are only nominally Buddhist. These communities live in higher ranges, follow the worship and appeasement of spirits and the dead (attached to place, family, or kin), and are constantly impacted by healers, diviners, and shamans.

The *Lao Loum* (lowland) rural society is largely autonomous, managing its own affairs without much centralized government interference. The wat—the center of village life—is managed by a committee of people (sometimes former monks) known for their integrity and morality. The Lao Loum, the backbone of Laotian Buddhism, go to the wat for meetings, prayers (based on the lunar calendar), festivals, and ceremonies. Children being educated in the village wat are taught both the basics of Theravada and secular subjects; even the introduction of an elaborate national system of secular education has not truly diminished the importance of the wat as an education center.

The *Lao Theung* (mostly midland) are divided into several ethnic groups of varying size (for example, the Kammu community has more than four hundred thousand people). Although they are often more receptive to the gospel than the Lao Loum, the Lao Theung are animists, who highly value shamans and healers, who are, it is believed, adept at protecting people from illness and healing those who do become sick. They are also believed to have greater spiritual power than Lao Loum shamans. The male or female healer identifies the disease(s) caused by the spirits and applies the powers that he or she earlier obtained both through personal spirit-caused sickness and through trances and other manifestations. These healers are originally visited by the spirits and become ill; they are eventually healed by other shamans, and then a process of training begins under a senior shaman, during which the powers obtained are established and sharpened.

Spirits, as in Thailand, are called *phi* and are found everywhere, even in specifically designated monastic huts. The clergy does not discourage the laity from this belief; they recognize the existence and operation of good phi, and some are well-known for their mastery over evil phi (often through ceremonies of placation).

The Lao Theung are particularly given to the worship and appeasement of ancestor spirits; on every important familial occasion, ancestors are invoked (their spirits are considered to be benevolent). There are clear biblical injunctions against the worship or appeasement of spirits in general, including ancestor spirits. Leviticus 19:28 commands, "Do not cut your bodies for the dead or put tattoo marks on yourselves. I am the LORD." In Deuteronomy 18:10–11 we read,

> Let no one be found among you who sacrifices his son or daughter in the fire, who practices divination or sorcery, interprets omens, engages in witchcraft, or casts spells, or who is a medium or spiritist or who consults the dead.

Psalm 115:17–18 declares, "It is not the dead who praise the LORD, those who go down to silence; it is we who extol the LORD, both now and forevermore." We are warned against approaching the dead in Isaiah 8:19: "When men tell you to consult mediums and spiritists, who whisper and mutter, should not a people inquire of their God? Why consult the dead on behalf of the living?" This is even compared to adultery in Proverbs 2:18: "[The] house [of the adulteress] leads down to death and her paths to the spirits of the dead."

The Hmong People and Opium

Among the *Lao Sung* (highland) there are several sizable groups; the Hmong group is the largest (comprising nearly two-thirds of the Lao Sung). Hmong are also widely found in Vietnam and Thailand, and many have moved to the United States as refugees. The Hmong are family-oriented people whose lives center around the village wat. Your evangelistic focus, then, should be on the family of your friend rather than on the entire community. When the head of a family changes his heart, his entire family may also accept Jesus as Lord and Savior (the Lao Sung are generally the most open to Christ).

The Hmong cultivated opium for medicinal and ritual purposes before they came under the twentieth-century colonial occupation of the French, who encouraged its proliferation for commercial purposes. Hmongs then commonly began to use it for their own enjoyment, and there was very little resistance from civil or religious authorities. Many of the Hmong are still under this bondage. Pray earnestly for their spiritual and physical liberation. Hmongs frequently recognize the ill effects of drug abuse, but in the absence of a strong theological resistance against its addictive power, they experience overwhelming practical helplessness.

Substance Abuse and the Word of God

The focus on keeping our body holy is strongly emphasized in the New Testament. The gospel of Jesus Christ makes it plain (in contrast to Buddhism) that the body is not a burden, an evil thing, or a source of bad karma (see 1 Corinthians 6:15); it is weaker than the spirit (Matthew 26:41) but is nevertheless the residence of God's Spirit: "Do you not know that your body is a temple of the Holy Spirit, who is in you, whom you have received from God? You are not your own; you were bought at a price. Therefore honor God with your body" (1 Corinthians 6:19–20).

> "Everything is permissible for me"—but not everything is beneficial. "Everything is permissible for me"—but I will not be mastered by anything. "Food for the stomach and the stomach for food"—but God will destroy them both. The body is not meant for sexual immorality, but for the Lord, and the Lord for the body. (1 Corinthians 6:12–13)

Multiple Spouses

Another problem among Hmongs (and in other Southeast Asian Theravada communities) is the practice of having more than one wife (or sometimes more than one husband) at the same time. Although this is not rampant, society at large seems to condone it, and the Hindu *Mahabharata* (one of two highly regarded ancient epics that impact the lives of all Hindu classes) has a prominent character that has five simultaneous husbands. Scripture is clearly against these practices: "Do not take your wife's sister as a rival wife and have sexual relations with her while your wife is living" (Leviticus 18:18). In Deuteronomy 17:17 we read, "[The king] must not take many wives, or his heart will be led astray." The Lord saw that this would be abominably practiced by some rulers.

The prophet Malachi reports,

> Another thing you do: You flood the LORD's altar with tears. You weep and wail because he no longer pays attention to your offerings or accepts them with pleasure from your hands. You ask, "Why?" It is because the LORD is acting as the witness between you and the wife of your youth, because you have broken faith with her, though she is your partner, the wife of your marriage covenant. Has not the LORD made them one? In flesh and spirit they are his. And why one? Because he is seeking godly offspring. So guard yourself in your spirit, and do not break faith with the wife of your youth. (Malachi 2:13–15)

Continuation of Buddhism

Theravada, which came to Laos in the eighth century, has been the religion of Laotian elitists for over twelve hundred years. It took six more centuries for Buddhism to become the nation's most widely practiced religion. (There is no missionary urgency in Buddhism, due to the perceived power of samsara. The Word of God, in contrast, clearly says that we have only one life, and the Lord Jesus has commanded us to take the Good News of salvation to the ends of the earth in His name.) The Buddhist strategy, again, has been first to establish themselves as a distinct group and then penetrate into their adopted society through the amalgamation of local beliefs and practices.

So we have two tasks. *First,* we need to pray and then examine the futility of folk practices and beliefs; *second,* we need to answer the genuine concerns of orthodox Buddhists at their theological level. We also must understand the role of Theravada as synonymous with nationalism and loyalty and respond to this by showing that being a follower of Jesus Christ does not keep us from being attached to our national identities and demonstrating our patriotism.

Ironically, communist rule helped Laotians to look at their religion from a different standpoint. The enforced socioeconomic reforms somewhat eroded the influence of Buddhism in both Laos and Cambodia (perhaps more prominently in Laos); nevertheless, Theravada is so ultimately entwined with Laotian culture that the communists had to gradually allow for the practice of Buddhism, and since the 1990s there has been a great resurgence. More wats are now open, more people attend the festivals and other religious activities, and more people join monasteries.

At present, Theravada Buddhism is moving upward in popularity among Laotians, in particular among the majority Lao Loum. You now have an excellent opportunity to share the gospel of Jesus Christ in your person-to-person contacts. Laotian culture needs tremendous financial, moral, and prayer support to build infrastructure, and its society needs modernization through science and medicine. One immediate question is, will the Laotians and Cambodians relinquish faith and become secularized, or will they retain Buddhism while at the same time trying to receive the tools of materialism from the West?

REVIVING THERAVADA: NEO-BUDDHISM IN INDIA

The Maha Bodhi Society, an organization devoted to the spread of Buddhism, was founded in Calcutta, in 1892, to help spread the message of Buddha among the Indian Hindu majority. This society began to work toward the renovation of shrines in Bodh Gaya, where Gautama Buddha first realized his nirvana, and was instrumental in the celebration of his twenty-five hundredth birthday throughout the world.

Many nations have helped in renovating Buddhist shrines in India, including a beautiful Buddhavihar constructed with the help of Japanese Buddhists in the state of Orissa in eastern India, where the emperor Asoka repented of his violent war against the people of that region (this began his conversion to Buddhism). While the shrines continue to be a great attraction for Buddhist pilgrimages, efforts at substantially reviving Buddhism among Hindus in India in a significant manner have not been fruitful.

Meanwhile, the Hindu elitist classes presently recognize the massive Buddhist contributions to their ethics and philosophy. For more than one thousand years they have been slowly assimilating Buddhist thought and practice as their own, even as they have sometimes violently fought against Buddhist influence in various regions of India, ensuring that there will not be any distinct and separate Buddhist consciousness among them. (The process of assimilation is clearly seen in their preference for personal names taken from Buddhism, often without the origin.)

A breakthrough came in 1956, when a respected Indian political leader, Dr. B. R. Ambedkar, chose to convert to Theravada—"orthodox" Buddhism—as a protest to the society of caste. He believed that this was the only way the lower castes could be in a position to cast off their stigma and establish social equality. Ambedkar looked at Gautama Buddha mostly as a social reformer who fought against the domination of the upper castes in India.

This assumption is valid to some extent, but remember that even the earliest Buddhism recognized "superior" qualities in the Brahmans (see chapter 1), and the emancipation of the so-called lower Hindu castes is not emphasized within Buddhist theology. Nonetheless, revolt against Hinduism was a political act that brought the problem of Hindu discrimination worldwide attention, and at least three million people converted to Buddhism because of Ambedkar. Such voluntary and instantaneous adoption of a faith is virtually unheard of. Unfortunately, since most of the converts came from the so-called "untouchables," they have become a separate caste of neo-Buddhists, retaining (in the eyes of Hindus) the stigma of belonging to the lower castes.

Very recently there was much ado about the possibility of another million from the so-called lower Indian castes openly converting to Buddhism, and some Western Christian leaders saw this as a huge opportunity for these classes to embrace Jesus. The fact of the matter is that such conversions are prompted primarily by political motivation. Christian activists interested in fostering social and political alliances were excited by these developments, but most church leaders in India, who dedicate their lives to the spread of the gospel of Jesus Christ under very difficult and hostile circumstances, appeared to be amused by such enthusiasm.

When you come across a neo-Buddhist from India, please pray that he will understand that he has not liberated himself from the idolatry that dominated his Hindu life. Although he wants to develop a rationalistic perspective, the rituals that he adopts for the worship of Buddha are anything but reasonable. Pray that he will realize that the Brahman still occupies a superior position in samsara; how many countless times should he die and be reborn in order to obtain what he wants to achieve through his conversion to Buddhism?

Realize that while political alliances among neo-Buddhists, other so-called lower castes, Muslims, and Christians may be a necessary reality in India, it is not a sufficient condition for salvation. Political revolutions bring in more problems than they solve; spiritual revolution brings stability, peace, and prosperity. Pray that overenthusiastic Christian activism will not become a barrier to attracting Indians to the grace of our Lord and Savior, Jesus Christ.

MAHAYANA BUDDHISM

6

Mahayana Buddhism is widely prevalent in China, Nepal, Japan, Korea, and Vietnam. The Buddhism practiced in Bhutan, Sikkim (in India), Tibet, and Mongolia may be considered a variant of Mahayana; however, since this variety is dramatically different from Mahayana proper, we will treat it as a third category—Vajrayana—in the next chapter.

Mahayana, the largest Buddhist sect, was practiced in India and central Asia (mainly comprising parts of Iran, Afghanistan, western China, and eastern Turkistan, most of which is presently Islamic) for at least two thousand years. As already mentioned, "Mahayana" (in its most general sense) means "greater vehicle," meaning that it is believed to provide the way to nirvana to a greater number of people.

CHARACTERISTICS OF MAHAYANA

For one thing, there is only a subdued emphasis on monastic life in Mahayana—the laity as well as the clergy may attain nirvana. While Theravada does not encourage prayer (adoration and veneration of relics and images are common), Mahayana Buddhists pray to Gautama Buddha and others. On the other hand, Mahayana has introduced a number of Bodhisattvas who act as mediators to help people to overcome samsara in their journey toward nirvana.

Mahayana is more mythologically oriented than Theravada, focusing on narratives about Gautama Buddha and others in great detail. While Theravada also has its mythology, there is some hesitation to fully subscribe because of the desire to stick to the orthodox (canonical) Buddhist teaching. Mahayana, along with its amazing web of mythologies, also emphasizes magical acts, recitation of the sayings of Buddha and other scriptural texts in Mahayana, and folk practices.

Worship of multiple Buddhas, all with supernatural powers and ruling various heavens, is another Mahayana characteristic. Different texts suggest that all the Buddhas (some report one thousand, others several thousand) may be worshiped equally without discrimination. But the central figure for the present age is Gautama.

It is also suggested that Gautama Buddha has three bodies: a cosmic body that cannot be described or spoken of in words, a magical body that enables him to fully benefit from the merit that he generated before his nirvana, and a body that he assumes (in living form) to save people from suffering and lead them to nonexistence. Mahayana believes in a heavenly rebirth where there is only happiness. There are many heavens, and eventually people are born to continue toward total extinction.

While Gautama is considered to be the Buddha of this age, Mahayana believes also in a Buddha of the future—Maitreya, who will return to this world to restore the original orthodoxy (approved Buddhist ways of living). Devotees focus on birth in happier lands (or heavens) after their current life, and the Mahayana goal is to attain buddhahood. Mahayana distinguishes itself as *Bodhisattva Marga* ("the way of Bodhisattva"), in contrast to Theravada (called "the way of the disciples"). The ultimate intention, then, is to become a Bodhisattva (ever willing to help those who inevitably undergo suffering in this world), a stage toward eventual buddhahood. Bodhisattvas have several ideals, and since this is the goal for all Mahayana Buddhists, they are expected to acquire these virtues (such as extending help to others with no selfish motive, meditation, peace, patience, morality, right effort, supernatural insight, and a forgiving attitude) and may transfer their merit to others.

Another important characteristic of Mahayana is that it has numerous scriptural texts, and interpretations vary from one group to another. Adherents commonly focus on one text from among the many and then build their religious practices around it (to the exclusion of others). Mahayana in this manner lends itself to the development of a host of cults.

Some of the early Mahayana texts justify carnal desire as a process of compassion. As the realization of Gautama Buddha started with the denouncement of all desire, the position of accepting carnality is a gargantuan departure from his original teaching. The marriage of the monks is a widespread phenomenon in Mahayana now, and I cite this as an example to show how in Buddhism (as in other faiths), human reasoning easily comes to dominate practical living. In the absence of a standard and exclusive scripture, Mahayana Buddhism added magic, alchemy, and other disciplines to its belief and practice.

In contrast to the Theravada model, the various schools of Mahayana are very active in enlisting Western converts to Buddhism. The Mahayana Bodhisattva model encourages its followers to help others in their journey, which explains its expedited recruiting practices. Moreover, its open-ended approach to the widespread availability of salvation in this life—as well as its magical mysticism with magical powers—attracts more people than Theravada. From its very inception in northwestern India (including Afghanistan), Mahayana in its philosophical orientation was more interested in bringing people into its fold than establishing itself as an imperial religion. The Theravada characteristics of nationalism and loyalism are not strong among followers of Mahayana.

Recall that Theravada holds that the highest goal of becoming an Arhat is achieved only by leading the life of a monk, away from the shackles of this world. Gautama Buddha was an Arhat and a special one because, in addition to attaining nirvana, he attained parinirvana (total or perfect nirvana), by which he gained ultimate knowledge. Mahayana, on the other hand, celebrates (for clergy *and* laity) the ideal of Bodhisattva, who, after eons of samsara is ready to enter nirvana but, out of compassion for all living things, embraces a mission of helping others and therefore being involved with them. Mahayana claims that the Arhat model is selfish, while the Bodhisattva model is selfless and, thus, exemplary and allegedly exhibited in the life of Gautama Buddha.

Gautama is said to have remained, even after attaining nirvana, to teach the true knowledge and show his followers the means to achieve it. It is argued that numerous hidden scriptures written by Gautama Buddha reveal this truth (even though his early teaching may seem to be at variance), and he is continually reborn even now, rather than extinct. The nirvana that he is claimed to have attained in the Theravada scriptures is only an illusion, a model to the people so that they will be encouraged about the possibilities of their own future. With such deeply rooted differences in sectarian precepts, it is no surprise that even though they profess the same overall faith, communication between Theravada and Mahayana adherents is not extensive.

SCHOOLS OF THOUGHT WITHIN MAHAYANA BUDDHISM

The *Eclectic* (or *Comprehensive*) School considers all Buddhist scriptures authentic and adopts mystical initiation, silent meditation, and simple faith in all that has been said. People find truth by realizing their own identity with the universal reality, and enlightenment is available for all beings. The object of faith may be Gautama Buddha (the historical person), Amida Buddha (or "Amitabha"—a nonhistorical, mythological Buddha), Dainichi (the Supreme Buddha, nonhistorical and mythological), other Buddhas, or even non-Buddhist deities. *Living in unity with the universe is the goal.*

The *Esoteric* (or *Mystic*) School (also known as "Shingon") identifies the universe with the body of the Supreme Buddha, Dainichi, and has encouraged the unification of Buddhism with the native Japanese religion, Shinto, holding that Shinto deities are manifestations of the same eternal Buddha. There have been periodic attempts by Shinto followers to break from this syncretistic relationship between the two, but none have survived. According to the esoteric school,

> Other religions and other Buddhist schools of thought may be useful in man's lower stages of spiritual development, but the highest stage of true enlightenment, for which the inferior teachings have prepared the way, is found in the union of man with the universe by means of the mystical techniques transmitted in esoteric Buddhism. (Bentley-Taylor and Offner, 184–85)

The *Paradisic* (or *Pure Land*) School teaches salvation by faith through a simple recitation of the sacred formula that encourages belief in Amida Buddha, who obtained the merit to become Buddha but chose not to enter nirvana in order to help others attain it.

The *Zen* School has come to dominate many others and has been nicely packaged as the cure for all personal and social ills. Zen does not believe in the intercessory role of anyone, including the Bodhisattvas, and takes the exhortation of the historical Buddha seriously and literally: "Be ye lamps unto yourselves. Rely on yourselves, and do not rely on external help. . . . Look [not] for assistance to anyone besides yourselves" (Burtt, 49).

ZEN BUDDHISM

Zen Buddhism, the most popular elitist Buddhistic variety among people in the West, is extremely individualistic, encouraging everyone to strive for personal betterment and spiritual merit. Zen also has a methodical system of disciplines that appeals to the do-it-yourself cultures of the West, and it also excites people's minds through religious thoughts couched in appealing similes, metaphors, and riddles.

The simple philosophy of Zen Buddhism took roots in Japan in the twelfth century. It was embraced first by the military class, since "it called for action, for the most rigorous self-discipline, for self-reliance, for contempt of death" (Chang, 27). Zen seeks through meditation (dhyana) to hold "thought collected, not to let thought wander away from its legitimate path; that is, it means to have the mind concentrated on a single subject of thought" (ibid., 29).

There are various definitions of "Zen." One description is that "it liberates our natural energies and compels us to express our faculty for happiness and love." Another is that it "is the art of seeing into the nature of one's own being, and it points the way from bondage to freedom." A third is that it is "Enlightenment, but even so, Zen is not only Enlightenment, it is also the way to its attainment" (ibid.).

Zen has no respect for any sacred scriptures. It worships no supreme deity, nor does it follow ceremonial rites or believe in an afterlife or even in the existence of souls. There is no emphasis on the veneration of Buddha, nor is there any need to undergo pilgrimage. *Man is an end in himself*—he possesses the Buddha within, and he should realize this without intercession from anyone.

In some respects, Zen is a revolt against all other forms of Buddhism. It may likewise be characterized as a nihilistic philosophy, for apart from sharing the Buddhist view that earthly existence is senseless and useless, Zen also wants people to break from any tradition that may restrict innovative freedom and practice.

Zen practitioners aim at attaining enlightenment called *sattori*. The individual perceives for himself the Reality, whatever that reality may be, and regulates himself through various disciplines, especially through the use of the *koan,* which is a riddle, a paradoxical question, "a statement that is seemingly contradictory or opposed to common sense and yet is perhaps true" (*Merriam-Webster Collegiate Dictionary*). Even the solving of a single riddle is enough to open the Zen practitioner's mind to Reality (although traditionally the list of koans is at least a thousand). An aspiring Zen disciple may be asked to solve statements such as "Talk without your tongue"; "Play your stringless lute"; and "Clap with a single hand."

Here is an example of a Zen koan:

> Riko [Li-k'u], a high government officer of the T'ang dynasty, asked Nansen: "A long time ago a man kept a goose in a bottle. It grew larger and larger until it could not get out of the bottle any more; he did not want to break the bottle, nor did he wish to hurt the goose; how would you get it out?" The master called out, "O Officer!" [and] Riko at once responded, "Yes!" (The master said, "There, it is out!" This

was the way Nansen produced the goose out of its imprison-
ment.) (Burtt, 237)

What Is a Riddle?

A riddle is a brainteaser, a guessing game, a puzzle whose solution
requires specific mental acumen, which not everyone acquires. Riddles
are not exclusive to any one religion or community; they have been
used in folktales, folk literature, and literary works in all cultures. However, Eastern philosophies have developed the art of constructing and
solving riddles as a means of meditation. In descriptive riddles, for
instance, a disciple is given enigmatic, obscure, or glossed-over descriptions of an object or event and asked to give a correct answer. The
descriptions may even have multiple and/or misleading meanings,
requiring an intelligent guess (so to speak).

The second popular "riddle category" is composed of puzzles that
demand cleverness or shrewdness from the solver and that often focus
on the function of the object (or person) that forms the subject matter
of the riddle. Each category of riddle has several subcategories, some
based on numbers, some on letters, some on dates, and so forth.
Regardless, reasoned thinking and speed of response (to manipulate the
various possibilities of an answer to the riddle presented) are necessary.

Many religions have used riddles as a means to expound their meanings as well as to experience, control, and manipulate gods and humans.
Hinduism in particular has a long history of this. The earliest extant
Hindu Veda (the Rig Veda) talks of riddles as part of religious rituals.
Buddhism adopted this as a significant means for self-examination and
self-revelation. Often the riddles function as wagers for intelligent entertainment, and Buddhism imparts spirituality to these manmade puzzles.

During the Middle Ages, some clergy also used riddles to expound
on catechisms they were teaching to the laity (for example, "If God can
do all things, can He create a rock so heavy that He himself cannot
move it?"). Most religious texts that use riddles to expound on their
philosophy have employed the dialogue format. Human wisdom and
construction dominated all these efforts; obscurity and concealment are
important characteristics of riddles.

In Numbers 12:6–8, God talks about revealing himself through
visions and dreams but not in riddles that are couched in words that do
not clearly reveal the information intended. While dreams and visions
do need interpretation so that we can understand, these are not revealed
as brainteasers.

There are several straightforward riddles reported in the Old Testament, but all are devised by humans rather than suggested by God. The

tragic story of Samson and his wife (in Judges 14–15) involves a riddle that in some ways is no riddle at all because it demanded knowledge of a personal story that was kept secret. The queen of Sheba came to Solomon to test his wisdom with "hard questions" (riddles: 1 Kings 10:1; 2 Chronicles 9:1). The sayings and riddles of the wise are mentioned in Proverbs 1:6, and the psalmist sings, "I will turn my ear to a proverb; with the harp I will expound my riddle" (Psalm 49:4).

In several places in the book of Daniel, the use and understanding of riddles is mentioned. The king was told, "This man Daniel, whom the king called Belteshazzar, was found to have a keen mind and knowledge and understanding, and also the ability to interpret dreams, explain riddles and solve difficult problems" (5:12). It is also implied that a man who understands and solves riddles may function as a master of intrigue (8:23).

Nowhere in the Word of God is the riddle shown to be a spiritual device, a means to experience God, or a way to reach salvation. Although riddles were widely used in his time, Jesus used parables instead. Christ's teaching in John 6:53–60 is sometimes considered to be a riddle, but that the Lord did not intend it to be a riddle becomes obvious in subsequent verses when he admonishes, "Does this offend you?" (6:61).

There is one clear riddle in Revelation 13:18 regarding the number of the beast, but this belongs to what will happen in the future. The future is always a puzzle for humans, but for those who put their trust in God, it loses its value as a riddle. This is one reason the Word of God emphatically forbids us to indulge in divination; we can and should prepare ourselves to meet the future, but solving riddles is not the way.

God's ways are *mysterious,* but they are not *riddles* that need to be solved with human wisdom and training in rhetoric (consider Romans 11:33 and 1 Corinthians 13:12). While as humans we may not be able to exhaustively grasp the full meaning of His Word, none of His utterances qualifies as a riddle because *He was and is not intending to hide His meaning—Scripture is a revelation, not a concealment.* We have assurance that we will receive revelation in due course, not by solving riddles but by reposing our faith in the one true God.

In this context, point out to your Zen Buddhist friend that God is completely simple (uncomplex) yet also immeasurably majestic. He is at hand always, and we don't have to recite or solve riddles to experience Him. Oracles need to be alert in their pronouncements because they are not sure the things they predict will come to pass, and failures are easily avoided by presenting solutions in riddles with multiple meanings and possibilities. Our God is not an oracle to indulge in riddles as a means of communicating His intent; while life itself presents many paradoxes, God is not a paradox, for a paradox is not the same as a mystery.

Obscure Mysticism

Zen Buddhism may recognize nature as a supreme power, but it denies God as a person who is transcendent (away from us, beyond our full experience and knowledge) as well as immanent (close to us, within our experience and knowledge). Zen is given to obscure mysticism (to God's exclusion). While it is important for us to look inside ourselves when praying, this must not occur in isolation from the Lord. *The purpose of any meditation is the edification of one's soul, and this cannot be achieved without the help of God.* In addition, an "empty house," one without God's presence, is an easy and vulnerable target for evil spirits (see Matthew 12:43–45).

Zen Buddhism denies the need for God in our salvation; individuals must accomplish their own, and this is to be attained mainly through meditation based on riddles. However, since Zen leaves no room for the operation of God's grace, it is impossible for humans to be perfected, which Zen demands. All the talk about controlling the mind and canalizing it into spiritual matters is simply an ideal, never to be actually achieved. Since one inevitably fails to be pure in thought, deed, and word, it follows that humans will be reborn again and again to attempt to improve their lot and continue toward nirvana.

Zen does not see holiness anywhere—it is an unconventional pursuit that focuses on repudiating and eliminating all institutions, traditions, established practices, and beliefs. Zen does not recognize a leader (though in reality the Zen guru is highly revered). Zen does not recognize sin or the need for a mediator between God and humanity and, accordingly, acknowledges no necessity for repentance or change. These characteristics appeal to modern humans, especially those pursuing artistic and other professional careers.

Deep within, we all know that in every walk of life we need the help, understanding, and support of others. If this is true in day-to-day living, we can easily imagine how indispensable it is for us to have a mediator to lean on in our spiritual journey. The true Mediator is a self-sacrificing Shepherd who does not lead his sheep astray or leave them unprotected (see Mark 6:34; John 10:11–13). The guru or Zen Master does not offer help, direction, or safety.

Like the methods of meditation from other schools of Buddhism, Zen teaches us to focus on our inward nature and try to either improve or extinguish it without absorbing the qualities that the Lord wants us to receive and practice *by His grace and in His strength*. The apostle Paul wrote,

> You were taught, with regard to your former way of life, to put off your old self, which is being corrupted by its deceitful desires; to be made new in the attitude of your minds; and to put on the new self, created to be like God in true righteousness and holiness. (Ephesians 4:22–24)

The next verse says it all: "Therefore each of you must put off falsehood and speak truthfully to his neighbor, for we are all members of one body." The emphasis of God's Word is on being a body member rather than a selfish organism (Zen focuses on the individual to the exclusion of neighbor and community).

The nature of the enlightenment sought after in Zen Buddhism is not an uncovering of the truth but only an insistence on the use of the mind and the will. The Zen Buddhist engages his mind and his will in strenuous efforts to realize what he calls truth. This is a fundamental characteristic of Buddhism in general and has been developed into the main focus of Zen and other sectarian groups.

Is Meditation Based on Grit and Determination?

Ashvaghosha, the first-century Buddhist historian and poet, mentions in several places in his *Buddhacarita* (roughly translated "Buddha's biography") that the grit and determination of Gautama Buddha to realize "truth" and attain nirvana at any cost is the model to emulate. Mass media often portray these qualities as the reason for the success of individuals in reaching their arduous goals. What absolute individualism (anarchy) actually engenders is self-obsession, haughtiness, and pride, which go against the common good of community.

We come across so many situations in which, even with unimagined grit and determination, certain things cannot be achieved. Dependence on God does not mean that the individual should not do his best to achieve his goal; rather, it implies that we recognize the sovereignty of God over all His creation (Luke 12:7) and therefore apply our grit and determination to praying unceasingly.

> Then Jesus told his disciples a parable to show them that they should always pray and not give up. He said: "In a certain town there was a judge who neither feared God nor cared about men. And there was a widow in that town who kept coming to him with the plea, 'Grant me justice against my

adversary.' For some time he refused. But finally he said to himself, 'Even though I don't fear God or care about men, yet because this widow keeps bothering me, I will see that she gets justice, so that she won't eventually wear me out with her coming!' . . . Listen to what the unjust judge says. And will not God bring about justice for his chosen ones, who cry out to him day and night? Will he keep putting them off? I tell you, he will see that they get justice, and quickly" (Luke 18:1–8).

An important truth to impart to your Zen Buddhist friend is that the will of God ultimately prevails over ours. In response, he might present the theory of karma to explain why something is not achieved despite appropriate meditation. However, God our Father disciplines us even as He protects us from evil and blesses us with all that is good.

Karma is the consequence of previous lives, but God has promised to forgive and forget our past if we repent and return to Him (Hebrews 8:12). The shackles of karma are broken and eliminated when we turn from our sins with His help. This good news should be given to your Buddhist friend in all kindliness, never in a triumphant tone. Encourage him with other biblical accounts of God forgiving sinners (e.g., David and Bathsheba) when they approached Him with contrite hearts. God is all hope, and there is no room for pessimism when we deal with Him.

The Lord Jesus told us to pray that God's will would be done on earth as it is in heaven (see Matthew 6:10; Psalm 40:8). Although folk Buddhist practitioners realize that there are powers beyond what they can do, elitist Buddhism focuses primarily on the power of the individual. However, God's will is not karma; God's will is always for the good of His children (see Jeremiah 29:11; James 5:11). He intervenes on our behalf when we pray, and the process of prayer edifies and sanctifies the pray-er to God.

The apostle James informs us that while depending on oneself is boastful, depending on God's will is true devotion:

> Now listen, you who say, "Today or tomorrow we will go to this or that city, spend a year there, carry on business and make money." Why, you do not even know what will happen tomorrow. What is your life? You are a mist that appears for a little while and then vanishes. Instead, you ought to say, "If it is the Lord's will, we will live and do this or that." As it is, you boast and brag. All such boasting is evil. (4:13–16)

Mahayana Buddhism in China

China is the most populous country in the world, and its citizens consider themselves to be Chinese although they are diverse in their backgrounds. Central authority (under different dynasties), which knit various ethnic communities into a Chinese nation, ruled China for thousands of years.

Social Composition and Language

China, which declares itself to be a multiethnic nation, carries an undercurrent of ethnic rivalry. The government estimates that there are about sixty diverse ethnic minorities in the country, and this number is probably an incomplete reflection. The Han is the largest ethnic Chinese group and has the largest say in political and economic affairs. The Han may be considered an open-ended group that under various considerations admits people from other ethnicities into its fold, yet they do have their own distinctive characteristics.

Often you may hear the term *autonomous region*. In China this is a province-like administrative unit in which the majority of the people belong to one of the recognized national minorities. Such areas come directly under the central Chinese government rather than provincial authority. Tibet is an example of an "autonomous region"; although there is some amount of autonomy given to its minorities, over the years tension and conflict have developed with the central government, and minorities such as Tibetans and Uygurs consider the Han Chinese to be colonialists.

The Han Chinese are not a homogeneous community—its subgroups speak several mutually unintelligible dialects—but they are united under a single identity because of commonly shared values and a written language. The nature of the Chinese script system greatly facilitates this process. Chinese language characters focus on meanings and not on sounds, and these ideographs are a common ground for the diverse Han subgroups; that is, while people speak differently, they all write alike.

Buddhism and Confucianism

Confucianism and Buddhism share some common ground. For example, Confucius taught that heredity had no role to play in social status, and Buddhism, which preached against the caste hierarchy of the Hindus, resonated. According to Buddhism, individual effort (rather than dependence) is the main path by which the journey toward nirvana should be achieved; Confucius also insisted that individual effort is most effective in bettering one's lot.

Confucius asked his disciples to ignore (not adore) gods; orthodox Buddhism has a similar view. Scholarship was highly valued by Confucius, and Buddhism insists on rigorous training for its monks, both in spiritual and scholastic matters. The Middle Way (avoiding both self-indulgence and self-mortification, taking no extreme positions) is the bedrock of both Buddhism and Confucianism.

Since Buddhism is a religion of accommodation, it was never difficult to accept as its own the host traditions and knowledge practiced in Chinese society. Again, both Confucianism and Buddhism were imperial religions—both accepting the support of the nobility and assisting them in their role as guardians of society. Confucius did not highly value manual labor, and in Buddhism, activity (especially manual labor) adds to karma and needs to be avoided by monks. Confucianism does not look as favorably upon military service as civil authority; in Buddhism, killing any living being is wrong.

There are, however, certain aspects of Buddhism that run counter to Confucian practices. For example, Confucianism does not say that there should be a separate monastic class who should be celibate. Confucianism also validates the present life and encourages people to better their lots even now (more similar to Mahayana than to Theravada).

The Survival of Chinese Buddhism

Buddhism plays a compartmentalized role in the life of the Chinese. Unlike in the Theravada nations of Southeast Asia that happily adopted the Indian ideas and structures that arrived with Buddhism, the Chinese made several innovations to the fundamentals of Buddhism, and *that* type of Buddhism then became the standard for the eventual Mahayana nations.

Buddhism probably came to China in the first or early second century, but it did not become widely popular with the Chinese until the seventh century. We must recognize that Buddhism was never totally embraced or dominant in China throughout its history—China is not a Buddhist nation. Rather, Buddhism became a part of the other Chinese belief systems, such as Confucianism and Taoism.

There was a Buddhist decline around the ninth century; however, within the time it enjoyed imperial support, many texts were translated from the Indian originals into Chinese, and many scholars traveled between the nations. This scholarly interaction and the availability of the Buddhist texts greatly contributed to the spread and maintenance of Buddhism in China. People began to accept Buddhism mainly as an adjunct to their traditional Confucian and Taoist beliefs.

Buddhism began to assume importance in certain facets of life, such as funeral rites. Kenneth Latourette thought that the growth of Mahayana Buddhism might have been due to the fact that

> [it] presented conceptions of life after death in much more concrete forms than did beliefs then current in China. It offered vivid pictures, both in words and in paintings, of heavens of bliss and hells of torment. It therefore filled a void and gave answers to questions that men of all races and cultures seem always to have asked. (Latourette, 32)

In the process, the Chinese focused more on the heavens, their traditional belief, than on nirvana.

The Buddhism that was adopted by the Chinese elitist classes was from a variety of Indian schools, and the net result was that Chinese became a very important language of the Buddhist scriptures. From China, Mahayana spread to other countries in East and Southeast Asia.

Buddhists were persecuted in China in the ninth century; temples were destroyed and the monks and nuns were forced to become laypersons. This probably began the decline of Buddhism as an enterprising and economically powerful religion in China. (Its foreign origin was and is a great handicap for its total and unconditional acceptance among the Chinese.) At present, Buddhism survives in Chinese folk religion with a growing integration of Confucianism and Taoism: Buddhism has adopted the meditation techniques of Taoism while aligning itself as an effective means of providing a spiritual basis for Confucian thought. Zen Buddhism is not widely practiced in China, but it is exported in an effective manner from China and Japan to the West.

Chinese Ancestor Worship

Ancestor worship is the worship of deceased kinsmen (different from rites for the dead and beliefs about the dead in general). Ancestor worship is practiced in many religions, but it is most widely prevalent among (and is a hallmark of) Buddhists in East Asia.

Ancestor worship is not a *religion* but a *religious practice*. It does not have its own priesthood and is limited to the practice of an ethnic group. There is no attempt to proselytize or initiate others into it, and there is no formal doctrine—whatever is available in textual form is generally liturgical.

When I was a small boy, my father, a Hindu, used to take me to the riverside on an "auspicious" new-moon day in February or March to make offerings to the *pitr* ("forefathers") through the offices of a Brahman priest. The priest would set up his "shop" in the morning and would recite Sanskrit *slokas* (verses) in honor of the worshiper's dead ancestors, offering them uncooked rice, vegetables, pieces of new cloth, and other things. The priest was given a monetary offering for his services and was eligible to take all the other offerings given to the ancestors as his own. This was done once a year, and then the forefathers were generally forgotten. (Among the Chinese, the annual meeting with the ancestors is elaborate and is more significant. Moreover, the ancestors are worshiped every day in the family household shrine.)

The Chinese system of ancestor worship, which is also widely followed in Japan and other Southeast Asian countries, has the function of upholding the authority of elders, thereby exercising social control. This worship fosters conservative traditionalist attitudes and obedience to elders (both living and dead). Ancestors are believed to possess power similar or equivalent to that of a deity and are worshiped either in the home or in a public hall.

The process begins with the worship of recently dead parents and grandparents and is extended to all the ancestors of the family and clan, which indicates the belief that the dead are still living, that they can be contacted and their advice sought. This does not include dead or still-born children, miscarriages, or abortions, nor does it include those who die before marriage. Ancestor worship is a social institution linked to property inheritance and is primarily the responsibility of the oldest son. (Women are excluded from officiating roles.)

Confucianism greatly values ancestor worship and is concerned with the details concerning the content and arrangement of offerings, proper dress, gesture and posture, and order of precedence in appearing before the ancestral altars. Originally, Confucianism opposed Buddhism as a nirvana-focused religion but overlooked ancestor worship. Over the centuries, Buddhism not only incorporated this practice as its own but also encouraged it as plenary.

Anthropologist Francis Hsu identified three purposes for ancestor worship: (1) "to gain knowledge about the whereabouts of the dead, how they are getting along, and when they will be reincarnated"; (2) "to provide comfort for the dead"; and (3) "to invoke the dead to discharge the duties they performed while on earth, such as giving sanction on marriage and family division and acting as disciplinarian for the younger generations" (Hsu, 167).

Hsu's study shows that a family will make at least one memorial visitation every year to provide food, money, clothes, and wine to the dead. Dishes will be prepared and arranged before the two main tombs (the parents of the head of the family), a ceremonial offering before each tomb will be made, incense sticks and paper money will be burned, the head of the family will prostrate nine times before each tomb, and other male members will follow suit (one by one). Tombs of parents, spouses, and grandparents are visited in this manner.

Variations of Ancestor Worship in Other Buddhist Nations

In Korea, women do not worship the ancestors of their husbands, since those ancestors are antagonistic to them. The woman's position in her husband's household is not fully integrated, and she is treated as an outsider (ancestors are concerned only about the welfare of their own kin).

Ancestor worship in Japan is kinship-oriented, as in China, but it also becomes a means of expressing affection and respect to the dead in general. Hence, nonrelatives and people of other clans may also be included in the celebration.

In other countries, such as Sri Lanka, the rites include some aspects of Hindu ancestor worship. A mediating priest recites the sutras (verses) and transfers the merit of these rites to ancestors. In addition to household (domestic) rituals, this worship is an annual festival in Buddhist temples and becomes the largest revenue source for the Buddhist clergy.

Ancestor Worship in the Bible?

Is there any specific reference to ancestor worship in the Word of God? Some scholars have considered that the "teraphim" referred to in Genesis 31:19 ("when Laban had gone to shear his sheep, Rachel stole her father's household gods") could have been ancestor images. Deuteronomy 26:14 gives clear indication that giving offerings to the ancestors was practiced, for the tithe-giver was commanded to promise, "I have not eaten any of the sacred portion while I was in mourning, nor have I removed any of it while I was unclean, nor have I offered any of it to the dead."

There is reference to the burning of incense for the deceased in Jeremiah 34:5, and in Ezekiel 43:7–9 we read a strong condemnation of worshiping the dead. Isaiah 65:1–4 is a denunciation of the practice of according sanctity to the graves of family members, and consider once again Isaiah 8:19: "When men tell you to consult mediums and spiritists, who whisper and mutter, should not a people inquire of their God? Why consult the dead on behalf of the living?"

Christian Response to Ancestor Worship

At the outset, I would like to mention that ancestor worship is not based solely upon deference to deceased elders. *Respect for elders and the dead is not rejected in Christian thought*—the Bible insists upon venerating and obeying the wisdom of those in authority over us. However, *going beyond showing respect and obeying the wisdom of parents and elders, elevating them to the position of deity, is against the Word of God.* There is great joy in heaven when a sinner repents and comes to accept Jesus as Lord and Savior, and the dead rejoice over the progress of the living toward believing and trusting in the one true God. Evangelical Christians do not pray for the salvation of the dead but focus upon the salvation of the living.

Ancestor worship regards the dead as friendly or unfriendly, so its remembrance of the dead is not simply based on love. Often fear dominates, resulting in the living engaging themselves in the placation of the dead. Although some try to distinguish between worship and placation in certain forms of ancestor worship, in most cases they go hand in hand.

The conversations addressed to the ancestors attest to the fact that they are petitions for favors. The ancestral spirits are beseeched to give oracles for the future and for exigencies currently faced. This is not only idolatry but also contravenes the injunctions against consulting mediums (see Leviticus 19:31).

In some ways the practice of ancestor worship may strengthen family ties and give worshipers a cherished identity through lineage. Nevertheless, it is also true that even though family members may get together to worship their ancestors, there can still be internecine quarrels. Families may hold grudges against one another and continue to seek opportunities to take vengeance.

The entire relationship between ancestors and the living seems to be somewhat deceitful. For example, Chinese worshipers pretend to offer money by burning moneylike currency notes rather than real bills, believing that the ancestor sees these fake notes as authentic money and will accept their offering. This actually shows reluctance on the part of the living to honor and respect the dead. The primary motivation is to keep the dead ancestors pleased and prevent them from intervening in the present (and messing things up).

Spiritism

Although spiritism is not identical to ancestor worship, each tries to contact the dead for similar purposes. In addition to prominence in Mahayana areas, spiritism is widely prevalent among Buddhist converts in Western nations. Spiritist practitioners often believe in the possibility of communicating with the spirits of the dead *and* the spirits of the living—they frequently wish to receive messages from the former for the benefit of the latter.

Spiritism has a great attraction for the bereaved family whose members want both advice and to be certain the dead do not hold any grudge against them. Also, family members miss their loved ones and are not satisfied with fond memories alone—they want to hear, feel, and touch the departed, as well.

At death, the spirit is detached from the body and becomes independent, believed to have enormous powers in this state. For instance, it can enter another body and use it to communicate with other spirits and living beings. The person (medium) who receives the independent spirit becomes the intermediary between it and the humans who seek to communicate with it. Spiritism is possible only when a body is willing to receive the spirit and act as a medium; this is rare, but individuals all over the world have accomplished it and have practiced their "trade" with some success.

To make it a case of even greater confusion, there are a number of quacks in the field claiming medium status. Fraud is always a substantial possibility in these matters, since the ends of such dealings are personal profit. Consider the story of Simon, the Samaritan sorcerer (Acts 8:14–24).

Modern Buddhist spiritism (as with other animistic religions) cloaks itself in terms from psychology and other disciplines so that people are easily deceived and begin to believe that there may be truth in the spiritist's words. Mysterious happenings add color to the entire performance, but in the end, customers risk losing their money *and* their souls, for people become addicted to spiritism and slaves to these sittings, gradually living in a world of their own.

Again, the Word of God commands us not to turn to mediums or seek out spiritists (see Leviticus 19:31; Leviticus 20:6, 27; Deuteronomy 18:9–12; 1 Samuel 28; 1 Kings 22:18–23; 1 Chronicles 10:13). Revelation informs us that the spirits of demons will perform "miraculous signs, and they go out to the kings of the whole world, to gather them for the battle on the great day of God Almighty." It is no wonder that the leaders of public opinion—in fields such as entertainment, politics, and theology—give themselves over to spiritism.

The Bible (the Word of God, who cannot lie—Titus 1:2) offers guidelines for recognizing spirits:

> Dear friends, do not believe every spirit, but test the spirits to see whether they are from God, because many false prophets have gone out into the world. This is how you can recognize the Spirit of God: Every spirit that acknowledges that

Jesus Christ has come in the flesh is from God, but every spirit that does not acknowledge Jesus is not from God. This is the spirit of the antichrist, which you have heard is coming and even now is already in the world. You, dear children, are from God and have overcome them, because the one who is in you is greater than the one who is in the world. They are from the world and therefore speak from the viewpoint of the world, and the world listens to them. We are from God, and whoever knows God listens to us; but whoever is not from God does not listen to us. This is how we recognize the Spirit of truth and the spirit of falsehood. (1 John 4:1-6)

Evil spirits will not confess that Jesus is the Lord and Savior who died on the cross for our sins, though they may acknowledge Him and tremble when His name is uttered. Their goal is to deceive people as if they are part of Jesus' retinue, and people are often misled by their personal needs. In 1 Timothy 4:1-2 we read:

The Spirit clearly says that in later times some will abandon the faith and follow deceiving spirits and things taught by demons. Such teachings come through hypocritical liars, whose consciences have been seared as with a hot iron.

Revelation 12:9 says that Satan deceives the whole world, and Revelation 13:14 says that he does so by means of miracles, which he was given power to perform. Satan is able to get into human minds, even those of believers (Acts 5:1-4; 2 Corinthians 11:3; 1 Thessalonians 3:5). The external signs of such influence include, among other things, the reception of a different spirit and a different gospel (Galatians 1:6-9). James 4:7-8 commands us, "Submit yourselves, then, to God. Resist the devil, and he will flee from you. Come near to God and he will come near to you." Thus, the remedy to avoid and be victorious over the influence of other spirits is to draw closer to God and put on "the full armor of God so that you can take your stand against the devil's schemes" (Ephesians 6:11).

Evangelizing the Chinese

The Nestorians (followers of Nestorius, who believed that Christ was two distinct persons [divine and human], a position [thankfully] rejected by the church) were the first to preach the gospel in China, in the seventh century, but when the anti-Buddhist repression began in the ninth century, the Nestorians were also persecuted and eliminated.

There were several attempts in the early sixteenth century to preach the gospel to the Chinese. Francis Xavier, who pioneered the Jesuit mission into India, Sri Lanka, Tibet, and Japan, eventually died on a small Chinese island, and many Jesuits came to China to establish churches. The Jesuits were greatly successful in converting thousands of Chinese to Catholicism; they adopted a policy of accommodation (also called the policy of cultural adaptation) that was stoutly opposed by the mendicant Dominican and Franciscan monastic orders.

Matteo Ricci was the leading light of this policy of accommodation. Among other things, he and his Jesuit colleagues were accused of approving the idolatrous practice of ancestor worship: the rites observed in honor of Confucius included kneeling down before his image, paying obeisance to a tablet representing him, and offerings (including an animal slain on the spot, wine, silk, etc.) followed by a solemn banquet. However, Ricci concluded,

> All this has nothing to do with idolatry, and perhaps it can also be said not to involve any superstition, although it will be better to change this into giving alms to the poor where it is a question of Christians. (Dunne, 291)

Several popes had already banned the rites and the policy of accommodation.

George Dunne, sympathetically reviewing the work of the Jesuits and their reasons for accommodation, declared,

> By banning the ancestral rites, the Church was forced to assume a posture that seemed hostile to the Chinese environment. Instead of leaven Christianity became a foreign substance in the body of Chinese social culture. (ibid., 300)

At present, the Roman Catholic Church pursues a policy of tolerance.

Chinese Christians themselves raised serious questions about the form and function of *filial piety* (the responsibility of children to show reverence to their parents and ancestors) among non-Christian Chinese groups. There is now a greater understanding of the importance of filial piety among the Chinese Christians. With abundant caution, they try to adopt its features, so natural to Chinese and Southeast Asian societies, without compromising their worship of the Lord.

Robert Morrison, of the London Missionary Society, arrived in 1807, producing a dictionary of the Chinese language and a full Chinese translation of the Bible. The British victory over China at the end of the Opium War (in 1842) opened the door for the subsequent entry of Protestant missionaries. American Congregationalists, American

Episcopal Methodists, and English Anglicans were the earliest to arrive.

In 1865 Hudson Taylor founded the China Inland Mission. The missionaries pursued medical, educational, and other relief and development work along with evangelism. Christianity is widely viewed even now as an import from the West, but although the Chinese communist government has imposed restrictions against Christians, there is tremendous growth of (and faithfulness in) the church in China.

Christian Witness to the Chinese People summarizes the methods of evangelism developed by house churches as follows:

> (1) Sharing their faith with their immediate family and extended family members and introducing the gospel to trusted friends; (2) Incarnating the gospel in their lives and letting them speak for Christ; (3) Using public occasions, such as funerals, to witness for Christ; and (4) Testifying to God's power through the exercise of the gifts of healing and exorcism. (Lausanne Committee, Thailand Report, 6.14)

Watchman Nee's devotional writings offer insight into the pursuit of truth in China. The Bible is time and again declared to be the all-sufficient source of knowledge and through its constant reading the Chinese Christian avoids selectivity. An encounter with the living Christ and not the historical Christ is the basis of evangelization.

In his earlier thinking, Nee insisted upon "the geographical locality of the churches (one secular society: one local church administration)," but later on he accepted "migration evangelism" as a possibility (Kinnear, 302) because of dispersion of Christians in China in every direction under communist rule. The ground reality in China demands the planting of extemporaneous churches:

> one in Christ but scarcely at all organized, becoming increasingly versatile in its worship and witness, and learning from the Holy Spirit, not merely how to survive under fire in new situations but how, as one people, to do battle there for God. (ibid.)

There are *millions* of secret Chinese Christians. Recent migrants from China to Europe and the United States are often favorably inclined to listen to the gospel message. There are also substantial Chinese Christian populations in Singapore, Malaysia, Thailand, and Indonesia. Find out the ethnic background and the region of your Chinese friend. Talk to him about the healing powers of Christ. Narrate parables to show how Jesus encourages us to live righteously, helping the poor and the needy. Show your love in tangible ways.

Most Chinese have a favorable opinion of Christians—build on this. The Chinese are a polite and civil society, and Confucianism has helped mold their personalities for centuries. Your conversation should slowly veer around discussing the inadequacy of proper etiquette and behavior for our salvation. Show how magic and divination, so prominent in China, are mere delusions and will not bring contentment.

Western media have continually glorified the occult practices of Chinese civilization; martial arts and mythologies flood Hollywood movies. These trends have begun to impact the ever-curious Westerner with novel experiences in illicit spiritual practices, which, in turn, encourages the Chinese to believe that their occult practices have great benefits and truth value. Recognize that Chinese civilization has contributed many things to humanity, but at the same time share that practicing divination, idolatry, and the occult is against God's Word and demeans God's sovereignty.

The ministry of the Holy Spirit is currently remarkable in China. Millions will continue to come to know and experience the loving grace of Jesus as Lord and Savior. Pray that the Chinese church will become stronger in faith and, as the Holy Spirit moves among them, that the church will be founded on the Word of God and not on the idiosyncratic interpretations and dictates of political and religious leaders.

MAHAYANA BUDDHISM IN KOREA

Korea received Buddhism through China in the latter part of the fourth century and integrated it with local beliefs. Gods and spirits of the native Korean religion (Sinkyo) were given places inside the Buddhist monasteries, the folk symbols—dragon and snake—became protectors of the Buddhist faith, and the clergy began to uphold famous local ancestors as heroes and gods of Buddhism, as well. From the beginning, Korean Buddhist monks prayed to the Bodhisattvas for the protection of rulers, so a close relationship between Mahayana and the Korean elite was forged.

Syncretism

Religious belief in Korea is a collective amalgamation of Confucianism, Taoism, and Buddhism (all coming from China) with native Korean ideology. Buddhism adopted deities from native folk religion; Taoism contributed magical processes for geomancy (divination to identify the features of land), long life, fortune-telling, and alchemy; Confucianism introduced practices in support of secular ethics. This combination of the three major elitist religions accepted by Koreans is clearly revealed in their folktales—those from Confucian thought often are moralistic, focusing on socially appropriate behavior, while the Buddhist ones are mostly mythological, and native Korean stories focus on spirits.

Sinkyo is an animistic stratum in which humans, animals, and objects are believed to have spirits. The goal of Sinkyo followers is to make peace with the world of the spirits, best achieved by using the good offices of the professional spiritists or shamans (Korean women who commonly seek diviners, geomanticists, and alchemists). Shamanism is usually performed in small temples (with assistants, including drummers and singers), and though it was resisted and banned by several dynasties or governments, Sinkyo not only survived but influenced other elitist faiths (Confucianism, Taoism, and Buddhism).

One influential and flourishing cult is *Tonghak,* meaning "Eastern Sect" (in contrast to the *Sohak* sect—Christianity or Catholicism). Tonghak is generally marked by syncretism and relativism, and over time it has adopted selected features from Christianity, Confucianism, Buddhism, and Sinkyo.

Ethnic Identity

There has always been a strong sense of Korean identity as a distinct people group. They have been ruled over by more powerful countries such as China, Manchuria, and Japan, but this never deterred them from preserving their distinct nationalistic heritage. The Korean return to long-held beliefs (and their continued practice) may be attributed to this tendency. Your Korean Buddhist friend, consequently, will probably make no substantial distinction between Confucian, Taoist, Buddhist, Sinkyo, or Tonghak beliefs. These are integrated in his thinking and practice, and he strongly believes in nationalistic loyalty (a quality also emphasized by Korean labor movements).

Spread of the Gospel

Since the nineteenth century, belief in Jesus as Lord and Savior is growing more rapidly than any other religious faith in South Korea. Anthropologist Cornelius Osgood wrote (in 1951), "The influence of Christian ideals and ethics strikes the sophisticated observer immediately. The women who have gained a position of new respect and dignity, face one with quiet assurance" (Osgood, 128). The embracing of the gospel has stunningly transformed South Korean society—at present it is a developed country, leading in the production of many electronic goods and automobiles. The work ethics of Christians *and* the national loyalty found among all Koreans have combined to quickly make South Korea a culturally advanced nation.

Apart from the material benefits that come from hard work and proper stewardship of God-blessed resources, South Koreans are known for their zealous devotion to the worldwide spread of the Good News. Their churches are filled with large congregations, and they practice the gifts of the Holy Spirit for the edification of all. However, the grip of spirit worship and appeasement, supported by Buddhism for the last fifteen hundred years, is still continuing among those who follow native and amalgamated traditions.

Shamanism and Divination

Sinkyo has a variety (hundreds) of gods, mostly nature deities, such as the mountain-god, the earth-god, the animal-gods (such as the dragon-gods), and the disease-gods (like the smallpox-god). All have their own territorial functions, and they may help *or* harm people (for instance, enhancing or hampering household prosperity), depending upon whether they are properly and adequately propitiated.

The Sinkyo shamans, called *mudang,* are usually women. Some mudang are spirit-possessed, while others become mudang through heredity. When a woman becomes ill with symptoms such as violent behavior, sudden inability to speak, loss of memory, and/or going into a trance and not remembering it later, and when the treatment given to her does not heal her, people begin to suspect that she is spirit-possessed and on her way to becoming mudang—and her illness is no longer looked upon as a sickness. She then receives discipleship training (under another qualified mudang) through ritual, supernatural skill, reception of the ancestors, gods, and spirits, and going into trances through the descending of these spirits. Hereditary mudang come from the socially lower strata, and they may or may not become spirit-possessed but are, nevertheless, sought after for their skill in divination (see Osgood).

Divination (fortune-telling) is perhaps the most important function of Korean folk religion. Divination may be done by the mudang (in a state of trance) or by those skilled in horoscope reading (which greatly appeals to secular educated Koreans, who often look down upon divination through trances). Predictions based on horoscopes commonly appear to be scientific and follow a complicated method of calculating and assigning values to Chinese language characters. Palmistry, geomancy, and almanacs are also very popular among Koreans.

Remember that people from traditional Christian backgrounds all over the world often interact with some form of divination, even using techniques described above. For example, many Christians eagerly read what is hidden in fortune cookies in their favorite Chinese restaurants, and others peruse daily newspaper horoscopes, thinking nothing of it. Examine yourself to see whether you follow any of these practices—you may not be aware of them until you begin to consciously think about it. If your Mahayana Korean friend sees these elements in your life, you will become a classic example of a stumbling block, for he may think that Christianity has no conflict with these matters and thus wonder why he needs to change his beliefs. (We discuss the need to avoid divination and other ungodly spiritual activities, from a scriptural perspective, in chapter 13.)

Evangelizing Koreans

Christianity was first introduced to Korea in the sixteenth century, but it didn't start taking root for at least two hundred years. Catholicism reached Korea first; Jesuit opposition to ancestor worship then led to severe criticism (and a brief ban) of the Christian faith—a number of Catholics were executed. Toward the end of the nineteenth century, however, Protestantism started spreading all over Korea, and soon there were more Protestants than Catholics in the country. Historians have tried to explain the sudden growth of the Korean church in many secular ways, but the fact of the matter is that the Holy Spirit has moved mightily among them to show the power of God over all other spiritual forces.

Amazingly, despite the prevailing ethos of mixing various religions and forming an eclectic approach to spiritual matters, the Korean church, by and large, has adhered to the fundamentals of Christianity as revealed in the Word of God. This is a miracle and a blessing from the Lord. Our focus, then, is to impart this biblical dependence to our Korean Mahayana friend, a practitioner of an eclectic faith.

The spread of Christianity in Korea amid its powerful nationalism and syncretistic spiritualism is certainly of the Holy Spirit; we see, for instance, how difficult it is to share the gospel in Japan (a nation close to Korea). This gives you a greater responsibility for sensitivity to your friend—do not belabor theological points, and let the Holy Spirit move in His own way. *Tell the story of Jesus Christ as presented in the Gospels,* but never emphasize that Jesus was a Jew. Emphasize that although He was born and brought up as a Jew, and although He ministered among the Jews, He emphasized that His message is for the entire world and for all peoples.

Cults

Wherever the gospel of Jesus prospers, counterfeit movements spring up against the Word of God; dark forces put on innovative spiritual garments and imitate the truth. Korea is no exception. Since Christianity is popular, most Korean cults superficially adopt Christian practices and beliefs but strive to influence people to their own animistic and polytheistic faith. Sun Myung Moon's Unification Church is active among Koreans worldwide, as are other cults (including Jehovah's Witnesses and Mormons).

Your Korean Mahayana friend, by his very upbringing, is eclectic. Now he is more confused than ever because of the cults that parade before him as a version of Christianity that adopts Korean nationalism and Christian worship. Purely Buddhist cults are not popular, but when they are presented with a veneer of nationalistic Christian faith, they begin to attract Koreans.

Koreans are generally more spiritually inclined than the other nationalities surrounding them, and their search for truth is exemplified in their widespread acceptance of Jesus as Lord and Savior. However, as the past still lingers through folk religion and cult involvement, you must pray constantly for wisdom from above to communicate the truth.

A Korean Mahayana Buddhist may see his religion only in combination with Confucianism, Taoism, and Korean folk religion or new cults; he may or may not know that he is not truly practicing Mahayana, but by tradition he considers himself a Buddhist. Recognize that he is eclectic, animistic, polytheistic, and focused on magical powers. Pray to the Lord Jesus for wisdom and understanding to help wean him away from falsehood.

This wisdom and knowledge should come to you from the Word of God, not from scholars and analysts of social behavior. Remember that although social, political, cultural, and economic factors may appear to hinder the progress of the Good News, in reality it is dark spiritual forces that cause people's blindness. Our fight, then, is against *spiritual* powers; when these are countered and checked, social, political, cultural, and economic changes can follow.

Mahayana Buddhism in Japan

Mahayana Buddhism, which entered Japan (from China through Korea) in the sixth century, was quite unlike Shinto (the native Japanese religion). For instance, Buddhism had a deified and worshiped founder; Buddhism had an elaborate metaphysical system that governed its belief and practice; Buddhism made a distinction between clergy and laity; and Buddhism was in every sense organized compared to the free and unspecified system of Shinto. As elsewhere, Buddhism in Japan has absorbed elements of the host nation and culture as its own, merging with the existing local beliefs and playing a secondary role as a supporter of the established order.

Chinese civilization had a tremendous longstanding impact on all East Asian societies; Buddhism, which came through Korea but was clearly marked as a Chinese contribution (mixed with Confucianism and Taoism), had some prestige, then, as a religion coming from an admired civilization with an advanced culture. As in China and other countries where Mahayana entered as *the* Buddhist religion, Buddhism was never dominant in Japan—it had to share religious "space" with Shinto, Confucianism, and Taoism. In this process, however, Buddhism was able to carve a special niche for itself in the hearts of the Japanese by performing essential functions.

Japanese Buddhism remained largely Mahayana, but the Japanese enterprise did not stop there: they also absorbed the orthodox scriptures usually ascribed to Theravada. Nonetheless, monasticism did not take deep roots in Japan. In a sense, Japanese Buddhism is a marriage between two distinct sects, with the Mahayana elements taking a more prominent place.

Buddhism initially attracted royalty and nobility, just as it did in India, other Theravada nations, and China. From this aristocratic springboard, Japanese Buddhism soon began spreading among the common people (not without some resistance from those who viewed it as a foreign religion). Those who began to receive Buddhism and follow its practices began to look at Gautama as an important kami (one of the nature gods of Shinto) from another nation. The Buddha was (and is) viewed as a storehouse of magical power from whom strength could be drawn for personal benefit. Early in Japanese history there was admiration for the beauty of the Buddha's image, which resulted in the building of exquisite temples for him.

The Japanese were a practical society from ancient times, yet the introduction of Buddhism brought with it an attitude that looked upon this life as an illusion, calling upon the people to negate this world and seek an existence far beyond their death. This did not strike a sympathetic cord in the hearts of Japanese, even as Buddhism was absorbed into their society. Standard Japanese Buddhism is mostly a means to pray for their emperor and nation and to obtain personal favors from the gods (including Buddha).

Prominent Schools

Japanese monks began the process of indigenizing Buddhism by incorporating various strands of it into local beliefs and practices. There are at least five important schools of Buddhism that have a large following in Japan: Lotus Sutra, Shingon, Zen (extensively discussed earlier in this chapter), Pure Land, and Nichiren.

The *Lotus Sutra* School is so named after the text considered to be the culmination of all Buddhist truth. This school is *eclectic* (or *comprehensive*) in its belief, holding that all the Buddhas, including Gautama, are the same, are in unity, and may be worshiped with equal results. Likewise, all Buddhist scriptures have the same power for desired result, and several techniques (such as meditation, initiation, and recitation) may be used. As stated previously, *the goal is to identify oneself with everything.*

Adherents are proud that the Lotus Sutra recognizes all scriptures as having some truth, so if your friend is from this school, you should address this matter with care. It may be necessary for you to point out that even Gautama Buddha did not believe in all scriptures; for instance, he attacked the Hindu scriptures and hierarchy. If all Buddhist scriptures are equal, why has there been so much recrimination between monks, past and present? Why should there be Buddhist divisions (Mahayana, Theravada, and Vajrayana)? Why call Theravada a "lesser vehicle"?

Your Mahayana Japanese friend may not recognize these issues and may even counter them by citing the existence of the denominations within Christianity. The truth is that while Christian denominations *do* focus on certain distinctive elements around which members build their approach to faith and practice, denominations *do not* deny or move away from core affirmations (such as acceptance of the Trinity, the Virgin Birth, and the Resurrection). The primary difference is that in Buddhism the three major divisions are extremely divergent on many core issues, and communication between them is rare. Raise these points only when your friend has established some level of trust in you. Until then, controversial topics should be avoided; reiterate what you believe and hold strongly to your faith, focusing on love and servanthood.

The *Shingon* School teaches that there is no difference between the universe and Dainichi (the Supreme Buddha—not a historical person); Buddha is present everywhere, in every particle, and *mystical* (or *esoteric*) meanings are given to air, water, earth, ether, and other substances. In addition, Shingon believes in the pantheon of gods, some of which are originally from Indian Hinduism.

Shingon has two kinds of doctrines. The *secret* doctrines, orally transmitted and given to those who are specially initiated, are held to be superior and more effective in the attainment of nirvana. The *open* doctrines, preached to the public, are known to all and are based on the usual assumptions of Buddhism.

The Shingon School is a classic example of pantheism (Dainichi is the universe and the universe is Dainichi). Worship of a multiplicity of gods makes it polytheistic. Practice of secret doctrines for the benefit of the initiated elite makes it antisocial. Insistence that secret teaching is more efficacious than the profession of publicly known doctrines makes it esoteric.

The *Pure Land* (or *Paradisic*) School preaches that nirvana is attainable by a simple recitation of the scriptures that express faith in Amida Buddha (mystical). Prestigious scholarship, asceticism, secret rites, monastic living, and celibacy are not considered necessary. Because of its simplicity, *Pure Land* is extremely popular among the Japanese, and its outward appearance and assumptions raise comparisons to the Christian faith:

> This school's teaching regarding man's sinfulness and need for salvation, the horrors of hell and bliss of Paradise, the grace of Amida which assures man's entry into the Pure Land where Amida dwells and the simple faith, apart from any other conditions, which is the effective element in gaining salvation, has prompted reference to it as an Eastern version of the Christian gospel. (Bentley-Taylor and Offner, 186)

Your Japanese Paradisic friend will often compare his faith to yours because he sees that you depend on the grace of Jesus Christ. However, this is a deceptive similarity. For one thing, Amida Buddha is a mystical or mythological being, who has gone through thousands of births, deaths, and rebirths. On the other hand, Jesus is a historical person, the living Son of God, who was born as a human being, died only once, and was resurrected from the dead.

There is also no mechanical Christian formula—such as the recitation of verses—that ensures salvation. (This despite the fact that some televangelists ask their faithful viewers to cling to Scripture passages so that they get the results they desire.) God's Word edifies us but is not a means for getting material benefits. The Lord blesses our prayers if they are according to His will, but we should not downgrade Scripture to the level of mantra.

The Pure-Land notion of "sin" refers mainly to individual acts of commission and omission in this world. It does not consider sin to be an act committed against God (who is absent), and there is no need for repentance, as mere scriptural recitation and faith in Amida are adequate for nirvana. However, as Christians, we know that nirvana and salvation are not synonymous. Salvation follows repentance from sin and placing our faith solely in Jesus Christ. Our goal is not total extinction (or non-existence), or sensuous life after death, but rather *to be present before God and to fellowship with Him,* now and in the afterlife.

The *Nichiren* School is wholly and truly a Japanese innovation of and contribution to Mahayana. It rejects eclecticism (and all other schools), seeking to stand only on the revelation found in the Lotus Sutra (the culmination of all scriptures). Nichiren claims that other schools have corrupted the early teaching of Gautama, and that leaning on Lotus Sutra *alone* is necessary. The degeneration and humiliation of Japan, allegedly reflected in the result of World War II, was due mainly to the giving up of the original final teaching of Buddha in Lotus Sutra.

> The only object of worship permitted by the Nichiren purists is a *mandala* scroll [simply described, a graphic representation of the universe in the form of a circle enclosing a square, each corner of which depicts a deity], in the center of which are written in Chinese characters the words of the sacred formula with the names or titles of Indian and Japanese divinities around it, representing all classes of existence in their relationship to the cosmic truth. The sacred formula (daimoku), which is chanted enthusiastically by the adherents of this school, is an invocation addressed to the *Lotus Sutra* itself, 'Hail to the Lotus Sutra!' Repetition of this formula and worshipping before the Nichiren *mandala* is considered effectively to unite the soul of man with the Eternal Buddha Spirit. (Bentley-Taylor and Offner, 188)

The cults that adhere to Nichiren display single-minded devotion to Lotus Sutra (as an object with great supernatural powers), the mandala design, and mechanical recitation of the verses. The Nichiren School offers small-group experience to its adherents and is involved in social services for the benefit of the community. However, the Nichiren leaders preach a messianic form that may lead to political disaster and social cruelty.

Nichiren is strongly grounded in Japanese patriotism, and most recent cults (some of which have proved to be violent) derive their basis and strength from this school. These cults wish to bring about a new world and a new order, destroying the present, and violence may be a lawful means for this purpose. While nationalism in itself is not harmful, love beyond one's nation and ethnicity is essential if we wish to be children of God (Mark 12:28–31).

Japan has produced several prophetic schools of Buddhist cults. In an industrialized society, people seek relief from the anguish of commercial busyness, and while Shinto and Buddhism continue to hold sway, the cults stemming from them offer ambitious plans for mental peace and material prosperity. Many of these are "doomsday" cults (called "Puristic Prophetic Schools").

Shinto and Buddhism

If we are to understand Japanese Buddhism, we must also understand Shinto. The Japanese began to use the word *Shinto* ("the way of the kami"), from the Chinese language, to refer to their faith in contrast to "the way of Buddha" or "the way of Confucius." Again, *kami* (plural) are the spirits or gods worshiped and adored by the Japanese. They are extraordinary and basically innumerable, and they live in everything that is beautiful, magnificent, and awesome. Kami may be nature-gods or man-gods that live in natural objects and phenomena; they may be heroes or ancestors or even ideas personified.

Shinto does not believe humans are sinful against *God;* predominantly, "evil" means social or economic wrongs committed by humans against *others.* Breaking long-held tradition and belief is considered sinful, and rites performed in worship of the kami are commanded, for living in harmony with nature is Shinto's dominant theme. Nonobservance of social rules and etiquette is also sin. Ancestor worship is fundamental as is the worship of the gods and spirits that protect the community (each community may have its own).

Shinto and Buddhism gradually appropriated each other's beliefs and practices to bring together a distinctive way of life that was sometimes very different from what the Buddhist scriptures demanded. The kami were seen to be the protectors of the multitudinous Buddhas and treated as Buddhist gods (part of the pantheon), occupying certain heavens after their samsara and even becoming the incarnations (avatars) of Buddhas. Through this arrangement, Shinto shrines began to have Buddhist priests, and funeral rites mainly followed Buddhist practices. Even so, Japanese religious history is marked by violent and vituperative attacks by Shinto purists who consider Buddhism to be a foreign religion.

Shinto is pantheistic, animistic, polytheistic, nationalistic, patriotic, and ethnocentric (making the assumption that one's own community is superior to others); accordingly, Japanese Buddhism inherited these characteristics. Presently, of all the Mahayana nations, Buddhism is most entrenched in the Japanese subconscious because of its close cultural association with Shinto. In addition, Buddhist monks from Japan take their faith all around the world, igniting Buddhistic enthusiasm through their renovation and restoration of Buddhist shrines and their concentrated research in the Mahayana scriptures.

Japanese Buddhism-Shinto From a Christian Standpoint

Several limitations of Buddhism-Shinto spring mainly from its racial character. It has no universality of reach and no universal appeal. It tends to be ethnocentric, claiming to be the religion only of the Japanese. It has a superficial view of humanity and nature, making the false claim that man can become a god.

Christians must explain that divine immanence is not in the objects *around* them but *within* the heart.

> Once, having been asked by the Pharisees when the kingdom of God would come, Jesus replied, "The kingdom of God does not come with your careful observation, nor will people say, 'Here it is,' or 'There it is,' because the kingdom of God is within you" (Luke 17:20–21).

Highlight the importance of heart-purification through the Spirit's work.

Catholic Missions

Among Christian missionaries, Roman Catholics were the first to confront Japanese doctrines and nationalism. Francis Xavier, the Jesuit pioneer to Asia, went to Japan in 1549, and by the time he left in 1551, he had already established a Christian community of one thousand believers. He was fond of the Japanese, saying that there could be very few finer people. However, his approach to evangelism was overly direct. He condemned their idol worship and accused them of practicing sodomy and abortion. He demonstrated that the idols were powerless by trampling on them and even suggested destruction of the shrines, declaring that the Japanese had forgotten God and chosen to worship other forces. Such in-your-face practices do not generally endear others to us. Weaning people away from sin is essential, but it is important to first establish a bridge of friendship and connection.

Xavier believed that everyone in Japan respected China, so he decided that the Chinese should be evangelized first. He did not realize the potential for Shinto to revive itself and replace Buddhism and Confucianism, nor did he correctly assess the depth of national pride in the Japanese. In 1587 the Jesuits were ordered (by governmental decree) to leave Japan; there were severe restrictions on preaching the gospel, and several edicts were issued against Catholics, who were declared to be the enemies of kami and Buddha. Most native Christians were forced into apostasy in the course of continued persecution, and scholars documented that over 250,000 Japanese were martyred.

Protestant Missions

Japan was closed to missionary work for more than two hundred years. In fact, only Dutch and Chinese traders were allowed to enter the country during this period. Japan reopened itself to foreigners in 1858.

Subsequently, the first American Consul-General, Townsend Harris, was instrumental in obtaining permission for foreigners to worship and build churches in their areas of residence. The treaty between the United States and Japan said,

> Americans should not destroy the Japanese temples and shrines and never hinder the Japanese Shinto-Buddhist worship nor destroy the body of Kami or the image of Buddha. Neither people should discuss each other's religion. (Hume, 87)

Although this treaty appears to have shut the door to the gospel in Japan, God's children became subtle leaven to the Japanese community—"a little yeast works through the whole batch of dough" (Galatians 5:9; see also Matthew 13:33; 1 Corinthians 5:6).

Evangelizing the Japanese

There is conflict between Shinto imperial and idol worship and Christian focus on acceptance of Jesus Christ as *the* Lord and Savior. The Japanese consider ancestor worship (and love and respect for parents and elders) as the foundation of their culture and religion. That the love of God takes precedence over everything in the life of a Christian is often taken to mean that Christians are disloyal to the nation and disrespectful to their parents and ancestors.

The question of shrine worship will remain problematic: is it idol worship or just an expression of patriotism? Shrines are the abodes of kami, and in that sense shrine worship cannot be encouraged, yet in a society that highly values the roles of nature, beauty, duty, discipline, and, above all, reverence for the emperor, visiting shrines for purposes of social solidarity cannot be fully avoided. Early Catholic missionaries acknowledged that the Catholic Japanese did indeed destroy Shinto shrines and Buddhist temples because of their changed theological understanding. Such hasty actions should be avoided wherever an assembly of believers is established.

One important need is to impress upon your Japanese friend that Christianity does not favor one nationality over others. (We discuss this in the section on the status of "chosen people" in chapter 9.) There are other significant issues that can be discussed, as well, but my focus is on an introduction to the possible issues you may face when you wish to develop contacts with the Japanese Mahayana Buddhist. Your day-to-day interactions will reveal other areas for which you need to develop understanding.

Christianity is not the only faith that seeks to attract the attention of the Japanese. For various sociological, political, and economic reasons, Japan remains second only to the United States in fostering various cults. Competing with Christian missionaries are cults of all kinds, and both Mormons and Jehovah's Witnesses work overtime among the Buddhist-Shinto practitioners in urban centers. Their propaganda needs to be checked, particularly because their major target happens to be the new Christians among the Japanese.

Mahayana Buddhism in Vietnam

Vietnamese Buddhism is a mixture of elitist Mahayana and local folk beliefs. Vietnam also has practitioners of Theravada and adherents to Roman Catholicism, Protestant Christianity, Islam, and native religions. Nearly 90 percent of the population of Vietnam is Vietnamese; however, there are several significant minority elements, such as the Hoa (Han Chinese), Thai, Khmer, Hmong, and tribal groups. Know that when you ask most people from Vietnam about their ethnicity, they will call themselves Vietnamese to an outsider.

History and Society

In its early history, Vietnam was dominated by Chinese rule for a thousand years (until the tenth century). Despite this occupation, the Vietnamese retained their distinct identity even as they received the civilizing impact of Chinese culture, Confucian ideals, and advanced technology.

Vietnam apparently received Buddhism from two different directions, both through China and also through India and other neighboring Southeast-Asian (Theravada) nations. Most Vietnamese are Mahayana Buddhists, but there is a significant minority of Theravada adherents, as well. In the twelfth century, the royal family adopted Buddhism as their religion, which widely opened its way into the nation.

The vast majority of the Mahayana Vietnamese are largely animistic. Christianity has spread widely among the minority tribal groups that live in the highlands of Vietnam; traditional Vietnamese people consider them to be less "civilized." (The Khmer minority group follows Theravada.) Vietnamese society is still governed by Confucian rules of relationship (loyalty to the ruler, obedience to parents, elders, and older people, and mutual respect between friends), and the communist party has not succeeded in significantly changing this.

Moreover, the cult of ancestor worship is still very much followed by the Vietnamese, who fearfully consider it necessary to keep restless ancestral spirits from harming their descendants. (Also, they believe such worship can ensure for them a better afterlife.) A household may have an altar for deceased parents and others, and through veneration and offerings the ancestors are informed about everything involving their living descendants.

Being married to more than one woman at the same time is still practiced in some parts of Vietnam. As in China and many other Asian nations, the male child is preferred over the female child because he is necessary for the continuity of the lineage and for ancestor worship. So parents generally desire to have at least one male child so that their afterlife will be taken care of by their descendant and his offspring.

The Vietnamese are aware of the general outlines of both Mahayana and Theravada. The knowledge of elitist Buddhism is very rare among common followers, but they are impressed with the need for and performance of the rituals and other activities connected with Buddhist worship. As in other Mahayana nations, the spirits and gods of native animistic religion are intertwined with those of elitist Buddhism.

Religious practice is not proscribed in Vietnam: people are allowed to practice their faith if they desire. However, everyone is warned against misusing religion to work against the government, and the implied threat has had great impact. Many people in urban centers do not even bother to visit temples, though the ancestor cult continues because it is an integral part of the society and culture.

Communist rulers try to regulate and control the activities of all religions in Vietnam. In the name of patriotism, Buddhist monks and nuns are asked to do manual labor, which goes against their belief. Their training is also regulated by the government.

There are at least two cults (based on Buddhism) that are popular among the Vietnamese: the Cao Dai is a combination of beliefs derived from Buddhism, Confucianism, and Roman Catholicism, and the Hoa Hao cult is based on Theravada. Both have a few million followers each and are under government control in the sense that appointments to religious hierarchy and other offices (even to the specification of what programs should or should not be conducted) are regulated.

Folk Religion

The Vietnamese use astrology, horoscopes, sorcery, and divination of various sorts (including geomancy). Diviners are in great demand for diagnosing illnesses that do not lend themselves to modern medical treatment. Astrologers are sought after to predict the success of ventures. Geomancy is used to construct buildings in a manner that is in consonance with the spirits and nature. Horoscopes are read before a marriage and before starting a venture or transaction. Palmistry is considered to be scientific by educated people. In the midst of all these practices sanctioned by both Mahayana and Theravada, worship of the native spirits and ancestors is quite common.

The Christian Church

There has been growth of the Protestant Church among the tribal populations who dwell in the highlands. They have suffered heavily because they have accepted Jesus as Lord and Savior through the efforts of American missionaries. At present, there is great enthusiasm to know Jesus, even among Buddhists. Roman Catholicism was encouraged for some time by the French colonialists, and there are many Catholics throughout the country (more in the former South Vietnam). Although links with the Vatican are allowed, there are government regulations that curtail the freedom of the Catholic Church.

Disconnection Between Buddhism and Patriotism

Unlike their counterparts in many other Southeast Asian nations, the Vietnamese do not look at their Buddhist faith as the backbone of their patriotism. Their long struggle to release themselves from the shackles of colonialism has enabled them to ignore religion as the basis of their nationalism. So your Vietnamese friend may not feel that Christianity is against his national patriotic fervor. However, he does see Christianity as a different way of life, and your focus should be on telling him that Jesus is Lord and Savior of all nations. Emphasize the love of Christ for all, and tell him that the superstitions of ancestor worship, rituals, and divination will not help him to experience the grace of God.

VAJRAYANA (TIBETAN) BUDDHISM

7

Vajrayana, the third major division of Buddhism, means "diamond vehicle"; the claim is that just as a diamond is strong, sturdy, and unable to be split, so the Vajrayana tradition is strong, steady, and a continuous thread. The term implies that there is an unbroken continuity between the guru (or master) and his disciple. The Vajrayana sacred texts are called *tantra*, which may be understood as a traditional thread of ritualized technique, continuous and unbroken, transmitted from master to disciple. Vajrayana is full of obscure and secret ritual practices that are designed so that only the initiated can be introduced to them (these practices are not open to the public, nor are they to be discussed in public).

Vajrayana is a further development or offshoot of Mahayana. However, practices followed in Vajrayana were found even in early Buddhism. Recitations or incantations of mantra and the performance of *homa* ("burnt offerings") were part of the Brahmanical rites in Hinduism, and these were transferred to Vajrayana with new meanings and elaborate rites.

Vajrayana assumes that body, mind, and speech may be regulated through proper rituals. This control helps the disciple to have power over spiritual forces and attain nirvana—even in this life—if he follows the secret practices handed down from his master.

Vajrayana first began in eastern India and slowly spread to other regions, notably northern India and China. Finally, it reached Tibet, where it became the most popular Buddhist school. Tibetan Buddhism derives most of its original characteristics from the declarations of the

Buddhist monk and scholar Nagarjuna, who lived in southern India in the third century. It emphasizes rituals and monastic disciplines and has appropriated certain shamanistic practices and beliefs of Bon (pronounced *Pon*—the word's meaning is unclear), a pre-Buddhist native Tibetan religion.

Tibetan Vajrayana rites are also practiced in parts of Mongolia, Nepal, Bhutan, and Himalayan (northeastern) Indian states. The meditative and ritual practices of Vajrayana, especially through missionary zeal, became very popular in the sixties with the emergence of the hippie and New Age movements in the Western nations, particularly the United States.

Wherever Vajrayana is practiced, a large number of people adopt monastic disciplines. The present Dalai Lama, who is the spiritual and secular leader not only of the sect but also of several Tibetan regions, is considered to be a reincarnation of the previous Dalai Lamas. (*Dalai* means "ocean" and *Lama* means "superior one, guru," suggesting a spiritual leader with an ocean of wisdom and compassion.) There are other powerful lamas who also are considered to be incarnations of the previous lamas of their sects; reincarnation, thus, is a fundamental characteristic of Tibetan Buddhism.

Magical Formulas and Divine Beings

Vajrayana magical formulas are usually composed of syllables with no apparent meaning. Like vending machines, they deliver power when recited repeatedly, with proper pronunciation, a specified number of times. Similar practices are commonly found in animistic, pantheistic, and polytheistic religions. (Other mystic groups also use this method, such as Sufism [within Islam] when reciting the names of Allah. Some Christian denominations encourage repetitive recitation of certain prayers.)

The powers thus generated by the recitation are used to drive out demons and other evil spirits and to derive personal benefits (both material and spiritual) for the practitioner. This enables an individual to be in personal contact with the gods and spirits and use them for his or her own purposes. Recitation of the name or names of Buddha, both historical and mythological, is followed for the same purpose.

The Vajrayana gods, spirits, and demons are many and varied. The follower of Vajrayana meditative techniques may choose a divinity as his or her own and, supposedly, through the use of recitation could temporarily become part of buddhahood. Recitation enables a person to visualize and to call the divinity to mind, and often he sees the "reality" of objects and experiences extrasensory perception.

Adherents to Vajrayana believe it is possible to become a Buddha in this life; in fact, there are said to be many Buddhas, even now. The goal is to become a Buddha through meditative practices given to them by their mentor guru. People can be in touch with the Buddha reality through their contacts with living Buddhas around them. (This is in contrast to Mahayana belief that those who have attained buddhahood allegedly live in a world of purity and complete happiness.)

In Tibetan Buddhism, three Buddhas are gratefully remembered: Padmasambhava, Atisha, and Tsong Khapa. Padmasambhava is supposed to have come from India to help establish Vajrayana and is believed to have had extraordinary powers with which he influenced leaders and overcame Buddhist enemies. Atisha also came from India (Bengal) and went to Java, bringing with him this doctrine. Tsong Khapa was a Tibetan who was identified as a Buddha even when he was a small child; by his wisdom, understanding, and sustained effort he helped shape the teaching and practices of Vajrayana. (All three are believed to have had remarkable magical powers.)

An active pantheon of gods and spirits, both male and female, characterizes Tibetan Buddhism. The most popular female deity is Tara, who may be depicted with more than two eyes. She is ferocious, compassionate, a protector of travelers (navigators), and a symbol of purity in her many incarnations. In Vajrayana, the historical Buddha, Gautama, is given rather a secondary position; Padmasambhava occupies the most prominent ritual status, visualized in several forms (such as a tiger-god, a perfecter of thought, or a god of wisdom).

Clergy and Laity

A problem with Tibetan Buddhism is that because it is an esoteric or secret practice, the laity is not involved. The role of Buddhism in Theravada countries (like Sri Lanka) has been to educate the laity even through secular education offered in the monasteries. In Vajrayana nations, monasteries become sacred places where monks live and practice meditation; the role of the laity is mainly to support the clergy to acquire merit and to receive the benefits of their magical powers. Laypeople, however, are extremely loyal, both seeking and obeying monastic leadership. The laity's attitude is that Vajrayana is a mystery, and that mystery is time-honored and used for the benefit of the whole community. The influence of the clergy on the laity has enabled the people to develop extraordinarily good manners and compassionate lifestyles.

The Tibetan region is known for its relatively low crime rate, and

Tibetan concern for the welfare of animals is legendary. At the same time, certain theological beliefs are occasionally taken to extreme ends. For example, butchers occupy the lowest societal stratum.

Congenital disorders are assumed to be the result of bad karma acquired in a previous life. Actually, anything that happens now is a consequence of past karma. Sometimes people justify (at least jokingly) their present wrongdoing against another as a tit-for-tat action for what that person did in a previous life!

Amulets and Other Prayer Mechanisms

Amulets and charms, usually attached to garments, are worn in abundance by Vajrayana Tibetan Buddhists. These function as a guard against demons who bring disease and misfortune; they usually have a Sanskrit word or phrase or even a sentence inscribed on them, and they may have relics inside (a piece of garment cloth, nail clippings, or even the dropped food) of living or dead lamas. Spiritual force or power is supposedly contained in these objects.

The lamas and diviners guide the lives of the Vajrayana laity from birth to death. Prayer flags for the dead and for spirits are hoisted everywhere for protection from evil. People look for omens, search for information on lucky and unlucky objects, events, times, and days, and consult with the Lama (who is considered to be adept at astrology and divination). People continually pray; often their prayers are either warnings to the evil forces (devils and demons) that the Buddhas will punish them or petitions to the Buddhas to save them from these evil forces.

Prayer wheels, an integral part of worship, are spun constantly during the recitation of the Sanskrit mantra, *"Om mani padme, hum!"* (which is said to possess power). This is an omnipotent utterance that saves the Buddhist believer and finally transports him or her to heaven, where Amida (Amitabha) Buddha has his abode.

One problem with the use of a prayer wheel is that prayers become rote. The repetition of a specific word, phrase, or sentence is accompanied by the belief that this action will bring desired results through magical powers, and the focus is more on getting material results than on experiencing spiritual growth. The Word of God does not teach us to worship God in a mechanical fashion. Jesus said,

> The true worshipers will worship the Father in spirit and truth, for they are the kind of worshipers the Father seeks. God is spirit, and his worshipers must worship in spirit and in truth. (John 4:23–24)

Demons and the Word of God

The Tibetan layperson sees demons everywhere and is mortally afraid of them. Demons engender many problems, bring sickness, cause drought conditions, and so on. Vajrayana followers seek the help of their Buddhas to save them and to kill these demons, but they are never sure that this request is granted, and so they propitiate the Buddhas annually. Doubt comes from their uncertainty about the karma that they have carried into this present life and also from their uncertainty about whether the Buddhas have listened to them and will intervene.

The Bible recognizes the existence of demons and cites ample incidences of Jesus driving them out. At the same time, the ministry of Jesus and His disciples was about the salvation of this sinful world and about our fellowship with God and worship of Him. Through the crucifixion and resurrection of Jesus, victory over demons is assured once and for all. Followers of Christ have the freedom not to be anxious about evil spirits taking possession of them or putting obstacles in the way of prosperity. We do not live in fear but in hope and with courage, and we rest in the assurance of Jesus' presence with us, come what may. So our focus is not on what demons can do to us but on what God will do in, through, and for us when we follow Him and His Word. Even when demons attack us, which they are capable of doing, we know that God is with us, and in spite of appearances we will ultimately succeed. God promises to "[work] for the good of those who love him, who have been called according to his purpose" (Romans 8:28).

Bon Religion

Vajrayana Tibetans recognize Bon (Pon), the native animistic religion that includes devil worship and allows animal and even human sacrifices. Dragon worship and sorcery are also common. For a long time most Vajrayana Tibetan monks did not approve of Bon practices because of the sacrifice of living beings, and even now the Buddhist hierarchy does not endorse Bon. However, people in Tibet and adjacent areas who follow Vajrayana do practice Bon religious rites, as well. As elsewhere, Buddhism in these nations has made accommodation for pre-Buddhist practices.

Bon temples, widely found, are noticeably dark inside and give non-Bon visitors a depressing feeling. (I can personally testify to this experience because I visited a Bon temple, or gompaz, in Ladakh, India, many years ago.) Bon temples contain numerous images of gods, spirits, and demons, most of which parallel the divinities and saints of Buddhism—the names may be different, but they look like the Buddhist idols.

So often (and sometimes strangely), Bon has adopted Vajrayana names, scriptures, and rituals to reflect Buddhism. The recited mantra reverses the Vajrayana "*Om mani padme, hum!*" to "*Muh em pad ni mo!*" Other Vajrayana symbols, such as the swastika, are also reversed by Bon (the swastika used by Hitler and his Nazi party closely resembles this). In some parts of Tibet, Bon claims a separate identity for itself, but there are many parallels with Vajrayana. Both traditions continue to coexist and impact each other, despite the disapproval of Buddhist clergy.

Meditation

Vajrayana monks undergo extremely grueling training in meditative practices. For example, after his yearlong residency in a monastery, Chang Chen-chi, a Chinese master of Buddhism, wrote that of the four main organizations (temple, seminary, meditation school, and hermitage) in a Tibetan monastery,

> the Meditation House is specially designated for the very strict training in Yoga practice of the Vajrayana; and the Hermitages are small huts and caves for those devoted yogis who have found even the monastic life too worldly for their practices. (Gard, 197)

Training in the meditation house

> lasts three years, three months, and three days. Anyone who enters the Meditation House must be prepared to be a "voluntary prisoner," observing silence most of the time, and meditating continuously for 16 hours a day—for three years, three months, and three days—without a single day's leave! He is permitted to doze, but not to sleep lying down, for only three or four hours a day. (ibid., 201)

Meditative practice consists of many prostrations in front of various objects (including human gurus) and two hours of silent meditation. The monk-students are asked to practice the outer visualization of the bodily form of the patron Buddha of the seminary, and then they will train themselves to visualize the inner form of the Buddha. The first stage lasts for six months, and the second stage for eighteen months (ibid.). Note that such practices may vary from one seminary to another.

Tantrism

Vajrayana is highly identified with tantric practices (specialized, technical, and secretive procedures given in manuals) that are not open to the public—even other co-participants may not be informed as to what someone else is doing or reciting. Absolute spiritual authority is vested with the monk-guru who orally initiates an individual. The practices are hardly ever "reduced" to writing, but in recent times, because of the influence of Western thinking, some attempts have been made to write out selected synopses.

Practitioners are forewarned that knowledge of tantrism does not automatically lead to its successful practice. As one commentator put it, one needs to "undergo difficult and lifelong trial of spiritual transformation." Although tantric practitioners proclaim that theirs is not black magic, something done in secret becomes black magic in its assumptions and principles. Tantrism is occultic in that the word *occult* means "hidden." It operates on the basis of the law of similarity and contiguity.

The practitioner is expected to have purity of body, speech, and mind, and Vajrayana declares that one may attain nirvana in this lifetime through diligent tantric actions. Simplistically described, the practices are fourfold:

1. Yoga that enables one to visualize first himself and then the spiritual force;
2. construction of sacred diagrams (mandala) that represent the universe and provide abodes for the various Buddhas and other divinities;
3. appropriate ritual hand gestures (mudra) and mantra recitation as paying worship to the spiritual forces; and
4. sexual union with a woman as a model of union with the spiritual force.

Sexual Teaching and Practice

One of the techniques that has been widely revealed and discussed (perhaps because of its level of difficulty) relates to the control of orgasm. (When I was very young I heard about it in relation to the great achievement of an undisputed caste leader who was credited with having attained this state—hence his great selflessness, indomitable courage, oratorical ability, and magical power.) The practice of this technique, it is claimed, enables the individual to stop the ejaculation of semen after he reaches full sexual arousal. (Supposedly, when semen is ejaculated, somatic and psychic energy is wasted.) A successful practitioner would not only be able to stop the ejaculation of semen but also "send it upward," which is said to help accumulate energy for nirvana. (Some even calculate the units of such energy that a person can accumulate in his lifetime.)

In general, this approach compares and contrasts human sexual experience with the divine bliss of conceptualizing and experiencing the union of gods and goddesses in divine embrace. Thus, in some teaching it is the control and regulation of human sexual experience that is significant in the path to nirvana, while in others total abandonment to the experience of sexual union is key.

Vajrayana teachers acknowledge that this has led to widespread misuse among people who claim to practice tantrism. They also bemoan the fact that several New Age groups abuse and misinterpret the original intent of such practices. Do not fail to tell your Vajrayana friends that any attempt to locate God or His powers in the experience or control of sexual urges is not only an insult to the One who instituted and blessed our sexuality, but it also corrodes our very social fabric by encouraging, condoning, and legalizing secretive experiments with unlawful sexual relationships.

Tantric bliss is defined as the process of losing one's separate identity and becoming one with God. The issues of our sinful nature, the need for repentance, and the importance of living a sanctified life are bypassed through manmade techniques. In many ways, sexuality *is* no doubt a mystery, but to elevate it as a tool for experiencing God and becoming one with Him is atrocious; it reduces God to the level of human existence, despite the claims of tantric practitioners to the contrary.

Sexual Metaphors

Sexual metaphors are common in most religions for describing the relationship between humans and God. In Christianity, too, such metaphors are easily found (in the Song of Solomon, for example); however, Christian sexual analogies of union are based on the firm belief that sexuality is a God-given gift. Such comparisons illustrate divine love from the pedestal of union between man and woman because such love is pure when divinely ordained.

> God said, "Let us make man in our image." . . . So God created man in his own image, in the image of God he created him; male and female he created them. God blessed them and said to them, "Be fruitful and increase in number" (Genesis 1:26–28).

Consider Matthew Henry's comments on the Song of Solomon:

> This book represents the love between Christ and his church of true believers, under figures taken from the relation

and affection that subsist between a bridegroom and his espoused bride; an emblem often employed in Scripture as describing the nearest, firmest, and most sure relation. . . .

There is no character in the church of Christ, and no situation in which the believer is placed, but what may be traced in this book. . . . Much, however, of the language has been misunderstood by expositors and translators. The difference between the customs and manners of Europe and those of the East must especially be kept in view. The little acquaintance with Eastern customs possessed by most of our early expositors and translators has in many cases prevented a correct rendering. Also, the changes in our own language, during the last two or three centuries, affect the manner in which some expressions are viewed, and they must not be judged by modern notions. But the great outlines, rightly interpreted, fully accord with the affections and experience of the sincere Christian. (from QuickVerse online)

It is indeed unfortunate that people (and the institutions they have built) try to use sexuality as part of ritual practice. They attempt to localize spiritual power in body, fertility, and sexual communion, making effort the basis of salvation rather than realizing that no amount of work can bring deliverance. We are saved by God's grace alone.

Some critics even from within Vajrayana criticize human effort as leading only to ego inflation for the practitioners of these works. Such attempts are common in several religions. Anthropologists report that some tribal societies in Australia and in other parts of the world practice ritual sexual union, believed to nurture communal cohesiveness and harmony. It is not just tribal societies that seek spiritual power in this way—the fact of the matter is that these beliefs give license to people to do what they please instead of subjecting themselves to the guidelines of God-ordained love.

The Word of God condemns sexual immorality in clear terms. I believe that by discussing with your Vajrayana friend the possibility of misusing and exploiting such sexual practices for personal pleasure, you may be able to make a foundation to further explore the topic. Reference to such delicate issues should be made only when your friend is comfortable with you. Other important matters—idol worship, day-to-day ritual, and belief in spirits, for example—may be first presented to your friend in relation to the ministry of Jesus.

BUDDHISM IN BHUTAN

Bhutan is a small landlocked Himalayan nation between Tibet (China) and India. The Tibetan Bhutanese, the Tibeto-Burman tribes, such as the Lepcha, and the Nepalese populate the country. According to government estimates, the dominant people group is the Bhotia (Bhutanese). The vast majority of Bhutan's people practice a combination of Mahayana and Vajrayana, closer to the practices of Tibetans, yet with some significant differences.

Buddhism came to Bhutan from Tibet in the seventh century. However, the eighth-century visit from India of Padmasambhava, considered Bhutan's patron saint, firmly established Buddhism. Padmasambhava, therefore, is the greatest of all Buddhist sages not only for the Tibetans but also for the Bhutanese of Tibetan origin.

Bon, practiced in Bhutan (as in Tibet), was absorbed into Bhutanese Buddhism, yet there is still a significant minority who practice this native religion. Bhutanese Buddhism is characterized by the search for omens, the appeasement of demons, religious monuments (such as stupa decorated with Buddha's eyes that simultaneously see in all directions), relics of kings and saints, the variable practice of polyandry (a woman being married to more than one man simultaneously), the extensive practice of polygamy, and rituals of bodily control.

Bhutan has seen much bloodshed in sectarian conflicts closely connected to its occupation by various powers (such as Tibet and Mongolia). Bhutan fought intensely in several wars to retain its independence, and for several centuries the Bhutanese king was vested with power as the religious head as well as the secular leader. Until recently, the Bhutanese king was considered to be a priest-king, and when he died, it was believed that he would be reincarnated in the body of a newborn baby. Presently, hereditary inheritance is the model of succession followed in Bhutan.

When compared to the size of the country, the number of Buddhist monks currently serving in various monasteries is rather astounding: five thousand or more appear to be in active service—approximately one monk for every four hundred people. Bhutan is indeed a priest-ridden country, just as Tibet was before the Chinese occupation. The practice of celibacy is not strong or widespread.

BUDDHISM IN SIKKIM

Buddhism practiced in the Indian state of Sikkim is similar to Tibetan and Bhutanese Buddhism, with a mixture of local animistic beliefs. There is some conflict between the original religion of the Lepcha people group and the adopted Buddhism. Hereditary priesthood is common in the pre-Buddhist religion, whereas in Buddhism the emphasis is on individual training. Lepchan shamanistic beliefs as well as Bon religious practices are accommodated within Sikkim Buddhism.

BUDDHISM IN ARUNACHAL PRADESH

Arunachal Pradesh, a northeastern Himalayan province of India, is largely Buddhist, following both Vajrayana and Bon. There are a number of Tibeto-Burman people groups of the Mongoloid race, and the focus of their popular religious life is on the worship of local deities, spirits, and the dead. The communities in Arunachal Pradesh are deeply concerned with what will happen to them in the afterworld:

> [The afterworld] is thought to resemble the land of the living, with villages and houses similar to those on the surface of the earth. The life the departed lead in that place is a reflection of their earthly life: rich men will be rich again, and the poor will be poor. (Furer-Haimendorf, 328)

BUDDHISM IN NEPAL

Nepal is a Hindu kingdom, but its religion may be described as a peaceful, cooperative mix or combination of Hinduism and Buddhism. Conflict between the two is very rare, mainly because of mutual influence. The Nepalese in general have respect for both; Buddhists worship in Hindu temples, and Hindus visit Buddhist temples.

Nepalese resistance to the Good News is motivated by their fear of the loss of identity and age-old traditions. In this context, assure your friend that the gospel is not against ethnic diversity or the retention of diverse cultures and linguistic allegiance. Jesus is not the God of any particular ethnic community but the God of all creation. He wants us to love one another, show respect to our parents and elders, be loyal to our nation and rulers, and seek to be righteous in everything we do. All this is agreeable to the average Nepali, who is friendly and willing to work with others, but his attachment to the deities of his religion is very strong. Start your conversation carefully, without hurting his feelings regarding his attachment to idols and rituals. There are several biblical points in chapter 10 that may help you to understand (and also be able to explain) why God wants exclusive worship.

Society and Religion

Nepal is made up of many distinct ethnic groups. The valley and plains are populated by the Indo-Nepalese. The Tibeto-Nepalese (Tibeto-Mongol) are found in the highlands, while the indigenous Nepalese people groups are found in the lower ranges. The Brahmans and Kshatriyas, from the Indo-Nepalese group, are the two upper Hindu castes, which dominate Nepali civil service, armed forces, and other professions. The Tibeto-Nepalese are primarily pastoral.

The people of Nepal are an international community; that Nepal is a small kingdom somehow conceals the fact that vast numbers of Nepalese live in other countries and regions. They live in India, in the Darjeeling Hills (in the state of West Bengal), in Bihar, and in the northeastern states of Arunachal Pradesh, Assam, and Manipur, and they are the majority in the state of Sikkim. They are also found in Bhutan (although they are not embraced by the government).

At present, while the Nepalese are concerned with retaining their identity, privileges, and traditions, people in large numbers have begun to support communist ideology. Meanwhile, Hindu laws have been relaxed only to a certain extent. In the past, religious conversion was not allowed, and even now Christians are only allowed freedom of worship. That is, they cannot openly evangelize, and believers among minority groups seem to be targeted by the law in this area. Churches must be registered with the government.

Your Nepali friend may be intensely conscious of his ethnic origin and his Hindu or Buddhist background. He is justifiably proud of the beautiful Himalayan range, and if he is a Hindu, he believes that the Buddha is an avatar of Vishnu and is very much aware that his nation is the home of Siddhartha Gautama, the founder of Buddhism (born in Lumbini).

He may be guided by caste hierarchy and rituals (both Hindu and Buddhist). He probably consults his horoscope, makes visits to diviners, shows interest in palmistry, and is an avid worshiper of the deity images. He considers the cow to be holy. He goes on pilgrimages to sacred places on the Indian subcontinent. He is industrious and works hard to earn his livelihood despite the difficulty and sometimes ridicule he faces from outside of Nepal. He is considered to be reliable in matters of security. It is possible that he indulges in marijuana and tobacco. (Some drinks consumed during festivals and holidays contain small or moderate doses of marijuana and other extracts that act as narcotics and hallucinogens.)

Substance Abuse

Simple beverages are ritually used in many religions. In some, such as the Hinduism-Buddhism practiced in Nepal, intoxicants play a special role in inducing trance, spirit possession, and exorcism (this is especially common in systems that encourage secretive practices). The shamans and priests, to bring themselves into a trance, regularly use opium, marijuana, hashish, and other herbal drugs.

Intoxicants bring dramatic and often violent changes in the behavior of shamans and priests. Their actions attract the undivided attention of the worshipers, who assemble in great numbers to witness exorcism and to hear and receive prophecies and cures. Those who drink or smoke these intoxicants often fall into hallucinations and start blabbering, which is taken to be the voice of spirits (or gods and goddesses).

For thousands of years, both scriptural and folk practitioners of Hinduism used hallucinogenic juices extracted from certain plants. The plants that have this essence of intoxication are also worshiped as powerful gods or spirits. It is a common practice in some northern Indian and Nepalese provinces to prepare and consume such drinks during momentous occasions, and the Hindu-Buddhist peoples of Nepal continue to follow this tradition. The use of hemp drugs for psychedelic experience is standard among the practitioners of various cults, whose leaders freely use plant essences to dope their followers to ensure that they will follow commands.

New Age dependence on drugs for the experience of calm, bliss, and visions is not new, and while the hippies who swarmed Nepal in the 1960s and 1970s are no longer welcome, their devastating impact on Nepalese youth is widely felt. In a society where older people smoked such intoxicants as a tradition, thousands of young people are now addicted to such habits. There is religious sanction for such use in both Nepal and India.

The use of intoxicants for spiritual experience enslaves. Talk to your Nepali friend about how people are destroyed in this way. The Word of God is against using intoxicants for any kind of experience: "Do not get drunk on wine, which leads to debauchery. Instead, be filled with the Spirit" (Ephesians 5:18). Consider the ridicule of drunken behavior in Isaiah 28:7–8:

> Priests and prophets stagger from beer
> and are befuddled with wine;
> they reel from beer,
> they stagger when seeing visions,
> they stumble when rendering decisions.
> All the tables are covered with vomit
> and there is not a spot without filth.

The Use of Wine and Other Intoxicants

There are many other passages in the Word of God that deal with drunkenness and the consequent loss of sense and propensity for evil behavior. The writer of Ecclesiastes says that he tried cheering himself with wine and embraced folly (2:3). Isaiah 5:22 condemns those who consider themselves "heroes at drinking wine and champions at mixing drinks." Modern chemistry has helped produce narcotic and hallucinogenic drugs, and the loss of fear for God and the practice of false religions has led to easy distribution and abuse.

Your friend will likely question why Western Christians drink alcohol and then condemn substances such as opium, hashish, and marijuana. There is really no justification. The status of wine is somewhat ambiguous, but consumption of wine in order to get high is certainly prohibited. The best course of action for your witness is to avoid alcoholic drinks.

Wine has always been a sign of abundance and life, treated as a gift and blessing of God (Genesis 27:27–28; Ecclesiastes 9:7; Luke 7:33–34; John 2:1–11):

> Do not let anyone judge you by what you eat or drink, or with regard to a religious festival, a New Moon celebration or a Sabbath day. These are a shadow of the things that were to come; the reality, however, is found in Christ. (Colossians 2:16–17)

We do not judge others by what they eat or drink, nor do we allow others to judge us by what we eat or drink. However, the Word of God clearly associates drunkenness and substance abuse with a lack of holiness and obedience to evil forces. For example, in Genesis 19, the daughters of Lot, fearing they would have no children because they were without husbands, coerced their father into drunkenness, slept with him on successive nights, and conceived. The sons born out of these incestuous relationships became the nations of Moab and Ammon, and the Moabites and Ammonites came to represent those who worshiped idols rather than God. The Israelites abandoned the Lord and indulged in immorality because of the seduction of the Moabites (see Numbers 25).

> Woe to those who rise early in the morning to run after their drinks, who stay up late at night till they are inflamed with wine. They . . . have no regard for the deeds of the LORD, no respect for the work of his hands. (Isaiah 5:11–12)

> Do not join those who drink too much wine or gorge themselves on meat, for drunkards and gluttons become poor, and drowsiness clothes them in rags. . . . Who has woe? Who

has sorrow? Who has strife? Who has complaints? Who has needless bruises? Who has bloodshot eyes? Those who linger over wine, who go to sample bowls of mixed wine. Do not gaze at wine when it is red, when it sparkles in the cup, when it goes down smoothly! In the end it bites like a snake and poisons like a viper. Your eyes will see strange sights and your mind imagine confusing things. You will be like one sleeping on the high seas, lying on top of the rigging. "They hit me," you will say, "but I'm not hurt! They beat me, but I don't feel it! When will I wake up so I can find another drink?" (Proverbs 23:20–21, 29–35).

Remember to tell your friend that desire for the consumption of alcohol and other drugs grows in us, enslaves us, and makes us seek stronger dosages every day that we continue our involvement with it. Soon the body benumbs, and excitement is possible only with greater quantities, along with which come the dangers of permanent depression and sickness. Finally, elevating the use of substances as an integral part of worship gives it a legitimacy, splendor, and magical power that causes us to be tempted to fall into Satan's trap; only God's grace can save us.

BUDDHISM IN MONGOLIA

Mongolia, a land of grasslands, mountainous ranges, and the Gobi Desert, was once a great empire, dominant in the history of humankind. At present, sadly, Mongolia is one of the least developed countries in the world. It is a closed nation, for all practical purposes, even after attaining its independence with the fall of the Soviet Union.

Mongolia is the last post of the Buddhist missionary movement that started two thousand years ago. Mongolia finally became a Buddhist nation with a strong shamanist base in the latter half of the sixteenth century, although Buddhist contacts were received from the fourth century onward. The Mongols were encouraged by the nobility to embrace Buddhism, who first adopted it cheerfully, expressing their acceptance through generous gifts. Shamanism, well entrenched in Mongolia despite blending and tolerating a variety of religious influences, was banned by the newly converted nobility on the grounds of animal sacrifice. Shamanism then went underground and resurfaced in the garb of Buddhist gods and sages and with fairly Buddhistic doctrine. Mongolia became predominantly Vajrayana by the mid-seventeenth century.

Spread of Buddhism

Among other reasons, the emphases on meritorious work and monasticism helped the spread of Buddhism. It is reported that more than one-third of the male population was at one time part of the strain of Buddhism that centered around the Mongolian Lama cult. Buddhism and Shamanism currently coexist and are mutually supportive; it is interesting to note that (as in Tibet) to ensure its adoption by the people, Buddhism had to ban native religion rather than absorb the spirits and gods worshiped in local practice. Pre-Buddhist religions (Bon in Tibet, Sikkim, and Bhutan, and shamanism in Mongolia) managed to survive by adopting a Buddhist veneer.

Shamanism

Mongolian shamanism is characterized by invocations and incantations to the spirits and idols, loud drum beating, worship of a variety of images, the appeasement of the spirits of dead ancestors, and use of triangular bones for divination. Exorcism of evil forces through a variety of rituals, including the burning of malevolent spirit effigies, is theatrical and creates fear in spectator-worshipers. Sign reading and reciting charms are also common.

Unlike orthodox Buddhism, which focuses on eventual total extinction, Mongolian shamanism (like all folk religions attached to Buddhism) seeks solutions to current predicaments and hostile environments. Herein lies the problem for the ordinary Buddhist layperson: he wants relief in the present, but there is no hope for it unless he goes outside Buddhism and accepts the help of shamanism.

Tell your Mongolian friend that Jesus is not only the God of the future but also the God of both the present and the past. He is here forever, and His compassionate mercy is always available: "He is good; his love endures forever" (2 Chronicles 5:13).

> Jesus Christ is the same yesterday and today and forever. Do not be carried away by all kinds of strange teachings. It is good for our hearts to be strengthened by grace, not by ceremonial foods, which are of no value to those who eat them. (Hebrews 13:8–9)

One of the most disturbing aspects of Mongolian shamanism is the trance (or ecstasy). Trance is induced by rapid repeated body movements; sensory bombardment using drums and shrilling pipes; loud, repetitive singing; and the consumption of intoxicants. Over the years, many practices of Mongolian shamanism have been incorporated into Mongolian Buddhism; shamanism cleverly appropriated the external appearances of Buddhism and began to demonstrate that it was, after all, close to (or a branch of) Buddhism.

Evangelizing Vajrayana Buddhists in General

Tibetan Buddhism is disseminated widely in many nations and among various people groups. Its essential features are animism, polytheism, secretive and sexual practices for nirvana, shamanism, divination, and meditation.

Marku Tsering, who works among Tibetan Buddhists, has suggested several steps for evangelism (paraphrased): Get a good foundation by examining your own commitment to Christ. Undergo a systematic study of the Bible and Christian doctrine. Learn all you can about Buddhism and how it affects its host culture. Consider the standards of behavior that Buddhists expect from those who profess to be religious. Remember that Christians share the gospel by their lives as well as by their words.

Understand and adopt local culture. Remember that "the person who has a plausible, non-religious reason for his or her presence in a country tends to be better accepted than the person whom everyone knows is there to preach a foreign religion." Be a gradual, thought-provoking, loving, powerful witness. Remember the necessity of repentance and prayer. Learn the language well. Think like a Buddhist. Understand the concepts of compassion, God, incarnation, salvation, and sin.

While selecting and adapting material for presentation, avoid offense—choose passages of Scripture that Buddhists will be able to grasp. Focus on spiritual issues. While applying the Word, adopt local styles: "Avoid informality, directness, lack of obvious reverence for God and the Scriptures, and overt displays of emotion" (Tsering, 149–55).

BUDDHISM AND CHRISTIANITY: MAJOR DISSIMILARITIES

8

ABSENCE OF A PERSONAL GOD

The first thing we notice in Buddhism is that it denies a personal God. At the same time, almost every shade of Buddhism deifies Gautama Buddha (or buddhahood), accepting and worshiping other gods, as well. Christians believe in only one triune God, but your Buddhist friend may question this claim because we maintain that God is three *persons* (and, therefore, *personal*).

The Trinity is a mystery even for those who meditate on the Word of God and are proficient with church history and theology, but Scripture does portray God in three persons with one essence. God the Father, Jesus Christ the Son, and the Holy Spirit are eternally existent together, and their ministries, although somewhat different in *human* historical terms, are of the same substance and function. This belief is not optional for anyone who claims to follow the Lord Jesus Christ, who clearly said, "I and the Father are one" (John 10:30).

> There is only one God; each of the three divine persons is recognized to be God; God's self-revelation recognizes distinctions among these three persons in that there are interactions among them; and these distinctions are not just a matter of revelation (as received by humans) but are also eternally immanent in the Godhead. (Myers, 1190)

Jesus said,

Anyone who has seen me has seen the Father. How can you say, "Show us the Father"? Don't you believe that I am in the Father, and that the Father is in me? The words I say to you are not just my own. Rather, it is the Father, living in me, who is doing his work. (John 14:9–10)

As for the Holy Spirit of God, there are references to His ministry throughout the Old and New Testaments. Jesus promised,

I will ask the Father, and he will give you another Counselor to be with you forever—the Spirit of truth. The world cannot accept him, because it neither sees him nor knows him. But you know him, for he lives with you and will be in you. I will not leave you as orphans; I will come to you. (John 14:16–18)

In these verses, the presence of the Holy Spirit is equated with the presence of Christ.

Throughout church history, attempts have been made to clarify Trinitarian doctrine through various descriptions, similes, metaphors, and examples from everyday experience. One explanation cited by Norman Geisler as an answer to Muslim concerns on this point is a mathematical analogy: The triune God is $1 \times 1 \times 1$, which results in 1, and not $1 + 1 + 1$, which results in 3 (Geisler, 262).

It must be stated, however, that human illustrations will not be adequate for nonbelievers from other religions to accept the Trinity: Faith in the triune God comes by the grace of the Lord and cannot be easily imparted through reason or metaphor. Let your Buddhist friend have his own objections and do not enter into argument on this account. Focus on prayer (to the Lord Jesus Christ) for his personal needs and expect miracles, but never suppress the fact that you are a Trinitarian believer—it is the loving presence of Jesus through the work of His Spirit that rescues us.

As I recommended in my book *Sharing Your Faith With a Hindu*, pray for your unbelieving friend in his presence and let him know that you will continue to pray on his behalf; not for your benefit, but for his. When your prayer is answered, give all the glory to God and *never* allow the impression that you are a god-man or god-woman with miraculous powers. Don't focus on the intensity or the efficacy of *your* prayer in such a way that your friend tries to give you credit.

IS CREATION WORTHLESS?

The Word of God says we have value and can be adopted as His children:

To all who received him, to those who believed in his name, he gave the right to become children of God—children born not of natural descent, nor of human decision or a husband's will, but born of God. (John 1:12–13)

We are not worthless in *any* sense—God wants to *live* in us! (1 Corinthians 6:19–20). His Word demonstrates that we are sinners but provides *forgiveness* and *redemption* through the grace of our Lord, who values us immeasurably. Buddhist belief, while insisting on compassion for all creation, nevertheless considers life in this world to be worthless—even precious relationships are regarded as inconsequential. Buddhism's teaching is that the intrinsic evil, corruption, and transitory nature of all things physical (material, tangible) are to be the focus of meditation.

While the Bible does establish that all things physical will pass away, it nevertheless does not despise the body; while it shows that we are weak in body, it helps us to overcome this barrier. Jesus wants us to be partakers of His tangible ministry (Matthew 26:26).

The apostle Paul often focuses on the body (its functions and the need to keep it holy), recognizing its obvious frailty, subjection to temptation, worldly perspective, and propensity toward (and cause for) sin. Nevertheless, he does not call for the destruction or denigration of the body, because it is an instrument in the hands of the God, who works His will in us. Paul, when made aware of his own weakness, cried out, "What a wretched man I am! Who will rescue me from this body of death? Thanks be to God—through Jesus Christ our Lord!" (Romans 7:24–25).

Therefore do not let sin reign in your mortal body so that you obey its evil desires. Do not offer the parts of your body to sin, as instruments of wickedness, but rather offer yourselves to God, as those who have been brought from death to life; and offer the parts of your body to him as instruments of righteousness. (Romans 6:12–13)

Since you died with Christ to the basic principles of this world, why, as though you still belonged to it, do you submit to its rules: "Do not handle! Do not taste! Do not touch!"? These are all destined to perish with use, because they are based on human commands and teachings. Such regulations indeed have an appearance of wisdom, with their self-imposed worship, their false humility and their harsh treatment of the body, but they lack any value in restraining sensual indulgence. (Colossians 2:20–23)

As long as we live in this world, our body is integral, and we can use it to bring glory to God and love to our neighbors. *The church is the body of Christ.* Paul wrote to the Philippians,

> I eagerly expect and hope that I will in no way be ashamed, but will have sufficient courage so that now as always Christ will be exalted in my body, whether by life or by death. . . . If I am to go on living in the body, this will mean fruitful labor for me. (Philippians 1:20–22)

Paul also clearly tells us, "In Christ all the fullness of the Deity lives in bodily form" (Colossians 2:9), and when we are resurrected from the dead we will have our own physical body, for "he who raised Christ from the dead will also give life to your mortal bodies through his Spirit, who lives in you" (Romans 8:11). We certainly should recognize the body's weakness, but instead of self-flagellation, we must consecrate it to glorify God:

> The body that is sown is perishable, it is raised imperishable; it is sown in dishonor, it is raised in glory; it is sown in weakness, it is raised in power; it is sown a natural body, it is raised a spiritual body. If there is a natural body, there is also a spiritual body. (1 Corinthians 15:42–44)

Desire

One of the cardinal declarations of Buddhism is that desire is evil, leading to the accumulation of bad karma that, in turn, leads to endless births, deaths, and rebirths. The Bible does not condemn desire as such, distinguishing between holy and unholy passions. *The Word of God abounds in assurance that the desire of the righteous will be fulfilled.* When we desire to do His will (Psalm 40:8), the Lord grants our heart's desire (Psalm 21:2). We are promised that "what the righteous desire will be granted" (Proverbs 10:24); "the desire of the righteous ends only in good" (Proverbs 11:23).

Worldly Activity

Buddhism frowns upon action or activity because it allegedly adds to the karma one has already accumulated, bringing bondage to this world for all. One of the effective ways to ensure better karma, then, is not to get involved or engaged, and in this sense there is a denouncement of human labor. While Buddhism does condemn evil deeds and exhort good deeds, every deed, right *or* wrong, adds to karma, and, as such, activity should ultimately be avoided in order to attain nirvana. While the laity are encouraged to be morally upright in all their duties, in their conscience labor is a kind of worldly slavery, a hindrance in the journey toward nirvana (total extinction). This sentiment, constantly expressed, is found, for example, in an eighteenth-century Tibetan text:

> Oh, to have given that care to those
> who were born of one's body—how pitiful!
> Relatives united and intimate friends,
> Children reared, and riches stored,
> All are impermanent, like an illusion,
> And nothing substantial is found in them.
> My mind has now forsaken all activity.
> So that I may keep constant to my vows. (Conze, 87)

On the other hand, good works are an essential part of being a true follower of Christ. God is active from the beginning; He created this world, and His Word calls it *work*. God likewise wanted the man to work "and put him in the Garden of Eden to work it and take care of it" (Genesis 2:15). *Work in itself is not a curse or sin.* God not only saw "all that he . . . made, and it was very good" (Genesis 1:31), but Jesus himself was a carpenter (Mark 6:3), and Paul also supported himself through manual labor (Acts 18:3). Righteous works are encouraged and demanded in Christian faith (see also Ephesians 4:28).

Each of us will have our works judged, both good and bad (2 Corinthians 5:10). That does not mean we are guided by works alone or that we carry our evil works without any scope for forgiveness while in this world. God makes us righteous, despite our evil works in the past, if we believe on Jesus Christ as Lord and Savior:

> Again, the gift of God is not like the result of the one man's sin: The judgment followed one sin and brought condemnation, but the gift followed many trespasses and brought justification. For if, by the trespass of the one man, death reigned through that one man, how much more will those who receive God's abundant provision of grace and of the gift of righteousness reign in life through the one man, Jesus Christ. (Romans 5:16–17)

Paul declares, "We are God's workmanship, created in Christ Jesus to do good works, which God prepared in advance for us to do" (Ephesians 2:10). In fact, the apostle James asks,

What good is it, my brothers, if a man claims to have faith but has no deeds? Can such faith save him? Suppose a brother or sister is without clothes and daily food. If one of you says to him, "Go, I wish you well; keep warm and well fed," but does nothing about his physical needs, what good is it? In the same way, faith by itself, if it is not accompanied by action, is dead. . . . You foolish man, do you want evidence that faith without deeds is useless? Was not our ancestor Abraham considered righteous for what he did when he offered his son Isaac on the altar? You see that his faith and his actions were working together, and his faith was made complete by what he did. . . . A person is justified by what he does and not by faith alone. (James 2:14–17, 20–22, 24)

At the same time, "it is by grace you have been saved, through faith—and this not from yourselves, it is the gift of God—not by works, so that no one can boast" (Ephesians 2:8–9). Your Buddhist friend has not reconciled the tension between works and grace, often believing that only if he can wear the yellow robe and become a monk is there any hope for salvation. Point out that even within Buddhist belief the need for the work of the laity is recognized, but it is given short shrift as something less spiritually worthy. This world is not illusory—it is real; but ultimately we are not of this world, and our citizenship is in heaven, praising the God of creation and fellowshiping with Him in His presence.

LIFE IS WORTH LIVING

The major goal of Buddhism, reflected in the endless cycle of samsara, is eliminating the suffering caused by desire, which can be achieved (for some) through following the noble paths and right conduct. That the world is full of suffering is recognized everywhere, but Buddhism denies that suffering has any relevant role. The Word of God says that life is His gift and is worth living *no matter what*. God is a God of life, and His covenant with us is "a covenant of life and peace" (Malachi 2:5). If we love Him (that is, if we serve and obey Him), God promises to both save and satisfy us (Psalm 91:16).

Life is not an end in itself: "Whoever finds his life will lose it, and whoever loses his life for [Jesus'] sake will find it" (Matthew 10:39). The Lord also teaches that you should not "worry about your life, what you will eat; or about your body, what you will wear. Life is more than food, and the body more than clothes" (Luke 12:22–23).

The gospel of John is about the life that flows from God: "Through him all things were made; without him nothing was made that has been made. In him was life, and that life was the light of men" (1:3–4). Jesus is "the bread of life" (6:35), who declares, "The Spirit gives life; the flesh counts for nothing. The words I have spoken to you are spirit and they are life" (6:63; see also 10:10). God himself *is* life and the Life-giver.

SIN

The Buddhist focus on karma leaves enough room to describe good and evil deeds, but the notion of sin is distinctly absent. Man needs to work out his salvation on his own, and his accumulated karma must be eliminated. He has not committed any "sin" against God or the gods, even though he has perpetrated deeds both favoring them and against them. Man inevitably suffers the inexorable and inflexible consequence of karma—there is no escape. Nonetheless, as we pointed out above, while the Word of God clearly says that we will be judged for our good and bad works, only the grace of the Lord makes our salvation possible.

This list of contrasts between Buddhist and Christian beliefs can be expanded with additional points through diligent conversations with your Buddhist friend. Remember, however, that such contrasts are for your understanding, not for debate. Confrontation and debate do not help bring about the conversion of the heart; in fact, they tend to harden people's hearts. Reasoning is important, but there are many other more significant facets. *Conversion of the heart is the job of the Holy Spirit,* so we must cooperate with Him and not hinder His work with our human arguments.

CHAPTER

EVANGELIZING
BUDDHISTS

9

In most of the countries where it is predominant, Buddhism is a government religion and is closely linked with political movements. Buddhist monks were at the forefront of the struggles against Western colonialism and even now get involved in political agitation. As mentioned, they often assume the role of the protectors of national interests.

Buddhism is currently identifying itself with anti-Christian forces. Although Hindu fundamentalists are opposed to Buddhist egalitarianism, and although they desire to reestablish the Hindu beliefs condemned by Gautama Buddha, they seek the collaboration of Buddhism's nationalist and radical elements. Buddhist renewal in modern times continues to have anti-Christian overtones; rejection of Christianity has become a cornerstone of contemporary Buddhist apologetics, though opposition to Christian faith varies among Buddhist factions.

In the past in Japan, Buddhists spied on Christians and missionaries under the guise of students. Refutation of Christianity became an educational subject, and children were given propagandist literature that showed Christians as anti-Japanese and supporters of "foreign religions." In several countries, defense of Buddhism became synonymous with the defense of the nation, and in some Southeast Asian nations, forcible prohibition of Christianity was (and is) demanded.

Buddhist monks see danger to their belief and practice through the spread of Christianity in their nations. They pressure governments to regulate and, if possible, ban Christian missionary activities. In addition, the war in Vietnam, the presence of American troops in some Buddhist nations, and the spread of secular education also foster resistance to the gospel.

However, the Lord is at work in all of these countries. As already stated, the spectacular growth of the church in South Korea has few parallels in evangelical history. I believe that through the influence of the South Korean church many in Southeast Asia will be attracted to the good news of Jesus Christ. I even expect a breakthrough in Japan, Buddhism's most industrialized and ethnocentric civilization.

STATUS OF JESUS

In the eyes of Buddhists, Jesus is not even on the level of a monk. Unlike Gautama, who was the son of a king, Jesus rose from a lowly birth as the son of a carpenter. Jesus ascended to His position suddenly, and then His disciples made Him look big, which, Buddhists argue, clearly shows the upstart (unplanned, unendorsed) nature of His ministry. They do not understand that the Bible not only prophesies about Jesus in the Old Testament but also foretells His saving work for all sinners.

This truth is difficult for everyone who is determined to resist the call of Christ, but the Holy Spirit continues to convincingly speak to individuals, groups of people, and even communities, bringing souls to salvation in Jesus. His humanity is there for all to see, and His divinity is demonstrated in His resurrection and His continuing ministry. Our Buddhist friends know well the mythology surrounding the birth and nirvana of Buddha (described as supernaturalism), but they are unwilling to accept the possibility that Jesus (who performed miracles) is divine.

Your Buddhist friend may even assume that Jesus was nothing more than a magician and that by His magic He gathered needy, worthless people around Him. This belief comes naturally, as Buddhists maintain that miracles are performed to overwhelm (and perhaps manipulate) those who observe them. For instance, a centuries-old Theravada biography of Buddha (Mahavastu) presents magic (or miracles) performed by Dipankara, predecessor to Gautama, in the following manner:

> Megha threw . . . five lotus flowers toward Dipankara, the Lord. The flowers remained sustained in the air, and formed a circle round the Lord's radiant head. The Brahmin girl also threw her two lotuses. They also stood suspended in the air, and so did those thrown by other people. This was one of the miracles by which the Buddhas impress people, to make them listen to the truth. (Conze, 23)

There are many similar examples in the biographies of the Buddhas and other sages, the purpose being to impress the laity and show the comparative greatness of "holy ones." A fifth-century text by Buddhaghosha claims that meditation leads to the acquisition of magical powers, such as becoming visible or invisible at will, going from being one to being many and from many to one, walking through barriers unimpeded, walking on water without sinking, floating cross-legged, having the ability to touch the sun and the moon, etc. (ibid., 123–29).

It *is* true that several church fathers resorted to narrating the miracles that were performed when relics of prominent Christian saints passed through towns and cities. These writers exaggerated the importance of these famous believers by chronicling their miraculous powers for the benefit of the laity. Fortunately for us, Christians throughout the ages objected to such tales and held on to the Word of God.

PRIMACY OF GOD IN HUMAN LIFE

Jesus cautioned:

> Do not suppose that I have come to bring peace to the earth. I did not come to bring peace, but a sword. For I have come to turn "a man against his father, a daughter against her mother, a daughter-in-law against her mother-in-law—a man's enemies will be the members of his own household." Anyone who loves his father or mother more than me is not worthy of me; anyone who loves his son or daughter more than me is not worthy of me; and anyone who does not take his cross and follow me is not worthy of me. (Matthew 10:34–38)

Buddhists see in this a revolt against national identity and are alarmed to hear of such teaching, but this is not justified, given the extreme individualism preached by Gautama Buddha. The focus of Jesus in these verses is on *the absolute primacy of God and the primacy of our love for Him over everything else in our life.* Fear of God leads to our love for God, and our love for God is the beacon that leads to all good things: "The fear of the LORD adds length to life" (Proverbs 10:27).

Jesus asked us to follow Him, taking up our cross daily (Matthew 16:24), making it clear that in *this* life, suffering is necessary and expected. Matthew Henry wrote,

> Our Lord warned his disciples to prepare for persecution. . . . Christ foretold troubles, not only that the troubles

might not be a surprise, but that they might confirm their faith. He tells them what they should suffer, and from whom. Thus Christ has dealt fairly and faithfully with us, in telling us the worst we can meet with in his service; and he would have us deal so with ourselves, in sitting down and counting the cost. . . . It appears plainly that all who will live godly in Christ Jesus must suffer persecution; and we must expect to enter into the kingdom of God through many tribulations. (Henry, on Matthew 16:42)

THREAT TO LOYALTY AND PARENTAL AUTHORITY

Buddhists also see in these (and similar) passages a threat to religious loyalty and filial piety. We elsewhere discussed the validity of worship of (or reverence for) the dead. It is sufficient here to say that the Word of God commands us to love, respect, and obey our parents. Parents must discipline their children and raise them in the fear and love of God.

> Children, obey your parents in the Lord, for this is right. "Honor your father and mother . . . that it may go well with you and that you may enjoy long life on the earth." Fathers, do not exasperate your children; instead, bring them up in the training and instruction of the Lord. (Ephesians 6:1–4)

Disobedience to parents is a dreadful thing that will become more prominent:

> Mark this: There will be terrible times in the last days. People will be lovers of themselves, lovers of money, boastful, proud, abusive, disobedient to their parents, ungrateful, unholy, without love, unforgiving, slanderous, without self-control, brutal, not lovers of the good, treacherous, rash, conceited, lovers of pleasure rather than lovers of God—having a form of godliness but denying its power. Have nothing to do with them. (2 Timothy 3:1–5)

When people are filled with wickedness, they disobey their parents (Romans 1:30); therefore, the Word of God strongly emphasizes obedience. (Again, Buddhist reverence for and worship of the dead is often maintained through selfishness, rather than selflessness.) While parents are loved and respected in every culture and theology—their authority over their young children is recognized, as are their duties to protect, discipline, and expect good behavior—Christian belief also emphasizes that their ultimate responsibility is to lovingly, patiently, and constantly reflect the Lord. The love, respect, and obedience that children give to parents is a model for following God, our Father.

MANY WORLDS, MANY HEAVENS, MANY LIVES

Buddhist apologists find the biblical creation story inadequate. There are numerous worlds and varieties of life-forms, gods, ghosts, and other species. How could this world and all it contains have been created in six days? What about the creation of other worlds that have existed for eons? Where do beings that live in different worlds go after death before they are born once again in this world?

However, there is no evidence that humanlike beings are found on other planets or imaginary heavens. (And, again, the Bible declares that we have only one life [Hebrews 9:27].) The nature and function of the Buddhist heavens revolve around samsara, and because Buddhist scriptures do not focus on God, Buddhists are unable to see the relevance of the creation presented in His Word—powers and works unimaginable to humans may be possible for a *pantheon* but not for a single, exclusive God.

That humans subsequently devise such ideologies is one reason God prohibits us from worshiping anyone or anything other than Him:

> You shall have no other gods before me. You shall not make for yourself an idol in the form of anything in heaven above or on the earth beneath or in the waters below. You shall not bow down to them or worship them; for I, the LORD your God, am a jealous God, punishing the children for the sin of the fathers to the third and fourth generation of those who hate me, but showing love to a thousand generations of those who love me and keep my commandments. (Exodus 20:3–6)

> Do not follow other gods, the gods of the peoples around you; for the LORD your God, who is among you, is a jealous God and his anger will burn against you, and he will destroy you from the face of the land. Do not test the LORD your God. . . . Be sure to keep the commands of the LORD your God and the stipulations and decrees he has given you. Do what is right and good in the LORD's sight. (Deuteronomy 6:14–18)

> Stop bringing meaningless offerings! Your incense is detestable to me. . . . When you spread out your hands in prayer, I will hide my eyes from you; even if you offer many prayers, I will not listen. Your hands are full of blood; wash

and make yourselves clean. Take your evil deeds out of my sight! Stop doing wrong, learn to do right! Seek justice, encourage the oppressed. Defend the cause of the fatherless, plead the case of the widow. (Isaiah 1:13, 15–17)

This is what the LORD says: "I will not turn back my wrath. . . . They have rejected the law of the LORD and have not kept his decrees. . . . They have been led astray by false gods, the gods their ancestors followed" (Amos 2:4).

Matthew Henry observed,

Considering how many temptations we are compassed with, and what corrupt desires we have in our bosoms, we have great need to keep our hearts with all diligence. Those cannot walk aright who walk carelessly. Moses charges particularly to take heed of the sin of idolatry. He shows how weak the temptation would be to those who thought aright; for these pretended gods, the sun, moon, and stars, were only blessings which the Lord their God had imparted to all nations. It is absurd to worship them; shall we serve those that were made to serve us? (Henry, on Deuteronomy 4:1–23)

Henry also noted,

The rejection of the Messiah by the Jewish nation is the continuance of their ancient idolatry, apostasy, and rebellion. They shall be brought to humble themselves before the Lord, to repent of their sins, and to trust in their long-rejected Mediator for salvation. Then he will deliver them, and make their prosperity great. (ibid., on Deuteronomy 5)

The jealous nature of God, exhibited extensively in the Old Testament, is the background of His exasperation with His chosen people, the Israelites. On many occasions He warned them to be obedient and refrain from worshiping false gods, that He is rightfully jealous and would not tolerate their idolatrous transgression.

In the New Testament, with the incarnation of Jesus Christ, the changed circumstances of the Israelites' fortunes, and the need for the gospel to be preached to all nations, there is greater emphasis on the *judgment* than the *jealousy* of God. The Father sent His Son to this world, and the ministry of the Holy Spirit is now in full operation, giving us tangible experience of God in Jesus Christ. God has moved toward humanity in mercy, forgiveness, and grace.

AN ARBITRARY AND CAPRICIOUS GOD?

Some Buddhists claim that God is inconsistent and irrational in His decisions. I do not see any substance to this criticism. The Old Testament is full of instances in which God gave thorough warning before actions against those who were disobedient. The gospel of John shows how Jesus continually explained His status as the Son of God and passionately wooed sinners. When He saw that those who witnessed His miracles and heard Him preaching the kingdom of God did not believe, He declared,

> For judgment I have come into this world, so that the blind will see and those who see will become blind. . . . If you were blind, you would not be guilty of sin; but now that you claim you can see, your guilt remains. (9:39, 41)

Some Buddhists think that the portrayal of God as having emotions is a slight meted out to the Supreme Being, who, as a Buddha, is beyond emotions and existence. Because Buddha is presented as beyond all feelings, your Buddhist friend expects God to be bereft of emotion. The truth is that since God is a *person*, not merely a force, He relates intimately with and participates actively in His creation.

Some Buddhists consider God to be capricious or whimsical because Jesus allowed himself to be crucified. Some also feel that God chooses one community over another. Buddhism, they claim, is *truly* international and offers nirvana without reference to social division or ethnic preference.

Jesus allowed himself to be crucified because He knew from the beginning that He was to offer himself as the sacrifice for the sins of His creation. This is neither capriciously whimsical *nor* tragically heroic. Jesus was merely fulfilling the plan that was established for Him from all eternity (Matthew 26:24).

There is nothing whimsical, arbitrary, or capricious about what God did, does, or will do; Scripture gives reasons and explanations for the actions of the Father, Son, and Holy Spirit. However, comprehending, appreciating, and believing such teachings requires faith and wisdom from above, and "the fruit of the light consists in all goodness, righteousness and truth" (Ephesians 5:9). Show your Buddhist friend biblical examples of God speaking against and laying out consequences for sin.

IMMANENCE AND RELATIONSHIP

Though this is extremely difficult for Buddhists to accept, God has entered into a covenant relationship with His creation and maintains personal relationship. God has a personal name and personal attributes not associated with any magical power, unlike the recitations of Buddhist names and texts. Through His covenant, God assures us that He is committed to our welfare and protection, and while we call upon Him for our needs, His name must not be used for selfish reasons.

> Then the LORD came down in the cloud and stood there with [Moses] and proclaimed his name, the LORD. And he passed in front of Moses, proclaiming, "The LORD, the LORD, the compassionate and gracious God, slow to anger, abounding in love and faithfulness, maintaining love to thousands, and forgiving wickedness, rebellion and sin" (Exodus 34:5–7).

> It was because the LORD loved you and kept the oath he swore to your forefathers that he brought you out with a mighty hand and redeemed you from the land of slavery. . . . Know therefore that the LORD your God is God; he is the faithful God, keeping his covenant of love to a thousand generations of those who love him and keep his commands. (Deuteronomy 7:8–9)

> Then God said to Noah and to his sons with him: "I now establish my covenant with you and with your descendants after you and with every living creature that was with you— the birds, the livestock and all the wild animals, all those that came out of the ark with you—every living creature on earth. . . . Never again will all life be cut off by the waters of a flood; never again will there be a flood to destroy the earth" (Genesis 9:8–11).

God is never reluctant to establish an intimate relationship with us; it is *we* who keep our distance through our sins of commission and omission. God reveals himself constantly, describing himself to be the living God (Deuteronomy 5:26; Jeremiah 10:10), Father, Redeemer, and Master, who expresses anger, love, concern, patience, and jealousy because He is *personal*. He listens to us and is ever ready to be persuaded by our prayers.

In order to demonstrate that God is personal, His Word deliberately uses anthropomorphic language that presents Him in human terms. He is never portrayed as merely a force, an animal, or a ghost. We may not understand God in physical form, but we know that Jesus, God's Son, came to live among us and to minister to us in His humanity. We are also created in His image; we become His representatives through our intellect, will, emotions, and conscience.

Unfortunately, Buddhism cannot provide for such personal experience because, for one thing, it does not believe in God (although it references "gods," "spirits," and "deities" abundantly). Deities may be appeased in the Buddhist folk stratum, and they may be portrayed as performing certain functions in orthodox doctrine, but Buddhists are cautioned to work out their salvation on their own, apart from relationship.

God is gracious and compassionate, ever-forgiving and always at hand for those who seek Him. God loves *all*, whether or not they yet believe. Share this with your Buddhist friend and tell him also the stories of how Jesus lived with us and suffered on our behalf. Testimony regarding miraculous occurrences should come later on, especially if you are conversing with an educated Buddhist.

Miracles performed by Jesus Christ are important for the growth of faith in your friend, but he will first be employing human reason to find out how Jesus really fits in. He will probably compare Jesus to Bodhisattva or Arhat. Perhaps he will even claim that the archetype (original pattern) of Jesus is found in one of these two; for instance, that the concept of Bodhisattva (a selfless person not entering nirvana but staying back to help others) preceded the mediating role of Christ.

Differences between Bodhisattva and Jesus Christ are found on several levels. A Bodhisattva does not guarantee nirvana; it is the individual who should work for this solution. A Bodhisattva himself has undergone several births and deaths and will continue to undergo samsara. An Arhat does not wait for (or help) others to obtain nirvana (hence, the Mahayana claim that an Arhat is a selfish person).

Jesus promises eternal life not only beyond this world but also here and now. Jesus does not desire sacrifices of appeasement from us. He wants us to repent from our sins and to turn to a righteous and holy life.

DOES GOD PREFER ONE ETHNIC COMMUNITY OVER ANOTHER?

If God does not favor one ethnicity over others, why did he do so with Israel? Is this supposed preference still in effect? What does God do now among the nations?

Answers to these questions, when based on the Word of God, will help your Buddhist friend to accurately understand God's alleged partiality. It is important for you to use simple language and limited, carefully chosen, relevant words. Theological terms are technical, and your friend may either have no knowledge of them or even misunderstand them as referring to something that you didn't intend. Remember that Jesus, like Gautama, used not the elitist (sacred) language but dialects that were comprehended by those around Him. Fortunately, the long-maintained tendency to communicate the Word of God using classical languages and archaic words is no longer mandated. Buddhists still rely on once popular but now defunct classical languages, yet your Buddhist friend likely has been brought up with the firm belief that only the commoner's dialect is the best medium to communicate spiritual matters.

The notion of a "chosen people" is found in the Bible. Deuteronomy 7:6–8 says,

> You are a people holy to the LORD your God. The LORD your God has chosen you out of all the peoples on the face of the earth to be his people, his treasured possession. The LORD did not set his affection on you and choose you because you were more numerous than other peoples, for you were the fewest of all peoples, but . . . because the LORD loved you and kept the oath he swore to your forefathers.

This was not the only time God chose people; for example, other instances of this nature are found in Genesis 12:1 and Numbers 17:2.

Adam and Eve are part of the Israelite history: God chose to create Adam and Eve and to bless all their descendants. So naturally, as the descendants of the line of people who consciously and deliberately retained the knowledge and wisdom of God, the chosen status of the Israelites continued. With the expanded revelation of God's eternal plan in the New Testament (which was constantly prefigured and prophesied in the Old Testament), emphasis shifts from the exclusive status of the Israelites as the chosen people to the right of *all of us* to become children (part of the chosen family) of God:

> To all who received him, to those who believed in his name, he gave the right to become children of God—children born not of natural descent, nor of human decision or a husband's will, but born of God. (John 1:12–13)

> How great is the love the Father has lavished on us, that we should be called children of God! And that is what we are! The reason the world does not know us is that it did not know him. Dear friends, now we are children of God, and what we

will be has not yet been made known. But we know that when he appears, we shall be like him, for we shall see him as he is. Everyone who has this hope in him purifies himself, just as he is pure. (1 John 3:1–3)

This is how we know that we love the children of God: by loving God and carrying out his commands. This is love for God: to obey his commands. And his commands are not burdensome, for everyone born of God overcomes the world. (1 John 5:2–4)

We know that we are children of God, and that the whole world is under the control of the evil one. We know also that the Son of God has come and has given us understanding, so that we may know him who is true. And we are in him who is true—even in his Son Jesus Christ. He is the true God and eternal life. Dear children, keep yourselves from idols. (1 John 5:19–21)

The Lord said to Ananias that Paul was His chosen instrument to carry His name before the Gentiles (Acts 9:15). The Holy Spirit was poured out even on the Gentiles (Acts 10:45), who were likewise granted repentance through the door of faith (Acts 11:18; 14:27). The apostles were led by the Holy Spirit to contextualize the Good News for the Gentiles and to declare that they "should not make it difficult for the Gentiles who are turning to God" by insisting on Jewish laws (Acts 15:19). We also read,

The Scripture foresaw that God would justify the Gentiles by faith, and announced the gospel in advance to Abraham: "All nations will be blessed through you." So those who have faith are blessed along with Abraham, the man of faith. (Galatians 3:8–9)

This mystery is that through the gospel the Gentiles are heirs together with Israel, members together of one body, and sharers together in the promise in Christ Jesus. (Ephesians 3:6)

Is God the God of Jews only? Is he not the God of Gentiles too? Yes, of Gentiles too, since there is only one God, who will justify [both] through that same faith. (Romans 3:29–30)

[We] are all sons of God through faith in Christ Jesus, for all of [us] who were baptized into Christ have clothed [ourselves] with Christ. There is neither Jew nor Greek, slave nor free, male nor female, for [we] are all one in Christ Jesus. If [we] belong to Christ, then [we] are Abraham's seed, and heirs according to the promise. (Galatians 3:26–29)

Has not God chosen those who are poor in the eyes of the world to be rich in faith and to inherit the kingdom he promised those who love him? (James 2:5)

God chose the foolish things of the world to shame the wise; God chose the weak things of the world to shame the strong. He chose the lowly things of this world and the despised things—and the things that are not—to nullify the things that are, so that no one may boast before him. It is because of him that you are in Christ Jesus, who has become for us wisdom from God—that is, our righteousness, holiness and redemption. Therefore, as it is written: "Let him who boasts boast in the Lord" (1 Corinthians 1:27–31).

It is also clear from the Word of God that any amount of effort on our part to become His children is inadequate. God chooses His own, and He extends His grace to us through His choice.

Nor because they are his descendants are they all Abraham's children. . . . It is not the natural children who are God's children, but it is the children of the promise who are regarded as Abraham's offspring. . . . Is God unjust? Not at all! For he says to Moses, "I will have mercy on whom I have mercy, and I will have compassion on whom I have compassion." It does not, therefore, depend on man's desire or effort, but on God's mercy. (Romans 9:7–8, 14–16)

We need to be sensitive and responsive to God to become His children, but our deliberate effort to achieve this status through good works will not achieve our end. Our actions, rather than *achieving* our salvation, are the *response to* and *confirmation of* what God has done for us.

Therefore, as God's chosen people, holy and dearly loved, clothe yourselves with compassion, kindness, humility, gentleness and patience. Bear with each other and forgive whatever grievances you may have against one another. Forgive as the Lord forgave you. And over all these virtues put on love, which binds them all together in perfect unity. (Colossians 3:12–14)

Since God chose His people from eternity, it is clear that the chosen status given to the Israelites and highlighted in Scripture was bound to be superceded by the future arrangements in which everyone who put his trust in the Lord and kept His commandments would become His children:

> He chose us in him before the creation of the world to be holy and blameless in his sight. In love he predestined us to be adopted as his sons through Jesus Christ, in accordance with his pleasure and will. (Ephesians 1:4–5)

Tell your Buddhist friend that our response is a key element in becoming His children (Matthew 22:14). I also caution you not to enter into elaborate explanations or discussions on this subject, risking the impression that because your friend does not yet acknowledge Jesus as Lord and Savior, he is not valued by God. While presenting what the Word of God says about "chosen people" and "God's family," emphasize the Lord's mercy even to those who do not yet love and serve Him.

Praying that God will meet the needs of your friend is a great way to keep the door open even as you refuse to twist or add to the Word of God. This skill flows first from the love you have for God and for His creation. If you begin to have empathy and compassion for your friend, just as the Lord wants you to, he will sense it and perhaps begin to understand and appreciate your position.

It is neither in our hands nor through our works that anyone is saved. We are willing and cooperative instruments in the ministry of the Holy Spirit. A knife can be used to cut a sweet and delicious mango into edible pieces, but it can also be used to bring harm to others. We must rely upon God-given wisdom, not our own agendas.

THE CROSS AS A SYMBOL OF SUFFERING

Buddhists are appalled at the sight of a man hanging on a cross, blood pouring from his body. The cross symbolizes acute anguish to them; their goal is to escape suffering, but Jesus seems to be the pathway to it. How, then, can they accept and adore an agonized figure who invites all of us to share in His pain?

The cross was a symbol of humiliation, a place of execution reserved by the Romans for the vilest criminals. Muslims looked at the cross and wondered how Allah could allow his "sinless prophet" to endure such an ignominious death of shame; in response, they developed a theory that Jesus was made to *appear* dead on the cross, while Allah actually held him up. (Thus, the cross is perceived as a drama.) On the other hand, Buddhists understand only the physical suffering of Jesus, while ignoring or refusing to recognize the true reason for His crucifixion.

The Word of God, however, makes it clear that the death of Christ was already foretold (Psalm 22; Isaiah 53), and that by His crucifixion Jesus offered himself as a sacrifice to reconcile all people with God and to resolve the conflict between Jews and Gentiles (Ephesians 2:11–16):

> Let us fix our eyes on Jesus, the author and perfecter of our faith, who for the joy set before him endured the cross, scorning its shame, and sat down at the right hand of the throne of God. (Hebrews 12:2)

The glory of the cross as a representation of what God did for us is not easy to grasp (1 Corinthians 1:18), and that the cross would cause difficulty was predicted:

> Jews demand miraculous signs and Greeks look for wisdom, but we preach Christ crucified: a stumbling block to Jews and foolishness to Gentiles, but to those whom God has called, both Jews and Greeks, [it is] Christ the power of God and the wisdom of God. (1 Corinthians 1:22–24)

Jesus also says that we must take up our cross to follow Him (Matthew 16:24; Mark 8:34). Here is what Matthew Henry says "taking up our cross" means:

> A true disciple of Christ is one that does follow him in duty, and shall follow him to glory. He is one that walks in the same way Christ walked in, is led by his Spirit, and treads in his steps. . . . "Let him deny himself." If self-denial be a hard lesson, it is no more than what our Master learned and practiced to redeem us and to teach us.
>
> "Let him take up his cross." The cross is here put for every trouble that befalls us. We are apt to think we could bear another's cross better than our own; but that is best which is appointed us. . . . We must not by our rashness and folly pull crosses down upon our own heads, but must take them up when they are in our way. (Henry, on Matthew 16:24)

The cross certainly is a symbol of our suffering, but we need to tell Buddhists that suffering is ultimately overcome by Jesus Christ. The cross, finally, comes to represent victory rather than defeat, and when we remember how the victory was won we also remember in whom we are to place our trust. We do not adore or worship the cross, but be aware that some Catholics do—this confuses the minds of Buddhists and adds to their distrust of this symbol.

The cross continues to cause great disturbance among nonbelievers. They despise it; they do not see the function it performed (and performs) in our lives; they do not accept the truth of justification. Pray that your Buddhist friend will come to see the purpose and beauty of the cross and will begin to cling to it in faith (though, of course, not as a talisman or charm, thought to contain energy or power).

TOTAL EXTINCTION OR ETERNAL LIFE?

In the context of showing that Jesus died only once, sacrificing His life for our sake, the Word of God clearly states that we have only one life to live:

> Nor did he enter heaven to offer himself again and again, the way the high priest enters the Most Holy Place every year with blood that is not his own. Then Christ would have had to suffer many times since the creation of the world. But now he has appeared once for all at the end of the ages to do away with sin by the sacrifice of himself. *Just as man is destined to die once, and after that to face judgment,* so Christ was sacrificed once to take away the sins of many people; and he will appear a second time, not to bear sin, but to bring salvation to those who are waiting for him. (Hebrews 9:25–28, emphasis added)

No one is reborn into this world, in any form. All of us are immortal: Those who accept Jesus will enter heaven, and those who do not will enter hell. There is life after death, but samsara is not included: The choices are eternal perfection and eternal condemnation (see Matthew 25:46).

> Everyone who believes in [Jesus] may have eternal life. For God so loved the world that he gave his one and only Son that whoever believes in him shall not perish but have eternal life. For God did not send his Son into the world to condemn the world, but to save the world through him. Whoever believes in him is not condemned, but whoever does not believe stands condemned already because he has not believed in the name of God's one and only Son. (John 3:15–18)

Inheriting eternal life is based on our faith in Christ, and He wants us to live a holy, selfless life that reflects the truth:

> As Jesus started on his way, a man ran up to him and fell on his knees before him. "Good teacher," he asked, "what must I do to inherit eternal life?"
>
> "Why do you call me good?" Jesus answered. "No one is good—except God alone. You know the commandments: 'Do not murder, do not commit adultery, do not steal, do not give false testimony, do not defraud, honor your father and mother.'"
>
> "Teacher," he declared, "all these I have kept since I was a boy."
>
> Jesus looked at him and loved him. "One thing you lack," he said. "Go, sell everything you have and give to the poor, and you will have treasure in heaven. Then come, follow me" (Mark 10:17–21).

Your Buddhist friend may tell you that it is precisely for this reason that Buddhism declares that only monks who have given up everything will be able to achieve nirvana. However, Jesus did not ask the young man to leave this world; He wanted him to be part of this world while serving God rather than money. Remember: God is no respecter of persons. He loves us all as His creation, and He does not favor people based on the institutions they support, the community they belong to, or the rituals they practice.

Make sure your Buddhist friend knows that eternal life is not relegated only to future life in heaven. The kingdom of God is already here (Matthew 13:18–23), and through our trust in the Lord Jesus we partake of it even now. Eternal life has no end or time—it is qualitatively different from the lives of those who do not put their faith in the saving grace of the Lord Jesus. As Paul says, "If anyone is in Christ, he is a new creation; the old has gone, the new has come!" (2 Corinthians 5:17). Already in our eternal life, we "with unveiled faces all reflect the Lord's glory . . . being transformed into his likeness with ever-increasing glory, which comes from the Lord, who is the Spirit" (2 Corinthians 3:18).

Beyond this life,

> God "will give to each person according to what he has done." To those who by persistence in doing good seek glory, honor and immortality, he will give eternal life. But for those who are self-seeking and who reject the truth and follow evil, there will be wrath and anger. (Romans 2:6–8)

> Now that you have been set free from sin and have become slaves to God, the benefit you reap leads to holiness,

and the result is eternal life. For the wages of sin is death, but the gift of God is eternal life in Christ Jesus our Lord. (Romans 6:22–23)

"The one who sows to please his sinful nature, from that nature will reap destruction; the one who sows to please the Spirit, from the Spirit will reap eternal life" (Galatians 6:8). Paul testified, "I was shown mercy so that in me, the worst of sinners, Christ Jesus might display his unlimited patience as an example for those who would believe on him and receive eternal life" (1 Timothy 1:16). Knowing God is always a necessary element in obtaining salvation. Jesus prayed to the Father,

> You granted [me] authority over all people that [I] might give eternal life to all those you have given [me]. Now this is eternal life: that they may know you, the only true God, and Jesus Christ, whom you have sent. (John 17:2–3)

HEAVEN

Buddhist texts speak of a number of hells and heavens, transitory camps of sadness or bliss for people who eventually come back to this world and continue the consequences of their past karma. Again, Buddhism offers no assurance that one will (or can) gather enough good karma to eliminate bad karma and attain nirvana.

To give one brief example, Ashvaghosha's first-century biography of Gautama mentions the journeys of Buddha to various heavens:

> His miracles caused the people of Shravasti greatly to honor and revere him. He, however, departed from them, and rose in glorious majesty miraculously above the Triple world, reached the heaven of the Thirty-three where his mother dwelt, and there preached the Dharma for her benefit. His cognition enabled the Sage to educate his mother. He passed the rainy season in that heaven, and accepted alms in due form from the king of the gods who inhabit the ether. Then, descending from the world of the Gods, he came down in the region of Samkashya. (Conze, 57)

Kamaloka is a heaven inhabited by kings and gods who manifest their sensual experience. *Rupaloka* is a heaven where the beings have forms. *Arupaloka* is a heaven of mind. When Gautama Buddha attained nonexistence, he immediately entered into *Tushita,* a heaven where enlightened Bodhisattvas and Arhats live after their nirvana. (Each of these heavens or worlds are further divided into various levels.)

In contrast, the heaven portrayed in the Word of God is His dwelling place where the faithful go and continually worship Him and enjoy His presence. In the New Testament, heaven is presented as an inheritance of the gift of God's grace to the faithful: "In his great mercy he has given us new birth into a living hope through the resurrection of Jesus Christ from the dead, and into an inheritance that can never perish, spoil or fade—kept in heaven for you" (1 Peter 1:3–4).

> The day of the Lord will come like a thief. The heavens will disappear with a roar; the elements will be destroyed by fire, and the earth and everything in it will be laid bare. Since everything will be destroyed in this way, what kind of people ought you to be? You ought to live holy and godly lives as you look forward to the day of God and speed its coming. That day will bring about the destruction of the heavens by fire, and the elements will melt in the heat. But in keeping with his promise we are looking forward to a new heaven and a new earth, the home of righteousness. (2 Peter 3:10–13)

You may tell your friend that Buddhist heavens are qualitatively different from the heaven of your belief. Tell him that heaven is not a transit camp for the dead but rather the place we enter into the presence of God. Heaven is not a place for the earthly high and mighty to rule over us; there is no social discrimination or economic disparity. The Lord Jesus is the way to heaven, and He compassionately welcomes us all:

> Come to me, all you who are weary and burdened, and I will give you rest. Take my yoke upon you and learn from me, for I am gentle and humble in heart, and you will find rest for your souls. For my yoke is easy and my burden is light. (Matthew 11:28–30)

WORSHIP

Your Buddhist friend may be surprised at the simplicity of Christian worship (though some churches do introduce spectacular practices lacking in reverence). The Buddhist is accustomed to elaborate rituals and ceremonies, and in the absence of an idol or image of Jesus Christ before the worshipers, he will almost certainly feel that our worship of the Lord is without any awe of His presence. He is accustomed to the kind of worship and adoration given to the Buddhas, Bodhisattvas, and spirits.

Buddhistic rituals and sacrifices are in sharp contrast to what Scripture repeatedly tells us: God does not want our sacrifices but our contrite heart (Psalm 40:6; 51:17) and the exclusivity of our attention and worship.

> You alone are the LORD. You made the heavens, even the highest heavens, and all their starry host, the earth and all that is on it, the seas and all that is in them. You give life to everything, and the multitudes of heaven worship you. (Nehemiah 9:6)

The psalmist says that his soul finds rest in God alone (62:1), that God alone is to be feared (76:7), and that His name alone is exalted (148:5). Our sins can be forgiven only by God (Mark 2:7), and no one is inherently good (Mark 10:18) or holy (Revelation 15:4). Salvation comes from Him alone, and "everyone who calls on the name of the Lord will be saved" (Romans 10:13). Jesus said, "I am the way and the truth and the life. No one comes to the Father except through me" (John 14:6).

Even though we have no need to appease or placate spirits, Christians are not passive against evil. Paul ordered,

> Put on the full armor of God so that you can take your stand against the devil's schemes. For our struggle is not against flesh and blood, but against the rulers, against the authorities, against the powers of this dark world and against the spiritual forces of evil in the heavenly realms. Therefore put on the full armor of God, so that when the day of evil comes, you may be able to stand your ground, and after you have done everything, to stand. (Ephesians 6:11–13)

Nor does Christianity support disrespect of authority or disobedience to it (disobedience is to occur only when by obeying an earthly command we could not be faithful to God).

> Everyone must submit himself to the governing authorities, for there is no authority except that which God has established. . . . Consequently, he who rebels against the authority is rebelling against what God has instituted, and those who do so will bring judgment on themselves. For rulers hold no terror for those who do right, but for those who do wrong. Do you want to be free from fear of the one in authority? Then do what is right and he will commend you. For he is God's servant to do you good. But if you do wrong, be afraid, for he does not bear the sword for nothing. He is God's servant,

an agent of wrath to bring punishment on the wrongdoer. Therefore, it is necessary to submit to the authorities, not only because of possible punishment but also because of conscience. This is also why you pay taxes, for the authorities are God's servants, who give their full time to governing. Give everyone what you owe him: If you owe taxes, pay taxes; if revenue, then revenue; if respect, then respect; if honor, then honor. Let no debt remain outstanding, except the continuing debt to love one another, for he who loves his fellowman has fulfilled the law. (Romans 13:1–8)

MAINTAINING ETHNIC IDENTITY

As for the maintenance of ethnicity, the action of evangelical Christians is matchless. For one thing, evangelicals insist upon having the Word of God translated into indigenous languages. They encourage worship within the boundaries of native familiarity, as well. The Word of God clearly states that there will be representations of all people groups in heaven:

They sang a new song: "You are worthy to take the scroll and to open its seals, because you were slain, and with your blood you purchased men for God from every tribe and language and people and nation." . . . There before me was a great multitude that no one could count, from every nation, tribe, people and language, standing before the throne and in front of the Lamb. (Revelation 5:9; 7:9)

As the Samaritans said, "Now we have heard for ourselves, and we know that this man really is the Savior of the world" (John 4:42). John confirmed, "We have seen and testify that the Father has sent his Son to be the Savior of the world. If anyone acknowledges that Jesus is the Son of God, God lives in him and he in God" (1 John 4:14–15).

Jesus came to set everyone free from the shackles of placing God in a specific ethnic, social, or political milieu. He wants us to be like Him, for we are made in the image of God. So if in our behavior there is racist insinuation or a superiority complex based on social and economic standards, then we are acting against the Word of God. Jesus healed, ate with, listened to, and had compassion for all kinds of people, irrespective of background.

A major problem that Buddhists face in regard to the acceptance of Jesus is Christianity's insistence that every individual must confess his sins and repent. In cultures that are largely inward-focused, confession is a foreign concept. A person becomes a Christian as an individual, but then she is expected to be a member of the believing community. In other words, conversion of the heart can be taken to mean the mandatory ending of long-standing relationships. Although sometimes spatial and/or emotional separation must occur, church leaders encourage new Christians to continue to maintain relationships with family and friends.

Moreover, the new believer (or potential convert) may be intimidated through language that is sometimes adopted by Christians. Terms such as "winning over" or slogans like "Myanmar for Christ" can cause misunderstanding and also be taken as an affront against the new Christian's community, nation, and ethnicity. We must be intentionally and constantly sensitive, and even when we are, the convert's process of learning and adjustment is extremely difficult and must be achieved by the grace of the Holy Spirit.

What Edward Bollinger says of Okinawans is largely true of Buddhists everywhere:

> The idea of One Transcendent God, Creator of Heaven and Earth, and the idea of the need for a restored relationship with God because of human sin are strange to [them]. Further devotion to ancestral spirits reinforces the particular loyalties of the individual and militates against the adoption of a universal faith which recognizes all people and all nations as potentially the family of one God. . . . In short, the concepts of human nature and destiny taught in the gospel are very different from the ideas which make up [Buddhist] religious orientation . . . and the fruit of the gospel is often hidden from view or not even present when the lives of those presumed to be Christians are observed. (Bollinger, 283)

CONVERSION: A GIFT FROM THE HOLY SPIRIT

As we have seen, conversion of the heart is an involved and mysterious process. We *must* make ourselves available to the ongoing ministry of the Holy Spirit. No one method should ever be suggested, and our efforts will only be effective if they are co-operational, relying on the Holy Spirit for wisdom, discernment, and guidance.

One important way to make us fit vessels for this task is by diligent fasting and prayer. Pursue visits with your Buddhist friends as frequently as possible. Care for their well-being through words and actions. Establish friendship and understanding, from which trust can be built.

Again, it is not right for us to focus mainly on his or her acceptance of Jesus as Lord and Savior. If it is the will of the Lord, your friend *will* take this step. God enables us to sow the seed, but we might not reap the harvest. Even if the Good News is not immediately embraced, your continued friendship, love, and concern will result in your Buddhist friend having a window through which to see God.

MISSIONS

Regarding worldwide *Buddhist* missionary activity, be aware that monks do not declare themselves as missionaries, preaching nirvana; they focus on those who are troubled in their spirit and are seeking peace. They politely suggest that their meditative techniques will enable those who are disturbed to overcome their distress. (At present, Buddhism is opening meditation shops around the globe.) They target individual conversions, and then, when society begins to accept their teaching, they accommodate local practices in order to minimize conflict.

General practitioners of *Christian* evangelism among Buddhists recommend that you engage in Bible study with your Buddhist friend, as this often creates an inclination in him or her to seek information about your faith and a willingness toward mutual dialogue. When this is established, I would say that the Holy Spirit has opened a door for you to get closer to your Buddhist friend and share basic elements of your faith. Enter this opportunity carefully, putting your trust in the Lord, and pray continuously that this door would continue to remain open and even open more widely.

Relief and development work in nations such as Sri Lanka, Myanmar, Cambodia, and Laos is greatly appreciated because they have urgent needs. People from these countries (especially Cambodia and Laos) are concentrated in certain U.S. cities, and our involvement in meeting their needs can help to open doors. Often relief and development happen to be just that—recipients are deeply blessed by your work but don't demonstrate willingness or readiness to receive Jesus. *Let us not lose hope.* It is God who is at work.

Another effective means for reaching Buddhists is through radio and print ministry. There are hundreds of communities in various Buddhist nations that do not have writing systems, and hardly any books are printed in their vernaculars. Oral communication is broad in its impact, and radio ministries help to develop and sustain community art forms. Many Myanmar communities, for instance, have benefited from such efforts; we need to help others in Buddhist nations, including China.

However, our *ultimate* goal is to share the Bible in familiar language to facilitate discipleship and maturity in understanding God's Word.

This will be accomplished if we undertake linguistic studies of unwritten and less developed languages, if script systems are provided, and if language learning and other educational materials are developed. Enterprising, devoted missionaries around the world have bestowed countless lasting contributions upon hundreds of communities.

Fast when you are compelled to do so (Matthew 6:16–18). Pray for the raising up of servants of God who minister in the demonstrative operation of spiritual gifts. Pray that the Lord will do miracles in the lives of Buddhists so that their eyes will be opened to see the glory of the only true God.

As we have seen, idol or image worship plays a prominent and approved role within scriptural or high Buddhist religion (just as in Shinto and Hinduism). The word *idol* is derived from the Greek *eido-lon,* meaning "a likeness to the object it represents." An idol, for this purpose, is a similitude of a supposed deity; idolatry is closely connected with, springs from, and supports polytheism and animism, which contributes to the perception that idols are the abode of spiritual beings. Buddhists who have had contact with Roman Catholic practices often wonder why they receive so much criticism for their worship, adoration, and visual representation of Buddhistic images.

The first-century Buddhist poet and historian Ashvaghosha, in his biography of Buddha (*Buddhacarita*), explains early examples of this practice:

> Sweet-scented barks and leaves, aloewood, sandalwood, and cassia they heaped on the pyre, sighing with grief all the time. Finally they placed the Sage's [Gautama Buddha] body on it. Three times they tried to light the pyre with a torch, but it refused to burn. This was due to Kashyapa the Great coming along the road, Kashyapa whose mind was meditating pure thoughts. He longed to see the remains of the holy body of the departed Hero, and it was his magical power which prevented the fire from flaring up. But now the monk approached with rapid steps, eager to see his Teacher once more, and immediately he had paid his homage to the Best of Sages the fire blazed up of its own. Soon it had burnt up the Sage's skin, flesh, hair and limbs. But although there was plenty of ghee [melted butter], fuel, and wind, it could not consume His bones. These were in due time purified with the finest water,

and placed in golden pitchers in the city of the Mallas [the name of a people group as well as a dynasty]. And the Mallas chanted hymns of praise over them: these jars now held the relics great in virtue, as mountains hold their jeweled ore. No fire harms these relics great in virtue; like Brahma's realm when all else is burned up. These bones, His friendliness pervades their tissue; the fire of passion has no strength to burn them; the power of devotion has preserved them; cold though they are, how much they warm our hearts! For some days they worshiped the relics in due form and with utmost devotion. (Conze, 64–65)

One Buddhist text, *Questions of King Milinda,* clearly indicates that Gautama himself prohibited the clergy from worshiping relics but did not discourage other classes—nobles, agriculturists, traders, etc.—from doing so. There are many other texts that speak of the necessity and merit of image worship.

It is perplexing for your Buddhist friend to even imagine that he could be religious and spiritual without adoring the images and idols. He also probably believes that what the Word of God wants him to do regarding idol worship will lead to the elimination of Buddhism altogether. This is one area that will require substantial prayer on your part.

Some monotheistic religions practice image-like worship within their *folk stratum;* for instance, Islamic grave visitation, Catholic saint worship, and Judaistic dependence on charms and talismans. Their *scriptural teaching,* however, does not approve of idolatrous practice. Again, in Hinduism, Shinto, and Buddhism, idolatry is both doctrinal *and* mainstream.

In the beginning, only Gautama's turban, footprints, throne, begging bowl, and bodhi tree were depicted and worshiped as symbols and relics. In due course, though, idolatrous representation of the Buddha became well established. Legends of his birth and life and narratives of his work were depicted in bas-relief (in which the surface surrounding the engraved picture is either not projected or projected only lightly so that the engraved material becomes more prominent). At this stage divine qualities were added to the representations of Buddha, and the idols came to represent his "thirty-two attributes." Worshipers offer flowers, incense, lights, food, drink, and many other things, and they are cautioned to focus on the attributes of Buddha rather than on the material objects.

All this is done despite the fact that Buddhist theology (especially Theravada) assumes that Buddha no longer exists, having reached total extinction. How can he then receive worship, and how can he be of any help? If these practices are intended to demonstrate that worshipers are making offerings to Gautama, they seem to be logically inconsistent—Buddha has attained his nirvana and therefore cannot receive (and does not need) any of it. What this means is that devotees are seeking merit for their own benefit in the next life.

SPREAD OF IDOLATRY IN BUDDHIST NATIONS

In China, Japan, and Korea, it was through Buddhism that a pantheon of deities was concretely represented. This introduction and worship of images resulted in regional pre-Buddhist religions adopting idols and other forms for their own gods and spirits. While Japanese Shinto is not fully involved in the representation of kami through images (Shinto uses real objects—comb, broomstick, etc.—as symbolic divine representations), other nations quickly and unreservedly embraced the creation and worship of idols. (*Buddhist* personages are, however, given idolatrous representations in Japan, which has some of Buddhism's most mammoth images.)

In Tibet and other Vajrayana and Mahayana nations, in addition to the usual postured representation of Buddha, various others—including Bodhisattvas, gods, demons, and spirits—may be represented in idolatrous or iconic forms. Moreover, people want numerous smaller carvings of these personages in their homes—the amulets and charms they wear may carry such miniature shapes.

Bon (the pre-Buddhist religion of Tibet) has adopted Buddhistic shapes for its gods and spirits. As explained earlier, preparation of idols, portraits, charms, and amulets is an important industry in all these nations; divinities are distinguished from one another through unique characteristics of dress, posture, color, and implements held in his or her (variously numbered) hands. Note that there is significant similarity between Hindu and Buddhist iconography.

A MISGUIDED HUMAN EFFORT

Idolatry is a folk practice that is biblically condemned and must be avoided. In idol worship, direct contact with God is exchanged in favor of direct contact with an image supposed to be divine. This is clearly illustrated by the Israelites in the wilderness, who felt that their leader, Moses, was not available to lead and counsel them (he had gone onto Mount Sinai to take care of business with God). In desperation, they took things into their own hands:

When the people saw that Moses was so long in coming down from the mountain, they gathered around Aaron and said, "Come, make us gods who will go before us. As for this fellow Moses who brought us up out of Egypt, we don't know what has happened to him."

Aaron answered them, "Take off the gold earrings that your wives, your sons and your daughters are wearing, and bring them to me." So all the people took off their earrings and brought them to Aaron. He took what they handed him and made it into an idol cast in the shape of a calf, fashioning it with a tool. Then they said, "These are your gods, O Israel, who brought you up out of Egypt."

When Aaron saw this, he built an altar in front of the calf and announced, "Tomorrow there will be a festival to the LORD." So the next day the people rose early and sacrificed burnt offerings and presented fellowship offerings. Afterward they sat down to eat and drink and got up to indulge in revelry. (Exodus 32:1–6)

Idol-making as a religious pursuit is also a reversal of what God did by creating (animate) humankind in His image; humanity, in response, attempts to make (inanimate) gods according to its kind. Our view of God is often desperately skewed—even among the Israelites a divine representation was manifested as an animal (a calf). Polytheistic and pantheistic societies do not necessarily represent their spiritual beings (or Supreme Being) in human form; often they admire animalistic strength and depict their gods with unusual features to show their alleged power. However, the Word of God rejects all idolatry (see below), and, once again, *every* human being is given general revelation about Him:

What may be known about God is plain to [all], because God has made it plain to them. For since the creation of the world God's invisible qualities—his eternal power and divine nature—have been clearly seen, being understood from what has been made, so that men are without excuse. For although they knew God, they neither glorified him as God nor gave thanks to him, but their thinking became futile and their foolish hearts were darkened. Although they claimed to be wise, they became fools and exchanged the glory of the immortal God for images made to look like mortal man and birds and animals and reptiles. (Romans 1:19–23; see also Ecclesiastes 3:11)

Idols function as mediating objects to an underlying belief system, and if the link between the two is weak, idolatry itself is likely to be weakened. This connection (between image worship and paradigm) *was* broken among Christians in the Greek and Roman worlds; consequently, image worship is now a rare phenomenon in the West (although common among Catholics); even in primarily non-Christian nations, idols have instead become objects of art.

Buddhists claim that idols are not mere objects—they do not look to them for artistic or aesthetic experience. As we have seen, the images represent the *attributes* of Buddha and other divinities; they allegedly act as mediators, and their visual tangibility helps devotees to focus on divine experience, majesty, and presence. Some of these justifications are similar to those offered by the Eastern Orthodox Church in support of iconic veneration, while others resemble those offered by the Roman Catholic Church.

THE WORD OF GOD ON IDOLATRY

You shall not make for yourself an idol in the form of anything in heaven above or on the earth beneath or in the waters below. You shall not bow down to them or worship them; for I, the Lord your God, am a jealous God. (Exodus 20:4–5)

Why do the nations say, "Where is their God?" Our God is in heaven; he does whatever pleases him. But their idols are silver and gold, made by the hands of men. They have mouths, but cannot speak, eyes, but they cannot see; they have ears, but cannot hear, noses, but they cannot smell; they have hands, but cannot feel, feet, but they cannot walk; nor can they utter a sound with their throats. Those who make them will be like them, and so will all who trust in them. (Psalm 115:2–8)

Half of the wood he burns in the fire; over it he prepares his meal, he roasts his meat and eats his fill. He also warms himself and says, "Ah! I am warm; I see the fire." From the rest he makes a god, his idol; he bows down to it and worships. He prays to it and says, "Save me; you are my god." They know nothing, they understand nothing; their eyes are plastered over so they cannot see, and their minds closed so they cannot understand. No one stops to think, no one has the knowledge or understanding to say, "Half of it I used for fuel; I even baked bread over its coals, I roasted meat and I ate. Shall I make a detestable thing from what is left? Shall I bow down to a block of wood?" He feeds on ashes, a deluded heart misleads him; he cannot save himself, or say, "Is not this thing in my right hand a lie?" (Isaiah 44:16–20).

The Spirit lifted me up between earth and heaven and in visions of God he took me to Jerusalem . . . where the idol that provokes to jealousy stood. . . . I saw this idol of jealousy. . . . [Then] he said to me, "Son of man, do you see what they are doing—the utterly detestable things the house of Israel is doing here, things that will drive me far from my sanctuary?" (Ezekiel 8:3, 5–6).

Son of man, these men have set up idols in their hearts and put wicked stumbling blocks before their faces. Should I let them inquire of me at all? Therefore speak to them and tell them, "This is what the Sovereign LORD says: 'When any Israelite sets up idols in his heart and puts a wicked stumbling block before his face and then goes to a prophet, I the LORD will answer him myself in keeping with his great idolatry. I will do this to recapture the hearts of the people of Israel, who have all deserted me for their idols. . . . Repent! Turn from your idols and renounce all your detestable practices!'" (Ezekiel 14:3–6).

They would not listen and were as stiff-necked as their fathers, who did not trust in the LORD their God. They rejected his decrees and the covenant he had made with their fathers and the warnings he had given them. They followed worthless idols and themselves became worthless. (2 Kings 17:14–15)

Rebellion is like the sin of divination, and arrogance like the evil of idolatry. (1 Samuel 15:23)

All the gods of the nations are idols, but the LORD made the heavens. (1 Chronicles 16:26)

They made a calf and worshiped an idol cast from metal. They exchanged their Glory for an image of a bull, which eats grass. (Psalm 106:19–20)

They consult a wooden idol and are answered by a stick of wood. A spirit of prostitution leads them astray; they are unfaithful to their God. (Hosea 4:12)

Of what value is an idol, since a man has carved it? Or an image that teaches lies? For he who makes it trusts in his own creation; he makes idols that cannot speak. Woe to him who says to wood, "Come to life!" Or to lifeless stone, "Wake up!" Can it give guidance? It is covered with gold and silver; there is no breath in it. But the LORD is in his holy temple; let all the earth be silent before him. (Habakkuk 2:18–20)

It is my judgment, therefore, that we should not make it difficult for the Gentiles who are turning to God. Instead we should write to them, telling them to abstain from food polluted by idols, from sexual immorality, from the meat of strangled animals and from blood. (Acts 15:19–20)

About eating food sacrificed to idols: We know that an idol is nothing at all in the world and that there is no God but one. For even if there are so-called gods, whether in heaven or on earth (as indeed there are many "gods" and many "lords"), yet for us there is but one God, the Father, from whom all things came and for whom we live; and there is but one Lord, Jesus Christ, through whom all things came and through whom we live. (1 Corinthians 8:4–6)

Do I mean then that a sacrifice offered to an idol is anything, or that an idol is anything? No, but the sacrifices of pagans are offered to demons, not to God, and I do not want you to be participants with demons. You cannot drink the cup of the Lord and the cup of demons too; you cannot have a part in both the Lord's table and the table of demons. Are we trying to arouse the Lord's jealousy? Are we stronger than he? (1 Corinthians 10:19–22)

The acts of the sinful nature are obvious: sexual immorality, impurity and debauchery; idolatry and witchcraft; hatred, discord, jealousy, fits of rage, selfish ambition, dissensions, factions and envy; drunkenness, orgies, and the like. I warn you, as I did before, that those who live like this will not inherit the kingdom of God. (Galatians 5:19–21)

You must not associate with anyone *who calls himself a brother* but is sexually immoral or greedy, an idolater or a slanderer, a drunkard or a swindler. With such a man do not even eat. (1 Corinthians 5:11, emphasis added)

Do not be idolaters, as some of [the Israelites] were. (1 Corinthians 10:7)

Of this you can be sure: No immoral, impure or greedy

person—such a man is an idolater—has any inheritance in the kingdom of Christ and of God. (Ephesians 5:5)

Put to death, therefore, whatever belongs to your earthly nature: sexual immorality, impurity, lust, evil desires and greed, which is idolatry. (Colossians 3:5)

Dear children, keep yourselves from idols. (1 John 5:21)

Remember that Scripture says the battle against idolatry will continue until the very end of this world. Such is the force of deception that many will not change even after great tribulation:

The rest of mankind that were not killed by these plagues still did not repent of the work of their hands; they did not stop worshiping demons, and idols of gold, silver, bronze, stone and wood—idols that cannot see or hear or walk. Nor did they repent of their murders, their magic arts, their sexual immorality or their thefts. (Revelation 9:20–21)

The cowardly, the unbelieving, the vile, the murderers, the sexually immoral, those who practice magic arts, the idolaters and all liars—their place will be in the fiery lake of burning sulfur. This is the second death. (Revelation 21:8)

CONNECTING WITH IDOLATROUS CULTURES

It is obvious that idolatry in *any* form is against God. Those given to image worship believe that through their actions they are getting closer to their deities and often acquire a *strong* emotional attachment. Only when they accept Jesus Christ will our Buddhist friends begin to see why God detests image worship.

You can show how idols are treated like favor-disbursing vending machines. The thief and the nobleman seek success from the very same idol; image worship does not inculcate higher ideals or sanctify devotees as fit vessels for God. Explain how attributes and characteristics ascribed to the images are imperfect; you will be able to reach these conclusions directly if you courteously allow your Buddhist friend to speak without interruption. When the time is right, demonstrate how God wants us to worship Him in holiness and not depend on material objects. God is always at hand to help us in our efforts to please Him.

If your friend regularly performs rituals before the pictures or images, you can help wean him away from this practice through fervent prayer, seeking revelation for his heart and soul (ritual Buddhists typically need something miraculous in order to understand and accept the glory of God). Pray that his personal needs are met; the best way is to pray (in his presence) and trust that the Lord will answer your prayers in a fashion that demonstrates a link between your prayer and the fulfillment of his needs.

Don't forget that idolatry is not only the worship of carved images; *any act, idea, or object that takes our focus away from the Lord and onto itself is an idol* and is detestable to God.

People all over the world were shocked when the barbarous, militant Taliban leadership ordered the destruction of the Bamiyan Buddha statues in Afghanistan. These figures were carved more than fifteen hundred years ago, and Buddhist monks occupied the caves around them until Islam took over Afghanistan after several centuries. These statues were no longer part of an idolatrous culture, but the Taliban destroyed them anyway.

The removal of image worship, even after acceptance of the gospel of Jesus Christ, is a tremendous challenge. In the name of heritage preservation, culture-lovers and culture-mongers tend to retain idolatrous elements as objects of art. Violent demonstration of the powerlessness of idols by treading them underfoot (or mutilating them) will not solve the problem; this will only add to confusion or hatred between Christian and non-Christian. Often the new believer is not convinced of the need to dispose of these objects because they have given him comfort and direction in his past spiritual life.

Augustine (354–430), in his *Sermons on New Testament Lessons,* suggested the following:

> Many pagans have these abominations on their own estates; do we go and break them in pieces? No, for our first efforts are that the idols in their hearts should be broken down. When they too are made Christians themselves, they either invite us to so good a work, or anticipate us. At present we must pray for them, not be angry with them. ("Sermon 12," Schaff, 303)

Continual preaching from the Word of God, constant vigil kept by new believers concerning their own actions, and persistent prayer against falling back into idolatry will all provide help.

THE INFLUENCE OF ANIMISM, PANTHEISM, AND POLYTHEISM

11

ANIMISM

Animism, a belief system prevalent in many religions, is the worship of spirit beings, including the belief in and propitiation of the spirits of the dead and nonhumans. Many of us have some animistic behavior or another, but we may not qualify as "animists" because such involvement or perspective is only a small part of our life. However, in the non-Christian world (including Islamic nations), belief in spirits and their powers often comes to regulate the daily lives of most individuals. Everything revolves around the supplication of spirit beings.

Buddhism started as a meditative philosophy, but, as we have established, it rapidly adopted and assimilated the belief systems of the nations it entered. In this process, Buddhism has become an animistic religion.

Worship of an Infinite Number of Spirits

There are countless spirits in the animistic world. The gods of Hinduism number around 330 million, and the impersonal and nameless spirits are beyond counting. In Buddhism, too, there are many other worlds, and each of these has innumerable spirits. Scholars who have studied animistic religions suggest that there are five important kinds:

1. the creator spirit;
2. the chief spirits (for earth, sky, sea, animal life, fire, etc.);
3. deified ancestors;
4. evil or mischievous spirits;
5. common, insignificant spirits of forest, field, stream, et al.

(These are a nuisance and do not have any other particular function.)

Spirits Are Like Human Beings

Animists view the spirits as they view fellow human beings: there are noble and ignoble, good and evil, caring and indifferent. They have limited power in their areas of operation, and they cannot accomplish everything you desire. They may be unpredictable, deceptive, and greedy, and although there are good spirits, the animist is more concerned with (and frightened of) the evil ones. He seeks to protect himself from these unavoidable creatures by offering them appeasement, and he views the spirits to be closer to him than the gods.

The animist should not be regarded as a helpless man before the spirits—he knows how to handle them. More often than not, his focus is on placating them, realizing that they can be maneuvered by offerings of suitable bribes, conjuring with magical words, presenting blood sacrifices, or threatening them with the help of more powerful spirits. The animist performs elaborate ceremonies, carefully avoids tabooed objects or persons, and fashions charms and talismans to tap and store spiritual power.

Animists believe some objects or persons may possess intrinsic power, and they want to obtain this power for personal benefit. Potency is tested by the result that accrues after procurement. The powers of some objects or persons or places are beneficial, others malevolent.

The Power of Special Words

Animists believe in special words that have magical powers to bring about desired results. Through the incantation of magical words, powers inherent in objects or persons are tapped. Sometimes the words are inscribed on talismans and charms, and people wear them to ward off evil spirits.

Magical words have the function of petitioning the spirits; through repetition, power is generated. In the general meditative practices of Buddhism (and particularly in Vajrayana), proper and perfect pronunciation of words addressed to gods and spirits is supposed to please, influence, and release divine powers for personal gain. As the prayers are often in fixed form with fixed words, the meaning may or may not be known to the person who recites them. (The prayer wheel carried by Tibetan Buddhists is a clear example. This is a small embossed hollow metal cylinder with a handle for turning. The wheel contains sacred written mantra, and followers believe that turning the wheel by hand is equivalent to the oral recitation of the prayers.)

Sacrifices and Offerings

Sacrifices and offerings are important characteristics of animistic belief. The spirits and gods take part in the essence of objects offered to them, although they do not physically enjoy the things offered—this is a benefit of the shaman or priest and his family. Ceremonial killing is significant because through it the spirits partake in the essence of the victim. Where animal sacrifice is not followed or is prohibited, vegetation may be offered. Buddhism does not approve of killing animals as sacrifice; animism holds that there is a kinship between humanity and nature, and animists sometimes worship animals as spirits or divine beings.

Animists may also hold to some form of ancestor worship or veneration—caring for the dead, remembering them as if they were living persons, and seeking their counsel. Animists are typically afraid of the dead in their families. If the deceased person was bad before his death, extra care must be taken to appease him.

Idol Worship and Shamanism

Animists frequently fashion and worship idols. There are numerous images of Buddha, and the wheel is fundamental—among other things, it signifies the cycle of samsara and the operation of karma. Vajrayana abounds in various forms of idols, including the graphic design of mandala and the representation of sexual union. Animists cling to their charms and images with great fervor.

Shamans are self-proclaimed mediators of spirits. They have direct encounters in which they are visited and possessed. The initial possession is often the most painful and difficult: shamans fall sick, go through rites to make amends for (or extinguish) their wrong actions, and take on a new role in the community. When their initial sickness is diagnosed as due to the visitation of spirits, the illness becomes the sign of shamanhood. They come to occupy a precarious but powerful position—people are afraid of them because of the spiritual visitation.

In Buddhism, shamanism is a way of life for the laity. Monks are not shamans but are seen to have powers in warding off evil forces through the reading of scriptures and the performance of rituals. Shamans use various means to get into a trance, including drug use and sensory bombardment through loud music and drum-beating. This is quite common in the shrines attached to Buddhist monasteries (and especially in Vajrayana practices).

Magic, Witchcraft, and Sorcery

The use of magic is frequent; animistic worldview is governed by actual and assumed magical occurrences. White magic is performed for individual benefit, and black magic is performed for individual harm. Another characteristic of the animist is that he often seeks divination to determine the future or causes of events.

An animist may believe in the use of ordeals to determine guilt or innocence of people charged with crimes. I have seen several instances of this in my lifetime. The accused are forced to dip their hands in boiling oil or water to prove their innocence, or they may be asked to walk on burning coals. This is obviously a cruel practice, but preliterate animistic communities do not agree. While the modern animist might condemn such ordeals, he may devise others, such as putting the accused through a maze to determine guilt or innocence.

Witchcraft and sorcery are also quite common among animists. People reared in or who believe in the operation of spirits do not trust modern medicine, maintaining that cures thereby obtained are either incomplete or temporary. Complete recovery is possible only if the spirits are consulted and cajoled to heal the sick. (Sometimes animists classify illnesses in terms of those who can be cured by modern medicine and those who can be cured only by ensuring the participation of spirits through shamanism.)

Animism is not dying out—it simply takes on different incarnations! The New Age movement in Western nations is animistic and seeks to tap spiritual power through well-orchestrated propaganda. Neo-Buddhism, often observable in Western megacities, is mostly a reemergence of animism in the garb of refined meditative techniques. Elitists, businessmen, and leaders, out of insecurity, seek mental peace and power by following animistic practices. Mass media indiscriminately and cleverly glorifies animism in the names of artistry and freedom of expression.

Focus on Power

Animism as belief in dealings with spiritual power and using it for personal ends is illustrated in the case of Simon the sorcerer:

> When Simon saw that the Spirit was given at the laying on of the apostles' hands, he offered them money and said, "Give me also this ability so that everyone on whom I lay my hands may receive the Holy Spirit" (Acts 8:18–19).

Simon was asking for power he could manipulate at will; his perception of this power (the Holy Spirit) was that it is amoral and neutral, available to anyone for a price. This perspective truly reflects the understanding of spirituality among animists, whose thoughts are dominated by fear, propitiation, and manipulation.

The Holy Spirit is not for sale. There is no demand that we be fearful of Him, nor are we asked to propitiate Him in order to be blessed. The Holy Spirit is the Comforter, and He does not threaten or demand offerings. The fruit of the Spirit "is love, joy, peace, patience, kindness, goodness, faithfulness, gentleness and self-control" (Galatians 5:22–23), but the spirits of animism enslave and lead to a life controlled by the sinful nature: "When we were controlled by the sinful nature, the sinful passions . . . were at work in our bodies, so that we bore fruit for death" (Romans 7:5).

Biblical Illustrations

There are a few scriptural instances in which the power of God is shown to flow through material objects. These examples clearly demonstrate the sovereignty of God's purpose, but they do not act as models for us to draw on His power through mechanical or material means. God's power *can* be transmitted and demonstrated through objects, persons, and events—since He is Spirit, He can transcend all barriers to express and reveal himself to us. However, treating an object, person, event, or process as a storehouse of power *in itself* (which animism does) negates or cheapens God's glory, and seeking to demonstrate that such power is available at will is a lie, a mere production of divine imitation.

The story of the Shunammite's son being restored to life (2 Kings 4:8–37) illustrates the limitations of mediatory objects and highlights the living power of God through His anointed servants. The Word also contains an instance of intense unannounced faith in which a woman who had long been subject to bleeding was instantaneously healed when she touched the edge of Jesus' cloak (Luke 8:43–48). By this act of faith, she declared the glory of Christ, and He made it plain that her *faith in Him,* not His garment, had healed her. Jesus didn't demand shamanistic sacrifice, payment, or propitiation—His healing was freely given.

There are two other narratives in the Bible that compel some to suggest that the healing power of God is contained in material objects. In one case, people waited with the hopeful expectation that "Peter's shadow might fall on some of them as he passed by. Crowds gathered also from the towns around Jerusalem, bringing their sick and those tormented by evil spirits, and all of them were healed" (Acts 5:15–16). Seeking power through a shadow is animistic—the focus of this incident is on the growing popularity of the disciples, and there is no statement indicating that people were healed by Peter's shadow. *This is a description of the prevailing animistic beliefs of that time, not a model for us to emulate.*

In another case, an "extraordinary" miracle from the ministry of Paul concerns the handkerchiefs and aprons that had been in contact with him (Acts 19:11–12). The Word of God calls it "extraordinary" for a cautionary reason—the *carrier* through which the miracle was performed could be mistaken as the *source* of power, focusing attention on the vessel rather than on the Lord. The major purpose in using the adjective *extraordinary* is to warn that this kind of miracle (and the consequent behavior of the faithful) is not commonplace.

That we should emphasize and magnify God's name rather than objects or elements through which His power flows is highlighted in the humorous episode that follows the above cited "handkerchief" incident. An evil spirit jumped on some Jews and overpowered them when they tried to exploit the name of Jesus to heal the demon-possessed (see Acts 19:13–16). They did this without faith in the Lord and suffered this comic (for us) but tragic (for them) consequence.

PANTHEISM

Pantheism is equating the Godhead with the universe: God is all, and all is God. Pantheism holds that God is found in *everything*. God has millions of representations, but God is not the totality of these representations—each representation is itself God.

This view of God (and the relationship between God and the world) has been practiced by many historical religions. Although Gautama Buddha did not concern himself with God, the Buddhist theology that developed after him sees Buddha as the universe. Dissolution of self leads to the elimination of separation between persons and the world around them.

When pantheism focuses only on the immanence of God, the world becomes the only reality. When pantheism focuses only on the transcendence of God, the world becomes completely unreal. When pantheism focuses on both transcendence and immanence, total identity between God and the world is emphasized. This leads to the position that *every* object around us is God.

There is but a thin line between pantheism and polytheism. Polytheism accepts the existence of a multiplicity of gods, while pantheism holds to one God who manifests himself (or herself, or itself) in varied millions of forms. Since in pantheism everything is God and God is everything, it is difficult to maintain any moral position: everything becomes relative or equal in its effect, and the distinction between right and wrong is obscured.

Because God is everything, it is possible to contain Him in an object (a charm, an idol, a relic, an animal) and use it for our benefit. While pantheists claim that they recognize the omnipresence of God more than any other system of faith, they do not recognize that they are equating creation with the Creator, downgrading Him in the process (Romans 1:25). Humans thus worship (as God) not only what was created by God but also the things they have fashioned (Habakkuk 2:18).

The awesome natural world that God created *is* worthy of admiration, preservation, and enjoyment. Natural creation is a witness to the glory and presence of God among us. However, elevating it to the level of the Creator and equating it with God, giving it His identity, is a terrible falsehood.

God detests pantheism: "How can I let myself be defamed? I will not yield my glory to another" (Isaiah 48:11). "I am God, and there is no other; I am God, and there is none like me" (Isaiah 46:9).

By him all things were created: things in heaven and on earth, visible and invisible, whether thrones or powers or rulers or authorities; all things were created by him and for him. He is before all things, and in him all things hold together. (Colossians 1:16–17)

See to it that you do not refuse him who speaks. If they did not escape when they refused him who warned them on earth, how much less will we, if we turn away from him who warns us from heaven? At that time his voice shook the earth, but now he has promised, "Once more I will shake not only the earth but also the heavens." The words "once more" indicate the removing of what can be shaken—that is, created things—so that what cannot be shaken may remain. Therefore, since we are receiving a kingdom that cannot be shaken, let us be thankful, and so worship God acceptably with reverence and awe, for our "God is a consuming fire" (Hebrews 12:25–28).

Consider this admonition from theologian Alec Brooks:

[However,] while God is never to be confused with the world, neither must he be separated from it. The Bible makes it clear that God is personal and therefore relational. And what the first chapters of Genesis make plain is that while God is related to the world in general, he is related to man in particular. God cares for the world that he has made, and he made the world as the place in which man would enter into and maintain loving fellowship with him. (Brooks, 17–18)

POLYTHEISM

Again, animism is belief in multitudinous spirits that have control over human beings and must therefore be worshiped and placated. Pantheism is belief in an impersonal God, identical with the universe, who is everything. *Polytheism* is belief in and worship of many gods. Buddhism offers all these traits—there is one historical Buddha, but there are numerous other Buddhas to be worshiped.

The Bible shows that polytheism gradually developed from true faith. It recognizes the existence of polytheism even at the time of Abraham, making it clear that God wanted to save people from slavery to idolatry and false belief. Joshua ordered the Israelites to "throw away the foreign gods that are among you and yield your hearts to the LORD, the God of Israel" (Joshua 24:23).

In the book of Judges we read:

> They forsook the LORD, the God of their fathers, who had brought them out of Egypt. They followed and worshiped various gods of the peoples around them. They provoked the LORD to anger because they forsook and served Baal and the Ashtoreths. (Judges 2:12–13)

Polytheism entered because the existing social disorder meant there was no one to lead, supervise, and guide the people (see Judges 17:6). They had as many gods as they had towns (see Jeremiah 2:28): "The altars you have set up to burn incense to that shameful god Baal are as many as the streets of Jerusalem" (Jeremiah 11:13).

Polytheism plagued God's people in earlier times also (see Genesis 31:19). When the Lord commanded Jacob to return to Bethel and build an altar there for Him, Jacob told his household and "all who were with him, 'Get rid of the foreign gods you have with you, and purify yourselves and change your clothes'" (Genesis 35:2). Moses likewise waged a bitter struggle to remove polytheism and idolatry from the minds and practices of the Israelites, realizing that their corruption was due to their distance from God:

> [Israel] grew fat and kicked; filled with food, he became heavy and sleek. He abandoned the God who made him and rejected the Rock his Savior. They made [the LORD] jealous

with their foreign gods and angered him with their detestable idols. They sacrificed to demons, which are not God. (Deuteronomy 32:15–17; see also Romans 1:21–23)

Astoundingly, polytheism is being weakened around the globe. The impact, attraction, and rise of monotheistic religions (such as Christianity and Islam) are contributing to this condition; secularization and education based on Western models are also accelerating this process. At the same time, animistic practices relating to magic, divination, and spirit possession seem to be increasing in cities around the world due to migration from rural areas. For the sake of maintaining identity and culture, elements of polytheism are still widely retained and glorified, and polytheism has shown its tenacity for survival within folk practices (including those of Buddhists).

Polytheism is detestable to God, a mixture of falsehood and sinister demonic forces. Polytheism survives because of its errant claim that the gods meet the personal needs of their devotees, reflecting our human weakness and susceptibility to deception.

MAGIC

12

Magic is an integral part of both official and folk Buddhism. One Chinese Mahayana text (seventh or eighth century) defines an ideal Buddhist as one who has "done homage to the countless Buddhas of the past, doing many good works, attaining to acquiescence in the Eternal Law . . . a man of wonderful eloquence; exercising supernatural powers, obtaining all the Dharanis [magical spells]" (Burtt, 238).

THE PURPOSE AND SCOPE OF MAGIC

Amazing magical events are narrated in the Buddhist scriptures; one of these, *Mahavastu,* says that magic is performed to impress people, to make them listen to the truth (Conze, 23). As we saw earlier, the training of a nirvana-seeking monk includes his ability to see all his previous births—Gautama "recollected the successive series of his . . . thousands of births, as though living them again" (ibid., 49). The Buddha "acquired the supreme heavenly eye" to look upon the entire world; getting into a trance to see things in reality is an essential monastic experience.

Edward Conze, in the introduction to *Buddhist Scriptures,* wrote,

> It is indeed a cherished belief among Buddhists that meditation not only widens the range of our spiritual awareness, but also adds one dimension or more to our actual existence, by awakening our psychic and supernatural gifts. These occult powers of the more advanced saints are a stock item of all Buddhist writing. In deference to the skepticism of the present age I have chosen a particularly sober and restrained account. Tibetan sources are more exuberant. (Conze, 98–99)

Myriad magical powers are obtained through meditation, including:

1. "Having been one, he becomes many; having been many, he becomes one. . . . He becomes visible or invisible."
2. "Right through a wall, a rampart, or a hill he glides unimpeded, as through empty space."
3. "He dives into the earth and out of it."
4. "He walks on water without sinking into it."
5. "Cross-legged he floats along like a bird on the wing."
6. "Even the sun and the moon, powerful and mighty though they be, he touches and strokes with his hands."
7. "Even as far as the world of Brahma he has power over his body."
8. "The power of miraculous transformations."
9. "The power of producing mind-made bodies" (from Conze, 122–29).

People in industrially advanced societies often pretend not to have faith in magic, which they consider superstition. For them, "magic" usually refers to sleight-of-hand performance that serves as entertainment. On the other hand, even highly educated and cultured people in Buddhist nations desire magical power on their behalf. For folk Buddhists, magic is more or less synonymous with religion; they seek magical demonstration and are convinced of a religious experience's authenticity if there is something magical about it.

Magicians may adopt natural, sympathetic, black, and/or white magic. *Natural magic* uses herbs to influence the spirits and concocts potions that impact those who ingest them. *Sympathetic magic* assumes that an enemy may be made to suffer by performing operations on a representative wax or cloth doll or image. (A man's hair, nail-clippings, clothing, shadow, or name might be used against him.) *Black magic* is the most popular; its purpose is to cause harm to others. The goals of *white magic* are to protect oneself from harm that may be caused by others and to coerce the spirits to work for the one seeking help.

Society on a whole has seen a recent decline of faith in magic. One reason may be that people can control and regulate their environment more easily than in the past. The development of the "scientific temperament" and the lessons of European history have resulted in greater confidence in upward human progress. While the widespread ideology of inherent human goodness and self-improvement is unjustified, in a positive sense, over the centuries, the spread of education, the emergence of Protestant faith, the proliferation of transportation and communication, the establishment of modern production and distribution, the growth of statistics as a scientific discipline, the emergence of experimental psychology, and the developments in the field of medicine have all diminished belief in spiritual forces that cannot be scientifically proven.

WHY CHRISTIANS REJECT MAGIC

As we have seen, the Word of God stands against magic and magical practices:

> Let no one be found among you who . . . practices divination or sorcery, interprets omens, engages in witchcraft, or casts spells, or who is a medium or spiritist or who consults the dead. Anyone who does these things is detestable to the LORD. (Deuteronomy 18:10–12)

Magical power is clearly inferior to the power of God. The prophet Daniel, in every matter of wisdom and understanding, was ten times better than all the magicians and enchanters in Nebuchadnezzar's palace (see Daniel 1:20). Pharaoh's magicians failed to interpret his dreams, and while they performed magic (see Exodus 7:11–12, 22; 8:7, 18), they failed miserably to match the power of God: "[They] said to Pharaoh, 'This is the finger of God'" (Exodus 8:19).

We reject magic because it does not glorify God—it tries to usurp His position, misleading people as to who God is and as to His nature, character, and attributes. Magic enslaves and is conducted as a business transaction rather than a means to save and edify. Magic is also amoral; it attempts to temporarily and deceptively meet pressing needs, and its net results are neither individually nor communally good.

In condemning magical arts, the Word of God includes necromancy (consulting the spirits of the dead), exorcism, shaking arrows, inspecting the entrails of animals, divination, sorcery, astrology, soothsaying, divination by rods, and witchcraft. The Old Testament attests to the fact that both the Israelites and their neighboring communities willingly sought after magicians and that God fully opposed them (Micah 5:12–13). Wearing magic charms, amulets, earrings, and magic bands was likewise forbidden:

> Now, son of man, set your face against the daughters of your people who prophesy out of their own imagination. Prophesy against them and say, "This is what the Sovereign LORD says: 'Woe to the women who sew magic charms on all their wrists and make veils of various lengths for their heads in order to ensnare people'" (Ezekiel 13:17–18).

Remember that the book of Revelation predicts the continuation and survival of magic arts even after awful manifestations of God's wrath (9:20–21). The second death (eternal separation from God) includes "those who practice magic arts, the idolaters and all liars—their place will be in the fiery lake of burning sulfur" (Revelation 21:8). Jesus proclaims that, at the end of time, those who practice magical arts are sure to be excluded from His kingdom:

> Blessed are those who wash their robes, that they may have the right to the tree of life and may go through the gates into the city. Outside are the dogs, those who practice magic arts, the sexually immoral, the murderers, the idolaters and everyone who loves and practices falsehood. (Revelation 22:14–15)

The story of Simon Magus (also referred to as Simon the sorcerer) illustrates how people confuse the power of God with magical powers drawn from other sources. People of faith seek the power of God for His glory, whereas others look at it as a neutral power that can be manipulated for personal benefit. Simon thought the power of God could be purchased, just as magical powers are obtained by propitiating the spirits through various offerings. He also mistakenly believed that he could use the power of God at will, just as he could manipulate the powers of magic (see Acts 8:9–24).

MAGIC AND MIRACLES

The ministry of Jesus, as well as that of the disciples, is full of miracles, yet people often misread miracles as magical actions. Jesus' power over diseases and spirits is given to Paul and to all the believing children of God, and they may heal by the power of His name, but this does not mean that *Jesus* is an incantation to be used and manipulated at will. (There is likewise a clear distinction between prayer and magic: magic compels, whereas prayer persuades.)

So *are* magic and miracles one and the same? To begin with, the miracles presented in the Bible are not acts of magical conjuring; they were performed as part of the work of God in history for His people's salvation and with the understanding and acceptance of His message. A miracle is not a mere performance; it is a sign, a symbol that stands for something else. A miracle *is* remarkable; however, its importance does not lie in its ability to astound but in its function as a message from God. An ordinary magical act is neutral and attracts attention to *itself*; a miracle from God is "for the common good" (1 Corinthians 12:7) and to bring glory to Him.

In the Old Testament, miracles are associated with the deliverance of the Israelite nation and with the fulfillment of God's promise against all adversity, including sins committed. Another major occasion for miracles was when God used the prophets to give signs and work wonders. Miracles demonstrated God's saving power and faithfulness on behalf of His people.

Scholars classify New Testament miracles into three categories: *miracles of healing, miracles of exorcism,* and *miracles of nature.* While the first two were performed by Jesus *and* the disciples, it was only Jesus who turned water into wine, stilled the storm on the sea, and multiplied food for hungry crowds. It appears that Christ's nature miracles are in a special category because no outline of structural process can be gleaned from them. Gurus frequently claim that they perform miracles of nature, but in reality such events are only mythologically reported.

Miracles *do* happen every day. Faith is required of those *for* whom they are performed (Mark 9:22–24; Acts 14:9), and faith is required in those *through* whom they are performed (Matthew 17:20; 21:21; John 14:12; Acts 3:16). Miracles are often demanded by unbelievers (Matthew 12:38–39; 16:1; Luke 11:16, 29; 23:8), and the Bible shows how alleged miracles are performed by magicians (Exodus 7:10–12, 22; 8:7) and other impostors (Matthew 7:22). Scripture also teaches that miracles may be performed through the powers of evil (2 Thessalonians 2:9; Revelation 16:14), even in support of false religions (Deuteronomy 13:1–3), and they can be also worked by false christs (Matthew 24:24) and false prophets (1 Samuel 28:7–14).

It is perhaps noteworthy that Jesus never produced a miracle ("sign") at the whim of unbelievers—people who demand them would not believe even if many such miracles were produced (Matthew 12:38–39; Mark 8:11–12). Gurus, on the other hand, make it a point to generate "miracles" in order to impress and to create deadly fear of themselves and their art.

Encourage your Buddhist friend to talk about his or her past efforts in seeking benefit and assistance through magic, asking frequent questions, such as: Was it successful? Did it bring peace and success? Did the peace and success last or did the process have to be repeatedly revisited? Why was magic sought—because of tradition, habit, advice, desperation? Did searching for help through magic develop dependence on capricious spirits? Do you realize that your enemies may go to the same magician to cause harm, and that the magician is amoral about this? Do you lose hope if met with successive failure? Is there any other hope outside of magic?

DIVINATION

13

Through divination people seek to know the significance of present happenings and link the results with both the past and the future. Divination is also used to know what occurs in another place. A few occasional successful predictions keep divination a flourishing business—that the unsuccessful predictions are many is easily and quickly glossed over and forgotten. Today in the West we seem to see "Free Psychic Consultation!" as commonly as any advertisement or offer.

Buddhist clergy and laity both seek divination. Gautama Buddha's parents sought the help of the astrologers to predict his future. *Buddhacarita* says that Gautama had the ability to see the future as well as read the past. Every Buddha, Bodhisattva, or Arhat is believed to have the powers of divination, even though they are not often used.

Buddhists go to monks and shamans seeking for the divination of their future and the suggestion of remedies for present ordeals. Divination is common at all the stages of life, and fortune is often determined on the basis of astrology, which is highly respected and is considered to be lawful for monks to use. The drawing of lots and the use of dice for divination are also widespread.

Pre-Buddhist temple priests and priestesses pursue sorcery, and Buddhist monks do not object, though they are often present when this happens. When the priests and priestesses act as oracles, interpreting omens and dreams, spirits communicate the future and also reasons for the past. Often these temple officials are hereditary practitioners who perform their acts while in a trance. Divination manuals are available in annual publications. Divination does have an aura of science around it—remember that some of the present-day empirical sciences developed from earlier animistic practices of divination. Astronomy, for instance, has a direct link with past astrology; however, at present they look and move in different directions.

Divination often degenerates to the point that anything and everything may be used for its purposes: dreams, hunches, presentiments, involuntary body movements or actions (such as twitches and sneezes), ordeals, spirit possession, consulting the dead, observing animal and plant behavior, interpreting the flight of birds, making mechanical manipulations with small objects (such as dice, shells), using playing cards, decoding natural phenomena (through palmistry or phrenology or astrology), and postulating intuitive predictions are only a few examples.

PREMONITIONS AND DREAMS

Premonitions through dreams are attested to in the Word of God. The dream is one of the means through which God speaks to us, though not the only (or best) means. When Miriam and Aaron spoke against Moses, "a very humble man, more humble than anyone else on the face of the earth," God said to Miriam and Aaron,

> When a prophet of the LORD is among you, I reveal myself to him in visions, I speak to him in dreams. But this is not true of my servant Moses: he is faithful in all my house. With him I speak face to face, clearly and not in riddles; he sees the form of the LORD. Why then were you not afraid to speak against my servant Moses?" (Numbers 12:6–8).

Anyone may have dreams and visions—that is not biblically questioned. Perhaps this ability is part of the makeup of humanity as being created in the image of God. The most important thing to watch is what message the dreamer brings:

> If a prophet, or one who foretells by dreams, appears among you and announces to you a miraculous sign or wonder, and if the sign or wonder of which he has spoken takes place, and he says, "Let us follow other gods" (gods you have not known) "and let us worship them," you must not listen to the words of that prophet or dreamer. (Deuteronomy 13:1–3)

Each dream has a meaning of its own (Genesis 40:5). However, the interpretations belong to God, not to individuals (Genesis 40:8). People may be warned or given advance notice of what is going to happen through dreams (Matthew 2:12, 22), but people may also have dreams when they have "many cares" (Ecclesiastes 5:3). Like communication, much dreaming is useless when less would be adequate and effective (Ecclesiastes 5:7). In the last days, dreams and (by implication) messages from God will come to everyone through the outpouring of the Spirit (Joel 2:28).

The Word of God teaches that dreams may be deceptive and that false prophets often present false dreams in support of their claims: "The idols speak deceit, the diviners see visions that lie; they tell dreams that are false, they give comfort in vain. Therefore the people wander like sheep oppressed for lack of a shepherd" (Zechariah 10:2).

> I have heard what the prophets say who prophesy lies in my name. They say, "I had a dream! I had a dream!" How long will this continue in the hearts of these lying prophets, who prophesy the delusions of their own minds? They think the dreams they tell one another will make my people forget my name, just as their fathers forgot my name through Baal worship. Let the prophet who has a dream tell his dream, but let the one who has my word speak it faithfully. . . .
>
> "Therefore," declares the LORD, "I am against the prophets who steal from one another words supposedly from me . . . who wag their own tongues and yet declare, 'The LORD declares.' Indeed, I am against those who prophesy false dreams. . . . They tell them and lead my people astray with their reckless lies, yet I did not send or appoint them. They do not benefit these people in the least" (Jeremiah 23:25–28, 30–32).

DIVINATION BY ORDEAL

As previously stated, divination by ordeal (with boiling water, burning coals, etc.) is rampant in animistic societies. A suspect will be helped (by the divine spirit or Supreme Being) to win through the ordeal and not feel pain if innocent, while the guilty will be harmed in the process. This manmade method of justice is cruel, inhumane, and coercive. Its trust in the gods is misplaced, as the gods themselves are not without blame for their involvement in human activity. In addition, divination by ordeal goes against the Word of God:

> When a man wrongs his neighbor and is required to take an oath and he comes and swears the oath . . . then hear from heaven and act. Judge between your servants, condemning the guilty and bringing down on his own head what he has done.

Declare the innocent not guilty, and so establish his innocence. (1 Kings 8:31–32)

Do not deny justice to your poor people in their lawsuits.
Have nothing to do with a false charge and do not put an
innocent or honest person to death, for I will not acquit the
guilty. . . . Be careful to do everything I have said to you. Do
not invoke the names of other gods; do not let them be heard
on your lips. (Exodus 23:6–7, 13)

MEDIUMS AND SPIRITISTS ARE LIKE A CANCER TO THE BODY OF CHRIST

Again, God warns: "Do not turn to mediums or seek out spiritists,
for you will be defiled by them. I am the LORD your God" (Leviticus
19:31). Mediums and spiritists were a cancer in the body of the Israelites, and since the holy nation was losing its holiness, God even took
the strong step of calling upon the Israelites to execute those who were
making such horrific mockery of His glory (Leviticus 20:27). As we
have seen, in entering the land promised by God, the Israelites were
told (in Deuteronomy 18:9–13) not to follow the animists who
indulged in divination: "Do not learn to imitate the detestable ways of
the nations there. . . . These things [are] detestable to the LORD"
(including child sacrifice, sorcery, omen-interpretation, witchcraft, or
spell-casting, and necromancy).

Jesus taught, "If you hold to my teaching, you are really my disciples. Then you will know the truth, and the truth will set you free"
(John 8:31–32). Paul said that "the Lord is the Spirit, and where the
Spirit of the Lord is, there is freedom" (2 Corinthians 3:17). "It is for
freedom that Christ has set us free. Stand firm, then, and do not let
yourselves be burdened again by a yoke of slavery" (Galatians 5:1). We
lose our freedom in Christ when we become slaves to anyone or anything else (Galatians 2:4).

DRAWING LOTS

The drawing of lots, perhaps the simplest of all processes of divination, is common in both elitist and folk religions all over the world. In
Buddhist villages, people either go to the local temple and ask the priest
to draw lots for them or do so themselves, either in front of the idol or
in their homes. My pastor's wife in India was in the habit of drawing
lots to make decisions, such as when to have gospel meetings or
whether young people should marry. As a new believer, I was shocked
that a Christian would do this. When I asked why she drew lots, she

told me it was biblical, that if the apostles themselves did it, why can't we?

> "Therefore it is necessary to choose one of the men who have been with us the whole time the Lord Jesus went in and out among us, beginning from John's baptism to the time when Jesus was taken up from us. For one of these must become a witness with us of his resurrection." So they proposed two men: Joseph called Barsabbas (also known as Justus) and Matthias. Then they prayed, "Lord, you know everyone's heart. Show us which of these two you have chosen to take over this apostolic ministry, which Judas left to go where he belongs." Then they cast lots, and the lot fell to Matthias; so he was added to the eleven apostles. (Acts 1:21–26)

The disciples did this before the Holy Spirit came upon them at Pentecost. With the Holy Spirit as the Comforter and Director of our lives, there is no justification whatsoever for drawing lots to decide on any matter. We must pray to the Lord Jesus Christ and let the Holy Spirit speak to us, giving His direction.

Remember also that the lot is only a mechanical device—results may not be true. For instance, in the book of Esther, Haman plotted "to destroy . . . the Jews, throughout the whole kingdom of Xerxes" (Esther 3:5), and in his presence the lot was cast to select a day and month for doing so. It turned out, however, that "when the plot came to the king's attention, he issued written orders that the evil scheme Haman had devised against the Jews should come back onto his own head, and that he and his sons should be hanged on the gallows" (9:25). The remembrance of Purim is indeed the declaration of the defeat of drawing lots!

Proverbs declares that in spite of lots, decisions are from the Lord (16:33). Casting lots does not produce a message from God but is a manmade device to settle disputes (18:18), an unreliable medium even for evil spirits. Dependence on the Holy Spirit's leading brings understanding, wisdom, and a result that is in the will of the Lord.

ASTROLOGY

Astrology, again, comes to us under the guise of a scientific pursuit, the assumption being that the planets have an effect on us humans: celestial bodies decide the course of our lives, and everything happens according to their position, direction, and movement. Astrological belief and practice have been around for thousands of years.

As soon as a child is born, Buddhists call an astrologer and obtain a birth horoscope that charts out milestones, such as quality and length of life. Wherever there is malevolent planetary influence, the astrologer may suggest propitiatory action. Choice of spouse is also made based on the match between the horoscopes of the prospective bride and groom—some girls may never be able to wed because their horoscopes predict the death of their husband as soon as they marry, while others predict the death of their father-in-law or mother-in-law (propitiatory arrangements for overcoming these ill effects may be made, as well).

Astrology is extremely popular in Buddhist nations; in fact, it is a highly regarded discipline in all pantheistic and polytheistic societies, usually considered to be more effective than divination through mechanical means (such as dice or lots). The astrologer, who normally is well read, studies the position and movement of the stars and planets, does mathematical calculations, draws charts of the zodiac, and presents findings in a language that sounds empirical and well reasoned.

As our civilization becomes more and more individualized, the popularity of practices that employ pseudo-scientific elements and terms will increase. There are already dozens of magazines that reveal "what the stars foretell." Millions of copies of "birthday forecasts" are sold. People also identify with their zodiac sign (Gemini, Taurus, Leo, and so on).

DIVINATION HONORS OTHER SPIRITS AND DISTRACTS FROM GOD

The Word of God tells us that Christ is *the* gate (John 10:9). If we put our trust in Jesus, why should we give in to divergent curiosity? We must "live by faith, not by sight" (2 Corinthians 5:7), making it our aim to please the Lord (2 Corinthians 5:9).

There is no guarantee that the diviner is telling the truth. What *is* important is the ultimate truth, which we still see only in part (1 Corinthians 13:12)—there is a curtain between us and the future. Avoid the temptation to peer through the partition through dubious processes. Put your faith in *Jesus*—His body was the curtain that was opened by His sacrifice for us:

> Since we have confidence to enter the Most Holy Place by the blood of Jesus, by a new and living way opened for us through the curtain, that is, his body, and since we have a great priest over the house of God, let us draw near to God with a sincere heart in full assurance of faith, having our hearts sprinkled to cleanse us from a guilty conscience and having

our bodies washed with pure water. Let us hold unswervingly to the hope we profess, for he who promised is faithful. (Hebrews 10:19–23)

More often than not, through subjective divination the diviner allows himself to be possessed by (or assumes the personality of) spirits, making himself a suitable medium to receive and transmit messages. There is no acceptance of trance (or transfer of spiritual power) in the Word of God. His prophets must not allow other spirits to enter them, and they must keep their mind and will intact (1 Corinthians 14:32–33; 1 John 4:1–3). Consider the following instance from Paul's ministry:

> Once when we were going to the place of prayer, we were met by a slave girl who had a spirit by which she predicted the future. She earned a great deal of money for her owners by fortune-telling. This girl followed Paul and the rest of us, shouting, "These men are servants of the Most High God, who are telling you the way to be saved." She kept this up for many days. Finally Paul became so troubled that he turned around and said to the spirit, "In the name of Jesus Christ I command you to come out of her!" At that moment the spirit left her. (Acts 16:16–18)

A similar condemnation of sorcery is found in Acts 19:19.

The question is not whether divination is authorized by the church but whether it distracts our attention from total faith in the Lord. *Divination in any form gives prominence to forces outside of Jesus Christ.* Once we confess our sins and accept Jesus as our Lord and Savior, a new world opens before us. The spark that ignites our heart will become a bright and brilliant light, eliminating our darkness. Our initial steps may be faulty and faltering, but we know that the Lord is always with us and that His grace is always available.

CHAPTER

SPIRIT POSSESSION

14

Body, *mind, soul,* and *spirit* are often mentioned when we speak of or contemplate the composition or makeup of our being. While "body" is rather easily understood as the external form—a concrete object that decays when a person dies—the meanings of *mind, soul,* and *spirit* often overlap, and we get confused by the interchangeability.

"Mind" is a familiar concept, yet it is difficult to describe exactly what the mind is. At one level of meaning, mind is identified with memory as the state of remembering or being remembered. At another level, it refers to our inclinations, intentions, desires, wishes, and purposes. The mind is often considered to be that which reasons, the sum total of an individual's conscious state.

The "soul," in opposition to "body," survives physical death. However, in Buddhism, *jeeva, aatma,* or *aatman,* referring to "soul," is associated with "life" or "living being." Often the word *soul* is used in the sense of "self"; Buddhism views the soul as impermanent and, therefore, bound to suffer in this world. What remains after death is karma, not the self (or soul)—the physical and mental forces (or energies) associated with self in this life continue without the former self after death. These forces take a new form, operating within the rules of karma; the soul grows and matures every moment. This is not the same soul that is born again and again through samsara; one self is distinct from another, and this distinction is carried into every successive birth.

In the Mahayana tradition, the "Embryo of the Enlightened One" (often referred to as the "Buddha Mind" or "Buddha Nature") is in every being, and each individual seeks to discover it. A person gradually loosens the chain that attaches him to the wheel of rebirth. As a result, he eventually loses the thought that he exists.

"Soul" and "Spirit" in the Bible

The New Testament brings subtle changes to our view of "soul," raising questions such as "what good will it be for a man if he gains the whole world, yet forfeits his soul? Or what can a man give in exchange for his soul?" (Matthew 16:26; see also Mark 8:36 and Luke 9:25). Any topical Bible or concordance will show that references to individual spirits and the Spirit of God are abundant in the Old Testament, but the New Testament is the book of the Holy Spirit. (Also note that the writings of the apostle Paul do not *define* "spirit" but are largely focused on the *workings* of the Spirit.)

The Bible uses the word *soul* for the flesh/spirit connection of man (see Genesis 2:7 KJV). The soul is abstract, relating to the body at one end and to the spiritual dimension at the other; the soul is related to the body even as it is the window to the spiritual realm. *The soul is not identical to the spirit*—it is our spirit that is in communion with the Spirit of God, and it is our spirit within us that knows Him best. No one knows the thoughts of God except by His Spirit (1 Corinthians 2:14–16): "The wind blows wherever it pleases. You hear its sound, but you cannot tell where it comes from or where it is going. So it is with everyone born of the Spirit" (John 3:8).

The distinction between "soul" and "spirit" is more or less a revelation of God that often is not recognized in other religions. Hindus and Buddhists who practice or seek spirit possession for various purposes exploit the thin bridge between the soul and spirit of man to flood his soul with all kinds of spirits. God's Word plainly says that each has an identity, recognizable only with the help of His revelation:

> The word of God is living and active. Sharper than any double-edged sword, it penetrates even to dividing soul and spirit, joints and marrow; it judges the thoughts and attitudes of the heart. Nothing in all creation is hidden from God's sight. Everything is uncovered and laid bare before the eyes of him to whom we must give account. (Hebrews 4:12–13)

Your Buddhist friend will agree to the continuation of karma, but he will be hesitant to accept the continuation of soul. Since he believes that everything is impermanent, why shouldn't the soul also be? Politely inquire as to the need for the continuation of karma: How can karma continue beyond this life if everything is impermanent? Isn't karma, then, superfluous? If the force that distinguishes individuals in this life, giving them their unique identity, is carried into the next birth, does this not mean, then, that he has some belief in its permanence?

SPIRIT POSSESSION

Spirit possession is a state of consciousness induced in a person by an alien spirit, demon, or deity; another personality takes control, and the person is often not fully conscious during the process. The person possessed shows a dramatic change in physical appearance, action, voice, and manner, and frequently he or she remembers nothing of the possession. Behavior varies according to the kind and number of spirits involved.

Spirit possession is a common phenomenon among Buddhists; through a demonstration of spirit possession, a person shows that he or she is fit to be a shaman. Subsequent possessions often involve inhalation of incense or fumes, ingestion of drugs, and bombardment of noise. If a person seems to be involuntarily possessed, exorcism may be undertaken. People gather around and view the entire proceedings of possession and exorcism with awe and fear, sometimes inducing the spirits to leave with food or animal sacrifice.

Deliverance and healing from the clutches of spirit possession is one of Buddhism's most needy areas. Charms are frequently suggested to overcome the influence of demons, rivals, magicians, wizards, and enemies, but since spirit possession is an important factor in becoming a village temple priest or shaman, religious practices encourage spirit possession at one level and try to exorcise spirits at another. This is like trying to drive away the spirits using the spirits—as Jesus said, "How can Satan drive out Satan?" (Mark 3:23).

A person may be possessed by a multitude of spirits; in exorcisms I have seen, the possessed person often lists the names of the spirits tormenting her. Sometimes she may not know their names and says she is possessed by a horde. At times there are comical conversations between the shaman and the possessed person; in Sri Lanka, such exchanges are wildly relished by the audience, forming an integral part of the procedure. In Tibet, Bhutan, and Sikkim, the shamans, the spirit-possessed, and the other participants in the exorcism process wear masks. In most Buddhist nations, exorcism is a communal affair, followed by sacrifice and feasting.

As with other animistic groups, Buddhist women have always been spirit-possessed in greater numbers than Buddhist men. Traumatic experiences open doors for seeking the help of spirits, which, in turn, cause their own trauma. If you have a Buddhist friend who is in need of help, share some of David's psalms. David underwent unspeakable suffering in his life, but he held on to the promises of God, even putting into song how the Lord fortifies against all adversity. *Anyone in need can identify with the psalms of David.*

I know many Buddhist migrants to the United States who are willing to read or meditate on the Word of God because every attempt to improve their condition within their own religious traditions has failed. When an alternative is presented, their initial reaction is one of hesitation, but when they begin to see and feel your zeal for them, they usually consider suggestions. If this breakthrough is achieved by the grace of God, begin to pray with them when the opportunity presents itself.

Buddhist exorcism is actually not exorcism at all; it does not lead to a permanent cure but is only an attempt to replace one set of evil spirits with another. Driving out demons in the name of Jesus is annihilation of the authority of demons over the possessed. The animist uses one evil spirit against another, and when some accused Jesus of doing this (Luke 11:15), He answered:

> Any kingdom divided against itself will be ruined, and a house divided against itself will fall. If Satan is divided against himself, how can his kingdom stand? I say this because you claim that I drive out demons by Beelzebub. Now if I drive out demons by Beelzebub, by whom do your followers drive them out? So then, they will be your judges. But if I drive out demons by the finger of God, then the kingdom of God has come to you. (Luke 11:17–20)

THE WORD OF GOD, SPIRIT POSSESSION, AND EXORCISM

The Word of God tells us that God is Spirit (John 4:24) and He has left us His Holy Spirit (John 16:7–14). The Bible teaches that there are other spiritual beings and that there is a continuing struggle between the angelic forces and evil spirits in the spiritual realm. Satan is a tempter (Genesis 3:1–5; Matthew 4:1–11; 1 Thessalonians 3:5), the adversary and slanderer of God, a distinct, malevolent spiritual being who from the start has worked against God's plans.

Satan has always been evil (1 John 3:8). He leads the world astray (Revelation 12:9) and rules the minds of unbelievers (2 Corinthians 4:4). He is also called "the ruler of the kingdom of the air" (Ephesians 2:2), who tries to ensnare the new believer into captivity:

> He [an overseer in the church] must not be a recent convert, or he may become conceited and fall under the same judgment as the devil. He must also have a good reputation

with outsiders, so that he will not fall into disgrace and into the devil's trap. (1 Timothy 3:6–7)

Those who oppose him [the Lord's servant] he must gently instruct, in the hope that God will grant them repentance leading them to a knowledge of the truth, and that they will come to their senses and escape from the trap of the devil, who has taken them captive to do his will. (2 Timothy 2:25–26)

Satan himself masquerades as an angel of light. It is not surprising, then, that his servants masquerade as servants of righteousness (see 2 Corinthians 11:13–15). The evil one "prowls around like a roaring lion looking for someone to devour" (1 Peter 5:8).

The good news is that Jesus came to this world to overcome His archenemy and claim victory over death: "The reason the Son of God appeared was to destroy the devil's work" (1 John 3:8).

Since [we] have flesh and blood, [Jesus] too shared in [our] humanity so that by his death he might destroy him who holds the power of death—that is, the devil—and free those who all their lives were held in slavery by their fear of death. (Hebrews 2:14–15)

"He has rescued us from the dominion of darkness and brought us into the kingdom of the Son he loves, in whom we have redemption, the forgiveness of sins" (Colossians 1:13–14). And, "having disarmed the powers and authorities, he made a public spectacle of them, triumphing over them by the cross" (Colossians 2:15). Thus, victory is already ours—we need to appropriate it by faith in Jesus Christ (see Ephesians 6:10–18).

While we are victorious in Jesus' name, we must recognize that exorcism is not an end in itself:

When an evil spirit comes out of a man, it goes through arid places seeking rest and does not find it. Then it says, "I will return to the house I left." When it arrives, it finds the house unoccupied, swept clean and put in order. Then it goes and takes with it seven other spirits more wicked than itself, and they go in and live there. And the final condition of that man is worse than the first. (Matthew 12:43–45)

Note that the house (the person) was kept clean and put in order, yet the evil spirits were emboldened to return in strength. Cleanliness in the natural, *without the armor of God's Word,* is a welcome home for spirits. In those for whom we have prayed and whom the Spirit has delivered, the place the spirits occupied must be filled with God's Spirit.

Power is given to us, the disciples and children of God, to drive out demons in Jesus' name (Mark 6:12–13; 16:17). Even so, this authority is not for our personal glory. Jesus said, "I have given you authority to . . . overcome all the power of the enemy; nothing will harm you. However, do not rejoice that the spirits submit to you, but rejoice that your names are written in heaven" (Luke 10:19–20).

Jesus taught that we must have faith in order to be effective in casting out demons. When a boy was spirit-possessed and suffering greatly, the disciples could not heal him, but Jesus did:

> Then the disciples came to Jesus in private and asked, "Why couldn't we drive it out?"
>
> He replied, "Because you have so little faith. I tell you the truth, if you have faith as small as a mustard seed, you can say to this mountain, 'Move from here to there' and it will move. Nothing will be impossible for you" (Matthew 17:19–20).

Some demons can only be driven out through prayer:

> When the spirit saw Jesus, it immediately threw the boy into a convulsion. He fell to the ground and rolled around, foaming at the mouth.
>
> Jesus asked the boy's father, "How long has he been like this?"
>
> "From childhood," he answered. "It has often thrown him into fire or water to kill him. But if you can do anything, take pity on us and help us."
>
> "'If you can'?" said Jesus. "Everything is possible for him who believes." . . .
>
> The spirit shrieked, convulsed him violently and came out. The boy looked so much like a corpse that many said, "He's dead." But Jesus took him by the hand and lifted him to his feet, and he stood up.
>
> After Jesus had gone indoors, his disciples asked him privately, "Why couldn't we drive it out?"
>
> He replied, "This kind can come out only by prayer" (Mark 9:20–23, 26–29).

Note that demons do recognize the Son of God and His authority over everyone, including them.

When Jesus stepped ashore, he was met by a demon-possessed man from the town. For a long time this man had not worn clothes or lived in a house, but had lived in the tombs. When he saw Jesus, he cried out and fell at his feet, shouting at the top of his voice, "What do you want with me, Jesus, Son of the Most High God? I beg you, don't torture me!" For Jesus had commanded the evil spirit to come out of the man. Many times it had seized him, and though he was chained hand and foot and kept under guard, he had broken his chains and had been driven by the demon into solitary places.

Jesus asked him, "What is your name?"

"Legion," he replied, because many demons had gone into him. (Luke 8:27–31)

God's healing power is *always* available to us. The synagogue ruler was furious that on the Sabbath Jesus healed a woman who was crippled by a spirit for eighteen years:

The synagogue ruler said to the people, "There are six days for work. So come and be healed on those days, not on the Sabbath."

The Lord answered him, "You hypocrites! Doesn't each of you on the Sabbath untie his ox or donkey from the stall and lead it out to give it water? Then should not this woman, a daughter of Abraham, whom Satan has kept bound for eighteen long years, be set free on the Sabbath day from what bound her?" (Luke 13:14–16).

Praying in Jesus' name, rather than praying to other spirits, is the only effective answer to spirit possession. Methods of exorcism from Buddhism should never be used. Fasting, prayer, and reading the Word of God must fill the life of one who ministers to the spirit-possessed.

BIBLIOGRAPHY

Barrett, David, George Kurian, and Todd Johnson. *World Christian Encyclopedia* (2nd edition). New York: Oxford University Press, 2001.

Bentley-Taylor, David, and Clark B. Offner. "Buddhism" in *The World's Religions*. Norman Anderson, ed. Grand Rapids, Mich.: Eerdmans, 1975. Reprinted 1991.

Bollinger, Edward E. *The Cross and the Floating Dragon: The Gospel in Ryukyu*. Pasadena, Calif.: William Carey Library, 1983.

Brooks, Alec. *Where in the World Is God?* Tenkasi, India: Morningstar Book House, 1999.

Burtt, Edwin A. *The Teachings of the Compassionate Buddha*. New York: Mentor Books, New American Library, 1955.

Chang, Lit-sen. *Zen-Existentialism*. Philadelphia: Presbyterian and Reformed, 1969.

Conze, Edward. *Buddhist Scriptures*. Baltimore: Penguin, 1959.

Dunne, George H. *Generation of Giants*. South Bend, Ind.: University of Notre Dame Press, 1962.

Furer-Haimendorf, Christoph von. "Himalayan Religions" in *The Encyclopedia of Religion*. Vol. 6. Mircea Eliade, ed. New York: Macmillan, 1987.

Gard, Richard A. *Buddhism*. New York: George Braziller, Inc., 1961.

Geisler, Norman L., and Abdul A. Saleeb. *Answering Islam: The Crescent in Light of the Cross*. Grand Rapids, Mich.: Baker Book House, 1993.

Henry, Matthew. *Matthew Henry's Concise Commentary on the Whole Bible*. Quick Verse 6.0. Cedar Rapids, Iowa.: Parsons Technology, Inc.

Hsu, Francis L. K. *Under the Ancestors' Shadow*. Palo Alto, Calif.: Stanford University Press, 1971.

Hume, Robert E. *The World's Living Religions*. New York: Charles Scribner's Sons, 1944.

Johnstone, Patrick, and Jason Mandryk. *Operation World*. Minneapolis: Bethany House, 2001.

Kinnear, Angus I. *Against the Tide: The Story of Watchman Nee*. Fort Worthington, Pa.: Christian Literature Crusade, 1973.

Latourette, Kenneth S. *Introducing Buddhism*. New York: Friendship Press, 1956.

Lausanne Committee for World Evangelization. *Christian Witness to the Chinese People*. Wheaton, Ill.: Lausanne Committee for World Evangelization, 1980.

Lee, Kun Sam. *The Christian Confrontation With Shinto Nationalism*. Philadelphia: Presbyterian and Reformed, 1966.

Merriam-Webster Collegiate Dictionary.

Monier-Williams, Monier. *Hinduism*. London: Society for Promoting Christian Knowledge, 1911.

Myers, Allen C., ed. *The Eerdmans Bible Dictionary*. Grand Rapids, Mich.: Eerdmans, 1987.

Nicholls, Bruce J. "Hinduism" in *The World's Religions*. Norman Anderson, ed. Grand Rapids, Mich.: Eerdmans, 1975. Reprinted 1991.

Osgood, Cornelius. *The Koreans and Their Culture*. New York: The Ronald Press Company, 1951.

Roberts, Alexander, and James Donaldson, eds. *The Ante-Nicene Fathers*. Vol. 1. Grand Rapids, Mich.: Eerdmans, 1956.

Schaff, Philip, ed. "Saint Augustine: Sermon on New Testament Lessons, Sermon 12" in *A Select Library of the Nicene and Post-Nicene Fathers of the Christian Church*. Vol. 6. Grand Rapids, Mich.: Eerdmans, reprinted 1991.

Spiro, Melford E. *Burmese Supernaturalism*. Englewood Cliffs, N.J.: Prentice-Hall, 1967.

Tambiah, Stanley J. *The Buddhist Saints of the Forest and Cult of Amulets*. Cambridge: Cambridge University Press, 1984.

Thirumalai, Madasamy S. *Sharing Your Faith With a Hindu*. Minneapolis: Bethany House, 2002.

Tsering, Marku. *Sharing Christ in the Tibetan Buddhist World*. Upper Darby, Pa.: InterServe (Agent for Tibet Press), 1988.